A Vision of H...

The Fiftieth Anniversary of the United Nations

PUBLISHED BY
The Regency Corporation Ltd.
Gordon House
6 Lissenden Gardens
London NW5 1LX, UK
Tel: 44 (171) 284 4858
Fax: 44 (171) 267 5505

PROJECT DIRECTOR
Jane Gee

EDITOR
Jonathan Power

PICTURE EDITORS
Lucy Johnson
Francis Rockliff

SUB-EDITORS
Gillian English
Lynn Jackson
Maggie Maloney

SENIOR CONSULTANT
Brian Parrish

PROJECT CONSULTANTS
Khalid Amin
Tunji Obasa
Ian Stuart

**DISTRIBUTION
MANAGER**
Jeremy Kyle

**EDITORIAL DESIGN
& REPRODUCTION**
PDM Services Ltd.
12 Chapel Street
Tring, Herts. HP23 6BL, UK

**CORPORATE COPY
DESIGN & REPRODUCTION**
McLeod Warner Ltd.
16 Rothesay Road
Luton, Beds. LU1 1QX, UK

PICTURES

ECPA, France

IBRD, USA

Panos Pictures, London, UK

*Prince of Wales Business
Leaders Forum*
London, UK

Rex Features
London, UK

Sean Sutton, Oxford, UK

United Nations/Photo by Sygma
New York, USA

WWF, Switzerland

© The Regency Corporation
Ltd. 1995
All rights reserved
ISBN Sb. 0-95204695-4
Hb.0-95204694-6

ACKNOWLEDGEMENTS
The publishers would like to thank those individuals and
organizations who contributed articles and suggestions for
the book. In particular, thanks are due to:
Ajit S. Bhalla - Author
Mauricio de Maria y Campos - Director General, UNIDO
Noel J. Coghlan - European Commission
Alecia De Clercq - Author & Journalist
Thalif Deen - IPS News Agency
Hon. J. Hugh Faulkner PC - Executive Chairman,
Sustainable Project Management
Raymond Florin - Executive Director, World Business
Council for Sustainable Development, Argentina
Carlos Fortin - Secretary-General, UNCTAD
Mark Francis - Director of Information, Committee for
Economic Development
Farhan Haq - IPS News Agency
Mahbub ul Haq - Special Adviser to the Administrator, UNDP
Jonathan Hobbs - Director, Industrial Environmental
Forum of Southern Africa
Lucy Johnson - Journalist
Azizur R. Khan - ILO
Gil Loescher - Professor, University of Indiana, USA
Jack Martin - ILO
Rajat Nandi - Senior Director, Confederation of Indian
Industry
Jan Oberg - Director, Transnational Foundation for Peace
and Future Research, Sweden
Dhira Phantumvanit - President, Thailand Environment
Institute
Richard Reoch - Journalist
Ricardo J. Romulo - Chairman, Makati Business Club of
the Philippines
Pat Rooney - Executive Director, Environmental Forum
of Zimbabwe
Maurice Strong - Chairman, Earth Council
Christopher Wilkinson - European Commission

CREDITS
British Chamber of Commerce, Argentina
Cámara Nacional de Comercio de la Ciudad de México
Chamber of Industry, Costa Rica
Chamber of Commerce, Israel
Chamber of Commerce, Slovakia
Dawson UK Ltd.
Extel Financial Ltd., UK
Gale Research International Ltd., UK
International Association of Ports & Harbors, Japan
International Chamber of Commerce, France
Kuwait Chamber of Commerce & Industry
Leadership Directories Inc., USA
Lloyds of London Press Ltd.,UK
London Stock Exchange, UK
Marconi's International Register, USA
McGraw-Hill Business Information Center, USA
R.L. Polk & Co, USA
Reed Reference Publishing, USA
Singapore Trade Development Board
Sociedad Nacional de Industrias, Peru
Telegulf Directory Publications WLL, Bahrain
Turkish Chamber of Commerce
United Nations Development Business, USA
World Development Council, USA
World Economic Forum, Switzerland
Who's Who Edition GmbH, Germany
Who's Who in the Arab World, Lebanon

PRINT
*BPC Waterlow Ltd, Bedfordshire,
UK.*

BPC pursue development projects
to prevent pollution by reducing
process emissions.

PAPER & BOARD
*Robert Horne Paper Co. Ltd.
Buckinghamshire, UK.*

Text printed on Quattro Recycled
Matt, manufactured from 75%
reclaimed fibre.

INKS
*B.A.S.F. Coatings and Inks Ltd,
Sussex, UK.*
The inks are water insoluble and
use harmless pigments.

LAMINATE
Celloglas Ltd. Berkshire, UK.

The cover is laminated with
Clarifoil cellulose diacetate film
manufactured primarily from
wood pulp sourced only from
managed forestry.

00932

Contents

A Parker pen was chosen to sign:

The 1899 Spanish-American Peace Treaty.

The World War II Peace Treaties.

The 1987 INF Treaty.

The 1990 Agreement banning chemical weapons.

The 1991 Strategic Arms Reduction Treaty.

The 1993 Palestinian-Israeli Peace Accord.

For nearly a century we've been doing our small part

to bring Peace on Earth.

PARKER DUOFOLD. ONE OF THE FINEST CRAFTED WRITING INSTRUMENTS IN THE WORLD.

‡ PARKER
DUOFOLD

The DUOFOLD Pearl and Black Fountain Pen. Lifetime Guaranteed.*
For more information please write to: The President, Parker Pen Company, Parker House, Newhaven, East Sussex, BN9 0AU, England.

*This guarantee does not affect your statutory rights.

Introduction

His Excellency Boutros Boutros-Ghali
United Nations Secretary-General

Half a century ago, delegates from 50 states gathered together to give birth to the world Organization, the United Nations.

Since then, many critical ideas and events have altered the shape of international relations. The 50th Anniversary could hardly have come at a more appropriate time. For an organization going through a time of great change and momentous challenge, it offers an opportunity to celebrate achievements, review lessons of the past and chart a new course for the future.

There is one important aspect of the anniversary which I believe is especially important: improving public awareness of the UN, building a wider constituency and demonstrating the system's continued relevance in the years to come.

A Vision of Hope, informing its audience of the work of the UN towards peace, development and democratization, is a valuable contribution to promoting continued and enlarged understanding and support for the Organization.

THE
ARAB CONTRACTORS OSMAN AHMED OSMAN & CO.

As the world approaches the end of the twentieth century, we are witnessing the development of technologies that can meet any kind of human want and demand for those who have the resources.

However, for the greater part of the world, problems such as poverty and environmental devastation continue to worsen.

Recognizing that business has become one of the most dominant institutions of the modern world, it is clear that business has a responsibility to assist in bringing about the changes necessary to reverse global environmental and social degradation.

To bring about these changes we must promote international dialogue, understanding and cooperation between all sectors of society. This means putting people first - giving people a voice and a stake in their own future. It is only in this way that advances can be made for the development and future of all humankind.

After all, it is up to us to build a better tomorrow for our children by creating a safer world today.

The Arab Contractors
Osman Ahmed Osman & Co.
34 Adly Street
Cairo
Egypt

Tel. 20 (2) 3935011
Fax. 20 (2) 3925728 - 3937110 OSMAN UN

Foreword

Gillian Martin Sorensen
Under-Secretary-General
Special Adviser to the Secretary-General for Public Policy

The 50th Anniversary of the United Nations, a historic moment in the life of the Organization, offers an opportunity to reflect on the UN's past and consider its future. It is a moment to take pride in the UN's achievements and build upon its strengths as well as to acknowledge its flaws and learn from its failures. In this sense, 1995 is a defining moment for the Organization.

Though peacekeeping draws the lion's share of media attention, the greater efforts of the UN go to development, disarmament, democratization, humanitarian and refugee work, environmental action, human rights, health and family planning. For that reason, we welcome *A Vision of Hope* which gives a thoughtful overview of this broad agenda. It makes vivid and compelling the dire needs of so many and brings home to the reader the real work of the UN as it saves lives, changes lives and offers hope and opportunity to millions.

The UN reflects the will of its Member States. When that will is clear and united the UN is strengthened and possibilities for a better world are real. *A Vision of Hope* adds to the analysis that will renew and reinforce the UN, convey a greater understanding of its work and assist it to become more effective in its next half century.

A Sense of Proportion

The United Nations headquarters in New York.

~ shaping a credible strategy

© Paul Smith/Panos

- Changing perspectives
- New attitudes
- Successes and failures
- The United Nations' future

Fifty years is two generations. And two generations is long enough to measure whether there has been a substantial change of direction in how mankind orders its affairs. It is clear that there has. We have been spared a Third World War. The change has affected not only war and peace, but also society's attitude to poverty, economic progress, its habitats, and women and children. In all, there have been strides forward that at the time of the ending of the Second World War seemed barely conceivable.

Yet we have clearly not learned one thing – a sense of proportion.

We are too arbitrary in our measurement of suffering, too beholden to early prejudices and too easily manipulated by the exaggerated and relentless, but fickle, eye of television. The danger is cumulative. As we are fed a random diet of suffering, based on misleading criteria for what is most important, we lose over time not only our discernment but our confidence in our ability to set intelligent priorities.

Strangely, we make the same mistake with successes as with failures. Look at this recent comment of the oft-quoted economist, Robert Heilbroner. The Western world, he says, 'is experiencing the startled realization that the quality of life is worsening – that people who are three or five or ten times richer than their grandparents do not seem to be three or five or ten times happier or more content or more richly developed as human beings'.

But is this not, in large part, because we are fed selective information, by both media and politicians,

Defending the Economic Frontiers of Pakistan

Pakistan Water and Power Development Authority (WAPDA) has been a source of strength for the country's economy through its pioneering work in developing water and electric power sources. Within a period of 10 years, **WAPDA** has been involved in the construction of Tarbela, the world's largest earth and rock filled dam, spanning the mighty Indus River; Mangla dam; eight inter-river link canals, five barrages and a syphon involving one of the largest civil engineering works ever undertaken.

In 1947 when Pakistan came into existence, total electric power generation capacity amounted to around 30 megawatts (MWs). This increased to 119 MWs in 1959 when **WAPDA** took over the country's power system. Today, electricity production capacity stands at about 10,000 MWs in the hydro sector and over 5,000 MWs in the thermal sector.

WAPDA's vast nationwide integrated transmission and distribution network caters for the needs of 8.7 million domestic, industrial and agricultural consumers, including nearly 52,500 villages.

In the water sector, the Tarbela and Mangla dams, with their massive storage capacity, provide water through the world's largest irrigation system. Over 80,000 hectares of waterlogged and saline areas of land are being reclaimed annually.

WAPDA provides drainage infrastructure to nearly 6 million hectares and is currently implementing a drainage scheme involving another 2.5 million hectares, including a substantial scheme for the Left Bank Outfall Drain Project (LBOD). An equally ambitious project for the right bank of the River Indus is also being undertaken.

WAPDA congratulates the United Nations on its 50th Anniversary and hopes that it will continue to play a positive role in future world affairs, encouraging cooperation among the nations of the world to foster universal peace and progress.

Pakistan Water and Power Development Authority
Wapda House, Shahrah-e-Quaid-e-Azam, Lahore 54000, Pakistan.

"*a flimsy reckoning of mankind's achievements*"

that makes us more aware of our failures than our successes? Are we really living, for example, in a more environmentally degraded world than our grandparents, whose industrial cities imposed no controls at all on industrial effluents? And are we not living longer and with less physical suffering too?

For example, Britain is regarded, by some, as hobbled by an antique industrial structure, an imperial nostalgia and a sharp lack of a modern day work ethic. Yet figures published by the Central Statistical Office in January 1994 show that real disposable income – cash left over after taxes, National Insurance and pension contributions – was almost 80 per cent higher than in 1971 and life expectancy is increasing by about two years every decade.

Nowhere is this flimsy reckoning of mankind's achievements more apparent than the way the inhabitants of the wealthy countries of Europe, North America and Japan perceive the rest of the world – the so-called developing countries – which are widely caricatured as poverty-stricken disaster zones. For the overwhelming majority of the Third World most of it is just plain nonsense.

In reality, in little more than a generation average real incomes in the Third World have more than doubled; child death rates have been more than halved; malnutrition rates have fallen by 30 per cent; life expectancy has increased by about a third; the proportion of children enrolled in primary school has risen from less than a half to more than three-quarters; and the percentage of rural families with access to safe water has risen from less than

10 per cent to more than 60 per cent. The proportion of couples using modern contraceptives has risen from almost nothing to more than 50 per cent – in China it is 72 per cent and Brazil 66 per cent. Average family size is falling in almost every country.

Only a short 70 years ago, 20 years before the founding of the United Nations, child death rates in the cities of the industrialized world were higher than the average for Africa today. In 1990, the UN Children Fund's (UNICEF) World Summit for Children set a target of reducing child death rates to 70 per 1,000 births in all countries by the end of the century. Already, only five years into this timetable, well over half of the developing countries have reached it. In the 1960s, the under-five mortality rate in Europe was higher than it is in most of South America today.

Ignorance of what progress has been made extends right up to the highest levels of policy-making. If the quality of life can be improved so rapidly, how is it that Western aid agencies allocate less than 10 per cent of their expenditure to meeting the most pressing needs of the poorest – primary health care and education, clean water, safe sanitation and family planning? Developing countries themselves, too, are often just as culpable. They spend only 10 per cent of their budgets on these basics.

We lack a sense of proportion about either success or failure. If only we could face facts rather than accepting so glibly the misleading interpretations others choose to feed us, how much more productive – and happier – we would probably be.

However, it is not just on matters of social and economic development that we too often see the world through a glass darkly. War and peace preoccupy us seemingly more than ever despite the ringing down of the Iron Curtain and the ending of the Cold War.

Countless human beings have been killed in war from 1945, the end of what North Americans, Europeans and the Japanese like to call 'the last war', until the close of the Cold War.

If a massacre on this scale were to result from berserk technology, from a new strain of the plague or from the despotism of a ruthless tyrant, the global flood of human despair and outrage would be incalculable.

So why so much agitated concern in 1995? The world is not worse than it has been; it is probably better. Despite the headlines, we are not killing at Cold War rates. To read the forebodings of the politicians and pundits is to be plunged into the depths of despondency. The world, they appear to say, is spinning out of control.

It is simply not so. The world we live in today, despite Yugoslavia, Somalia, Cambodia, Angola, Afghanistan, Rwanda, Georgia, Tajikistan and Chechnya, has probably rarely, if ever, been so peaceful. Since the waning of the misnamed Cold War, which stirred up hot proxy wars all over the place, the number of conflicts has been on a steady decline. According to the Stockholm International Peace Research Institute, the number of wars in 1987 was 36; in 1988, 33; in 1989, 32; in 1990, 31; in 1991, 30; and in 1992, 1993 and 1994, down to 27.

The majority of the big 'post-war' killers were the direct consequence of communist-capitalist confrontation – Korea, Vietnam, Angola, Mozambique, Nicaragua, El Salvador, Afghanistan, Ethiopia-Somalia, to mention only the principal ones. Added to these there were the great anti-colonial wars, Algeria, Kenya, Cyprus, Rhodesia and, long before they became Cold War conflicts, Indo-China, Angola and Mozambique.

There were the big inter-state wars –Israel versus the Arabs, Pakistan versus India, Iran versus Iraq, and Iraq versus Kuwait and the rest of the world.

Finally, as there still are, there were numerous ethnic or tribal wars.

The Cold War is over. The colonial era is over. In 1994 peace was made between Israel and the Palestinians and amongst black and white in South Africa. Peace also came to Northern Ireland. Indeed, right now there are no all-out wars between nations. What then has brought about this awful sense of gloom that pervades the political discourse?

> *we look at problems rather than shield our eyes*

Our unnecessarily pessimistic reading of the state of the world reveals a positive aspect – these days we look at problems rather than shield our eyes.

One only has to go back to the great Irish famine of the 1840s, which was effectively brushed under the carpet by official policy-makers. Yet famine today is televised worldwide and scarcely anyone feels unmoved.

It is our perspective, our sense of responsibility and our ability to care that have changed most. And that alone is one of the big achievements of our age. We are members of feeling societies. The question today is how best to mobilize those feelings, where best to direct them and what tools to use. At the same time we have to be aware that often there are no speedy solutions, that persistence is often the most important of virtues and that results or success can come from the most unlikely quarter.

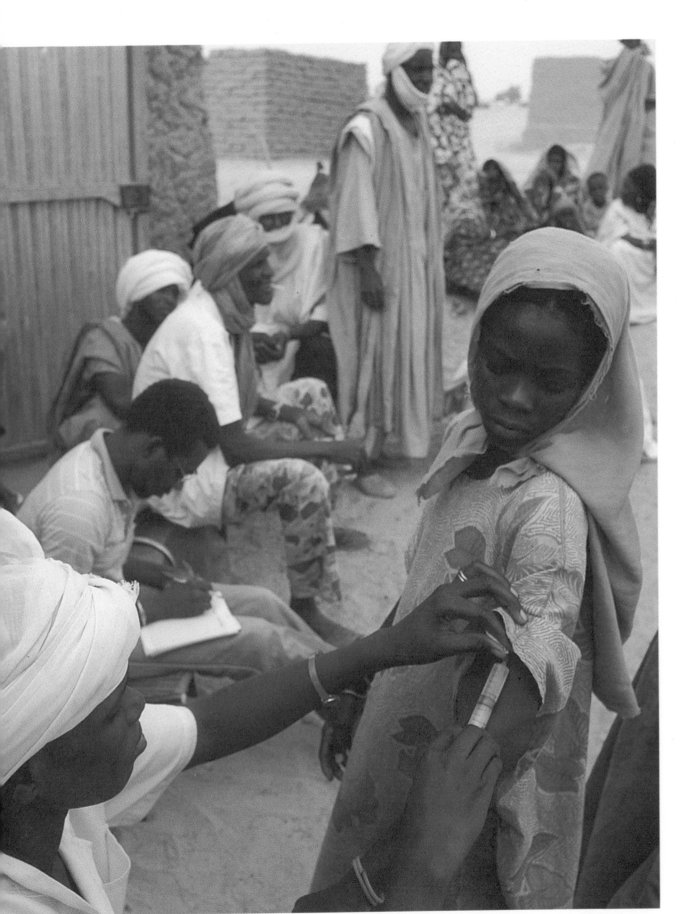

© *Jeremy Hartley/Panos*

In little more than a generation, child death rates in the developing world have been halved.
A child is vaccinated against meningitis in Mali.

STENA AB

To all companies within the Stena sphere and their employees it is essential to contribute to the development of human relations to create a society aware of our responsibility to future generations and the environment.

The complexity of today's society, together with our dependence upon efficient transportation systems to meet the needs of our highly specialized society and people's need to travel, has advanced a technical development in an area where, for many years, the environment was virtually neglected.

Stena started their recycling activities in 1939 and hold about 40% of the recycling market in Sweden today.

Extensive training programmes for our employees and continuous research and maintenance programmes for safer ships are part of our contribution to a safer and more environmentally friendly form of transportation.

As our sincere belief is that we only have a right to remain in business if we are best at what we do, we try to give each individual client our best attention and hope to provide a high quality of service.

Stena AB, S-405 19 Göteborg, Sweden.
Tel. 46 (31) 855000 Fax. 46 (31) 120651
Telex 2559 Stena S : Telegrams Stenaship

DAN STEN OLSSON
C.E.O.

"we may live in the best of times"

Since we are dealing with an intangible measuring rod – our perception – it is not easy to single out objectively the hardest-hit sectors of our world. So much depends on personal experience, which few of us have in sufficient quantity to make an informed judgement. The world is just too big. Instead of that we depend on the restless, but deceiving, eye of television which tends to be attracted by drama rather than some objective degree of suffering or need. The 'silent' emergencies pass it by. The distress it prefers is 'loud' and preferably opinionated.

Thus to make judgements on real need in this fast flowing, but poorly observed, world is not a task anyone, much less the layman, can find easy.

Nevertheless, 1993, 1994 and 1995 do not deserve the fashionable pessimism that has become dangerously pervasive. Unknown to ourselves, we may live in the best of times. Three single steps could help keep it that way – using the UN to tighten controls on the sale of arms and nuclear technology, to deploy the UN's peacekeeping machinery to more effect, and to step up the pace of the war on poverty. These days the economically advanced countries live peacefully together. Democracies, by and large, do not go to war with each other. War in the 1980s and 1990s is the prerogative of the poorer countries. Once capitalism was thought to be the source of international competition and conflict; the capitalist was thought the parent of war. No longer. These days it is the poor of the world who destroy each other. Poverty, too easily, makes them the prisoner of the dictator and the warmonger, who in turn can rely on the amoral pursuit of return by mainly Western arms salesmen.

The world *is* a better place. But such is the nature of life on earth that change, driven often by the technological motor of post-industrial life but also by wider education and new styles of life, constantly throws up new problems.

Daunting they often are, but compared with the problems that existed 50 years ago they are, on the one hand, of less draconian proportions and, on the other, more within our capacity to do something about.

When, for example, James Grant, former Executive Director of UNICEF, claimed that by the year 2000 we could, by inoculation, banish most childhood diseases the world over he was in fact, by both metaphor and illustration, underlining what remarkable resources contemporary mankind possesses. As for inoculation, so for many other problems and disabilities too. It is a question only of will and direction.

The UN has been at the heart of this sea-change in mankind's condition. Sometimes the instigator, often the referee and, at the least, the sounding board where opinions are shared and comparisons sought.

This book looks at the most important and interesting aspects of the UN's contribution. It is not, however, encyclopaedic. It offers a series of portraits into an organization at work, grappling with the unprecedented demands of contemporary history.

The UN is observed, a painting in process, where some strokes of the oil are still drying, others are uneven and unsure and, where the visage is clear, the furrowed brow as well as the more graceful features are obviously apparent.

© Sean Sprague/Panos

A credible blueprint

The next 50 years? That, for many, is perhaps the most relevant question and for this year the challenge is to fashion a credible blueprint.

'We the peoples of the United Nations' – the opening words of the UN Charter, an ambition, 50 years later, unfulfilled. Who among us, we can all ask, feels they are part of the defining force of this green skyscraper in New York, much less the sprawling buildings of Geneva, Rome and Vienna? Even our governments appear to keep their distance. It is, as the Carlsson/Ramphal commission observes, 'a global third party – belonging to itself, owned by no one except its own officials'.[1]

The single most necessary change that needs to be wrought is to change this perception, to involve governments and, not least, to involve their peoples. Only if this happens can the UN be effectively reformed so that it becomes the activist, muscular but lean, organization its founders envisaged.

Contrary to much received wisdom the present inadequacy of the UN is not all down to padded payrolls and turgid procedures although, in the opinion of some, all clearly play a part in slowing its activities down to what, too often, is a stately walk.

In many ways it is the legacy of the Cold War and the nuclear arms race. The Charter was negotiated in San Francisco, oblivious to the research on the atomic bomb being carried out a mere 1,000 miles away in New Mexico. The 'scourge of war' would not be removed, said the Charter, by a nuclear standoff, but by 'collective action in which armed force shall not be used save in the common interest'.

Indeed, the very first UN resolution, passed unanimously by the General Assembly, pledges nuclear states to total nuclear disarmament. And the United States suggested a series of measures to give effect to this, including bringing uranium mining, nuclear power generation and the nuclear bomb capacity of its own – the only one at that time – under inter-national control. The proposal was rejected by Stalin and an incredible opportunity lost. Within five years of the founding of the UN the nuclear arms race was under way.

The Cold War fuelled the nuclear race and rendered the UN impotent in a wide range of activities, making peace-enforcement for the most part impossible and restricting peacekeeping to the rarest of occasions. The Security Council itself became, but for the odd exception, one more arena for East-West polemics.

Now that the Cold War is receding into history and the remaining nuclear arsenals of the two superpowers only point aimlessly to the sky, the UN is ripe for reinvigoration. Already much is in motion. The Security Council itself is almost in permanent session. Reform is openly discussed and new ideas are being aired. It is not today a question of when or if change will happen, but how.

> *"reform is openly discussed and new ideas are being aired"*

The genocide in Rwanda and wars in Africa, Central Asia and Europe have overshadowed the post-Cold War decline in the number of conflicts.
Rwandan refugees at a makeshift market.

A Reliable Partner

Kazakhstan is determined to create the most favourable legal and economic conditions for the investment of foreign capital to develop modern technology and to utilize the country's mineral resources. At the same time, highly profitable but environmentally responsible industries need to be developed. This commitment is reflected in the country's recently adopted Law for Foreign Investments.

With a registered charter fund of 40 million Lenge and US$20 million, Alem Bank is one of the largest foreign dealers with a network of 22 branches in all leading regional centres and cities. Amongst its shareholders are the Cabinet of Ministers and many of the nation's international associations and corporations.

Alem Bank Kazakhstan has already gained vast practical experience in the areas of foreign investment, working in association with the leading banks in Europe, the US and Asia. As the first bank in Kazakhstan to join SWIFT, using REUTERS in its foreign exchange and money market operations and with its network linked by SPRINT, the reputation of the bank as a reliable business partner continues to grow. The Bank is also the leading dealer in state treasury bills.

The first bank in the Republic of Kazakhstan to become a full member of Visa International and Europay/Mastercard, Alem Bank issued its own credit card, AlemCard, in association with Visa, in October 1994.

MUTUAL TRUST AND SUCCESS
is the motto of Alem Bank Kazakhstan.

Erbol Zhamanbaev
Chairman of the Board

152/4 Moris Torez str. 480057 Almaty Republic of Kazakhstan Tel: (7 3272) 611 812/509 645
Fax: (7 3272) 509 632 Telex: 613390 ALEMB RU, 251206 AVAL SU S.W.I.F.T. ABKZKZKX REUTER ALEM

The Security Council itself is now the subject of intense scrutiny. Can it continue to be dominated by the five veto-wielding powers, the 'victorious' of the Second World War? In 1945 no one envisaged the demise of the Soviet Union, the creation of the European Union, the rise to great power status of defeated Germany and Japan, the economic awakening of large parts of Asia and Latin America, the wealth of the oil states or the birth of over 100 new nations.

contributions have the biggest say in budgetary matters. This is not democracy as practised anywhere and it is unfair to those who give as much in proportion to their national income as the larger countries.[3]

The General Assembly needs to be streamlined and rationalized, reducing its agenda to more manageable proportions yet, at the same time, providing a

> "*the General Assembly needs to be streamlined and rationalized*"

The 1945 *status quo*, as the Carlsson/Ramphal report says, with 'its unrepresentative character is the cause of disquiet leading to a crisis of legitimacy. Without reform it will not overcome that crisis. Without legitimacy in the eyes of the world's people it cannot be truly effective in its necessary role as a custodian of peace and security.'[2]

The General Assembly, the deliberative body in which every member nation has a seat, is the symbol of the UN as a universal and democratic organization. It has, however, always lived under the shadow of the Security Council and is, in many critics' eyes, nothing more than a frothy talking shop.

Yet its universality is its prime asset. It is why presidents and prime ministers regularly make their annual pilgrimage to address it and why it has been able to be the launch pad for important new ideas such as the Law of the Sea and the battle for human rights.

For the future it must develop a more coherent strategy for dealing with the budget of the organization, which is under its direct authority. This may mean resisting the traditional claim of the big donors that those who make the largest financial

forum for discussing the great controversies of the day that are the constant preoccupation of the Security Council. Only if the Assembly acts as a chamber constantly discussing the issues that confront the Security Council can it hope to influence it.

The Assembly, already more open than ever before to the growth of the now ubiquitous non-governmental organizations (NGOs), including those of the business community, needs to apply its mind to new ways of incorporating 'We the Peoples' into the deliberations of the main organs of the UN. Government participation alone is not sufficient if the Charter is to really come alive in our day and age.

In the future, once the Assembly itself is re-shaped and revitalized, consideration should be given to the establishment of an ancillary debating body, a constituent assembly of parliamentarians along with an annual forum of civic non-governmental groups, where there is an opportunity to hear the voice of activists in the NGOs. This, together with a Right to Petition for action to redress wrongs, would go a long way to give substance to the long-neglected opening lines of the Charter.

Around 50 per cent of couples worldwide lack access to family planning.
A family planning clinic in Africa.

© Rob Cousins/Panos

Some take the view that on the economic and social front the UN probably needs a new organ of responsibility. One that can bring under a single umbrella the many faceted activities of the UN played out in numerous autonomous or semi-autonomous agencies and conferences. The present segregation of trade, competition policy, environment, macro-economic and social policies no longer work as well as were originally envisaged.

There is now a serious debate under way about creating an Economic Security Council. One suggestion which has been put forward, is that while it should contain a representative mix of countries, it should be small and businesslike. Like the Security Council itself, it should have high-level representation although it would probably not possess the authority to take legally binding decisions. However it would, by its brief, range and standards of work, gain some of the standing and influence in relation to international economic matters that the Security Council has in the political field.

The extension of the rule of international law is perhaps the least understood element of the UN, yet in the long run it could be the most important. One day, as more and more swords are beaten into ploughshares, international legal institutions will become as important as domestic ones are in resolving disputes and punishing crime. Nations in dispute will no longer resort to war but to the courts.

International law is an essential part of the Charter. The founding fathers of the UN instituted the International Court of Justice as the 'Cathedral of Law' in the global system. But military power and economic strength have worked to sideline it. It now needs to be brought back to centre stage, with the universal membership of the UN accepting its compulsory jurisdiction. The Security Council for its part could make greater use of the Court as a source of advisory opinions, thus avoiding the frequent need to have to adjudicate an international dispute itself.

The Court should also be widened to take on responsibility for individual criminal matters, or else perhaps there should be established a separate International Criminal Court. Finally, the present

NATIONAL BANK FOR FOREIGN ECONOMIC ACTIVITY OF THE REPUBLIC OF UZBEKISTAN

Uzbekistan - A Country with a Great Future

When the UN was founded fifty years ago, a framework was established for international cooperation as a fundamental means of resolving disputes between countries. The collapse of the Soviet Union, of which Uzbekistan was a part, brought the period of confrontation to an end.

In September 1991 Uzbekistan regained its independence. From its inception, the country has striven towards integration in world affairs based on a belief of openness as an incentive for domestic growth. It is, therefore, not by chance that one of the first Decrees issued by the President of the Republic of Uzbekistan, Mr. I. Karimov, was the Decree on the Incorporation of the National Foreign Trade Bank. Signed on the sixth day of independence, 7 September 1991, the main aim of the Bank was to accelerate the integration of Uzbekistan's financial systems into international systems and to attract foreign investments.

The National Bank is one of the most dynamically developing institutions in Uzbekistan. Starting with just US$34, the bank's capital now totals US$234 million with assets of some US$2.5 billion. From a 1993 survey of the top 1000 international banks, The National Bank was placed 824 and in the leading 200 banks of Asia, it stands at 139th place.

The activities of the National Foreign Trade Bank are focused on the flow of capital and the allocation and servicing of foreign investments. At the same time it also functions as an export/import trade bank, a merchant bank as well as a reconstruction and development bank.

The main partners of the bank are: The European Bank for Reconstruction and Development, the International Finance Corporation and national export insurance agencies from countries including Belgium, China, France, Germany, Great Britain, India, Italy, Japan, Switzerland, Turkey and the US.

Uzbekistan is firmly resolved to establish itself not as a peripheral member of the world community but as a highly developed state standing together with the leading countries of the world. There are, indeed, grounds for this confidence. Uzbekistan possesses unique, incalculable resources of raw materials and an educated, hard working and enthusiastic workforce, a legacy to their forebears who contributed so much to world civilization.

In order to achieve these aims, Uzbekistan is implementing a series of profound social, economic and political reforms. These reforms are aimed at the creation of a typically Uzbek model of market economy based on the principles drafted by the President. They include:

- priority of the economy over politics

- the state as the main reformer and guarantor of economic transformation

- the supremacy of law in all areas of state activity

- social protection of the population as one of the main functions of the state in the period of transition to a market economy

- logical succession and development in the implementation of economic reform

Today the results speak for themselves. Uzbekistan is the first of the CIS countries to have overcome the difficulties of the transitional period and to have achieved a period of dynamism and economic prosperity.

We are convinced that our country has a great future, making its contribution to global cooperation and human progress.

Rustam Azimov,
Chairman of the Board of Directors

23 Akhunbabaev str., Tashkent, 700047, Republic of Uzbekistan
Tel. (7 3712) 336070 : Fax. (7 3712) 333200 : Telex 116371 RUNO SU: S.W.I.F.T. NBFA UZ 2X

ad hoc war crimes tribunal for former Yugoslavia and Rwanda should have its brief widened to allow it to consider war crimes cases in all areas of serious conflict.

The question of restructuring the UN Secretariat is one which has produced numerous, and often detailed, proposals now being discussed both within and outside the UN.

© *Jon Delorme/Panos*

In most developing countries, the lack of welfare often leaves the most vulnerable to fend for themselves.
A 'despatch rider' in Santarem, Brazil.

To refashion the UN we need to look deep into ourselves and see what kind of world we really want. As Barbara Ward wrote back in 1971: 'The most important change that people can make is to change their way of looking at the world. We can change studies, jobs, neighbourhoods, even countries and continents, and still remain much as we always were. But change our fundamental angle of vision and everything changes – our priorities, our values, our judgements, our pursuits. Again and again, in the history of religion, this total upheaval in the imagination has marked the beginning of new life, a turning of the heart, a "metanoia", by which men see with new eyes and understand with new minds and turn their energies to new ways of living.'

After 50 years, most of it consumed by the Cold War that froze so much of the life-spirit of the Charter, the UN is now slowly thawing. New seeds of endeavour, new shoots of opportunity can reach for air and light. We can make the world an even better place.

However, it will not happen without an immense application of political will. Any group of informed people can think of a hundred ways the UN can function better. But very few political leaders have the interest, the time, or the stature to really make an imprint on this immensely complicated vessel. The danger is that reform will only be tar slapped onto a weak hull, that most of the ship will be allowed to drift and that in the event of a big political gale it will take in water all too quickly.

What helmsman can drive his ship at speed in a condition like this? Secretaries-General can come and go but it is perhaps a near impossible command.

The present Secretary-General, Boutros Boutros-Ghali, has sought in all manner of ways to overhaul his boat but finance is restricted on the one side and resources, including personnel, in particular for peacekeeping, are withheld on the other.

The next two or three years are going to determine the course for the next 50. Will we use this time to give the UN the refitting it needs, knowing that in the Charter we have a remarkable blueprint that has stood the test of time and can probably take us through for another 50 years, given only a handful of amendments?

Education is the key to lifting societies out of poverty.
A school in Zimbabwe.

CEMIG
Companhia Energética de Minas Gerais

The UN has been a milestone along the road to global peace. In like manner, CEMIG has acted as a key participant in the development of the Minas Gerais State of Brazil.

Founded just seven years after the UN, CEMIG generates and supplies electric power to an area that has become the second largest energy market in Brazil. It has a generating capacity of 5.5 million kilowatts, produced by 36 hydroelectric power plants, one thermal plant and the first wind-driven generating plant in the country, as well as power purchased from ITAIPU.

CEMIG has four million consumers spread throughout 682 municipalities, covering an area of 580,000 square kilometres. Its power is supplied over the largest grid in Latin America, totalling more than 240,000 kilometres.

The company has been a watershed in the distribution of welfare and socio-economic development in the state. It has promoted industrialization, supplied quality energy in sufficient quantity to its market and extended the benefits of electric power to thousands of low-income residential and rural consumers. The company will reach 100 per cent of connected consumers within the next two years.

CEMIG is publicly-owned. The State of Minas Gerais, with 39 per cent of its stock, is the controlling shareholder. The remainder of the capital is distributed among 130,000 private Brazilian and overseas investors. In 1994, the company's gross revenue was US$1.8 billion, with a profit of US$698 million. With growth of 4 per cent forecast for the region, investment over the next four years should amount to US$2.5 billion.

Its technical staff are active in the search for renewable energy resources such as wind, solar power and biomass and, through its subsidiary company Gasmig, in the distribution of gas within the region. In partnership with private organizations, CEMIG is pioneering the formation of joint investment in the construction of new hydroelectric stations. In addition, the company is evaluating the exploration of a fibre optics system for data transmission and communication through its transmission and distribution networks.

The expertise acquired by the Company over a whole lifetime of learning and self-sustainable development within the energy sector has enabled it to intensify its operations through cooperation, transfer of knowledge and engineering solutions. In partnership with private enterprise, CEMIG has been able to provide assistance to utility companies in countries such as Bolivia, Canada, Costa Rica, Ecuador, Honduras, Indonesia, Malaysia, Panama, Paraguay and Uruguay.

Of vital importance to CEMIG is the preservation of the environment and the restoration of the native ecosystem. Its plan of action involves three major programmes: environmental preservation units, limnology and fish breeding, and the reforestation of water stream banks.

This has been CEMIG's approach in the search for harmony between progress and nature. Protecting life, extending knowledge and providing power to 16 million people throughout the State of Minas Gerais.

Carlos Eloy Carvalho Guimarães
President & CEO

Av. Barbacena, 1200 - CEP 30161-970 - Belo Horizonte - MG - Brazil
Tel: 55 (31) 349 2111 Fax: 55 (31) 349 4691 - Telex 311124

The way the decision will go will depend much on public opinion – what do we the people want to see from the UN? This brings us back to the central paradox of the UN. It was created in the name of the peoples of the world, yet it functions day by day in a manner that gives the impression that it is owned by no one.

Some way has to be found to start an interactive relationship between peoples and the UN that will impress on governments the need to participate in a much enhanced form.

The 50th anniversary could be the beginning of that. More articles are going to be written, more books published, more television documentaries made and more public meetings held on the subject of the UN, than in any other single year of its existence. Political leaders also have to play their part by using this opportunity to review their own policies towards the UN.

The essentials are already in place. If the last 50 years has not always been kind to the UN it has not been totally destructive either. The UN has developed in many positive and fruitful ways. Revolution is not needed. Reform is. Modest reform carried out purposefully and diligently could make the UN into what its founders wanted of it – an alternative to 'the scourge of war' that would 'promote social progress and better standards of life in larger freedom'.

> *"in the Charter we have a remarkable blueprint that has stood the test of time"*

Endnotes

1   *Our Global Neighbourhood* – Report of the Commission on Global Governance, chaired by Ingvar Carlsson and Shridath Ramphal. Oxford University Press, 1995.

2   Ibid.

3   The UN's total annual expenditure represents only $1.90 per human being alive in 1992. This does not seem a lot when measured against government military expenditures of $150 per person per year.

The Train is Back...

Colombia is placing its fully operational railway network at the disposal of the private, national and international sector through a system of franchises or concessions.

There are 1880 km of operational railway lines into which US$682 million is expected to be invested.

Lines to be franchised during the first stage:

- **Atlantis Railway: Puerto Salgar-Santa Marta (769km)**

- **Western Railway: Buenaventura-Medellín (651km)**

- **Atlantic Connection: Medellín-Grecia (198km)**

- **North-eastern Railway: Santa Fé de Bogotá-Belescito (262km)**

... it's the People's turn

Calle 31 No. 6-41, Piso 20, Santa Fé de Bogotá, Colombia
Tel: 57 (1) 288 3994

The Peace Process

The opening Declaration of the Charter of the UN places the quest for peace at the heart of the world body's mandate. The peoples of the UN, it says, are determined "to save succeeding generations from the scourge of war."

The Charter reaffirms "faith in fundamental human rights, in the dignity and worth of the human person, in the equal rights of men and women and of nations large and small."

To those who argue that this is the language of idealism, one need only point out that the Charter was the work, not of sages and saints, but of tough-minded warleaders: Churchill, Roosevelt and Stalin.

The vision of a world at peace remains the overriding ideal of the UN; achieving it in practice is fraught with turbulence. The very nature of disarmament, peacekeeping and human rights has often catapulted the UN into the epicentre of international and national conflicts.

Today, the UN is faced with unprecedented opportunities to act in situations of conflict and human suffering in which previously it would have been unable to intercede. Peacemaking now requires an approach that integrates political sensitivity, human rights monitoring, military logistics and development assistance. A world order is emerging which requires new policies, new expertise and new resources to meet the challenges of global peace and security.

Chapters

International Law,

Over 23 million refugees, fleeing conflict and environmental degradation, are scattered in camps and settlements around the world.
Rwandan refugees fetch water at dawn.

Universal Rights ~*the global dilemma*

- *Responsibility of government*
- *The bill of rights*
- *Investigations and remedies*
- *The world court*

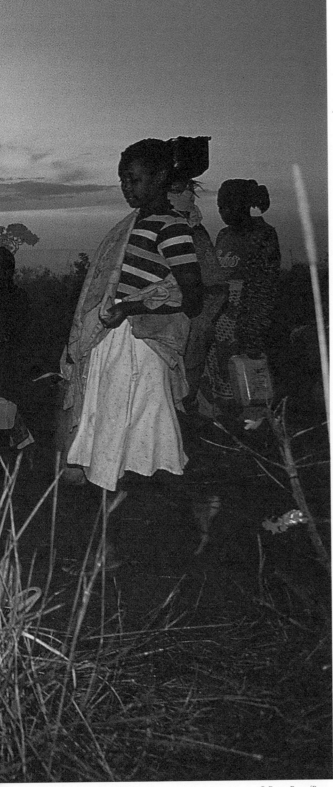

© *Betty Press/Panos*

To the dispassionate observer, the development of international law in the second half of the 20th century is one of the outstanding achievements of the United Nations. But the dispassionate observers are few and the critics are many.

Ironically, debate centres around a contradiction that no one disputes: virtually the entire body of international law has been created and enforced by those who stand most to gain from breaking it.

By definition, international law seeks to regulate the behaviour of governments. It is governments that must draft and vote for each piece of international legislation. It is also governments that must monitor their own compliance with international law and the extent to which it is respected by other states. Yet the very nature of politics makes it inevitable that it will be those same governments that seek to circumvent these obligations and in many cases openly flout them.

In the eyes of the most virulent critics, therefore, suspicion inevitably surrounds the rhetoric, resolutions and reports that follow in the wake of governments' statements about respect for international law.

But in the eyes of those who look upon international law as the only long-term underpinning for civilized behaviour among nations, the very fact that governments have begun progressively to commit themselves to common standards of decent behaviour is a remarkable and ultimately hopeful accomplishment.

Regulations and compliance

What is beyond question is that the body of international law is now immense. Almost all of it is the result of a mere half century of work, chiefly conducted through the UN. There is now a substantial body of treaties, declarations and other standards to which states have committed themselves. These range over a vast body of issues from the law of the sea, global, economic and social development, world trade, the political rights of women and, abolition of torture, right down to specific restrictions on the use of certain types of restraining implements in prisons.

That body of legislation is only part of the growing weight of international law. In addition, there is the ever-expanding number of findings and judgements that emanate from the many bodies whose responsibility it is to oversee and, in some instances, regulate the compliance of states with their international commitments. The International Court of Justice comes immediately to mind as the foremost of these bodies, but it is by no means the only one.

Today, however, the whole edifice of international law faces a crisis of confidence. It must survive this crisis if the global community is to rise to the challenge of managing the world in which we live.

Put simply, the crisis is this. For half a century some of the best and brightest legal and political minds around the world have devoted their energy to designing and constructing a splendid and unprecedented structure of international law. Now there is very little further drafting that needs to be done. The architectural work is largely complete; most of the essential construction is finished. The palace of justice is in place.

The question now is: who is it for?

Do the weighty treaties and declarations, so finely hedged with possibilities for exemptions and derogations, serve to keep governments effectively immune from the threat of serious and binding legal action by citizens and others seeking redress of grievances?

Is the entire framework purposefully skewed so as to bolster the economic, political and cultural interests of the North against the demands for justice and equity by the nations of the South?

Does the complex structure serve the interests of international experts in the maze of legal nuances?

In other words, does international law serve the interests of 'the peoples of the United Nations' in whose name the UN Charter was proclaimed in 1945? Or does it serve the interests of a dominant group of governments and an attendant élite of legal experts?

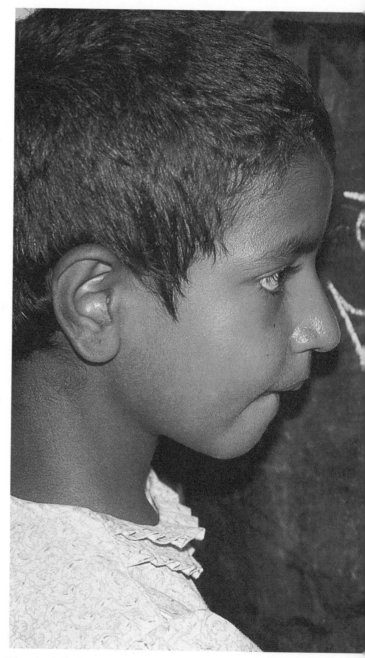

Education is the bedrock of human rights.

Universal human rights

Nowhere has this crisis in international law been more apparent than in the efforts to define and protect universal human rights.

When the fledgling UN rose from the ashes of the Second World War, one of the three main areas of its future work was to be the promotion and protection of international human rights. It was clear that any overall strategy for the creation of a peaceful world had to include a determined effort to ensure that fundamental human rights were secure for future generations. In October 1945, therefore, the UN Preparatory Commission recommended that the Economic and Social Council (ECOSOC) establish immediately a Commission on Human Rights. This was the body to be charged with drafting an international Bill of Rights.

Almost immediately the question arose as to whether the members of the Commission on Human Rights should serve in their individual capacity or be the representatives of governments? With hindsight the outcome of the debate was inevitable. The 18-member commission was to comprise governments and its members were to participate as representatives of government.

Over the years that fact has remained unchanged. It is only the size of the club that has grown. In 1962 the membership was increased to 21, in 1966 to 32, and in 1980 to 43. Its current membership is 53.

Work on the international Bill of Rights began in 1947. The Bill was to begin with a Declaration. That was to be drafted by a committee of eight: Australia, Chile, China, France, Lebanon, the United Kingdom, the United States and the USSR. The work was fraught with argument. The draft Declaration went through 81 ECOSOC meetings. Many observers at the time gave credit to the devoted work of the Chair of the Drafting Committee, Eleanor Roosevelt, for the fact that the Declaration survived the withering and often divisive deliberations.

Eventually, on 10 December 1948, the Universal Declaration of Human Rights was adopted by the UN General Assembly, with 48 votes in favour, none against and eight abstentions.

© Barbara Klass/Panos

"*the palace of justice is in place*"

50TH ANNIVERSARY OF THE UNITED NATIONS

electroperú s.a.

PROMOTING DEVELOPMENT
WITHOUT HARMING THE ENVIRONMENT

CEPRI-ELP

An extraordinary impact

Much has since been made of those eight abstentions, and it has been argued that, since the Soviet bloc, Saudi Arabia and South Africa abstained in the vote, the Declaration itself is somehow flawed or not fully legitimate. But the reality is that, were the vote to be taken today, it is unlikely that there would be anything other than consensus. The Declaration's provisions are enshrined in the constitutions and laws of numerous nations and it has been the constant reference point for the underlying principles of national, regional and international human rights standards ever since it was proclaimed.

Speaking before the UN General Assembly, Eleanor Roosevelt observed that the Declaration was 'first and foremost a Declaration of the basic principles to serve as a common standard for all nations. It might well become the Magna Carta of all mankind'.

The breadth of vision of the Declaration is unquestionable, even inspiring. Its preamble warns that 'disregard and contempt for human rights have resulted in barbarous acts which have outraged the conscience of mankind'. It describes 'freedom from fear and want' as 'the highest aspiration of the common people'.

It establishes that 'recognition of the inherent dignity and of the equal and inalienable rights of all members of the human family is the foundation of freedom, justice and peace'.

The Declaration covers two broad sets of rights. One set is known as Civil and Political Rights. The other set of rights is known as Economic, Social and Cultural Rights.

Under the heading of Civil and Political Rights, the Declaration requires all governments to protect the life, liberty and security of their citizens. They should guarantee that no one is enslaved and that no one is subjected to arbitrary arrest and detention or to torture. Everyone is entitled to a fair trial. The right to freedom of thought, conscience, religion and expression is to be protected.

Under the heading of Economic, Social and Cultural Rights, all governments are expected to try progressively to improve the living conditions of their citizens. For example, they should try to guarantee the right to food, clothing, housing and medical care, the protection of the family, and the right to social security, education and employment. They are to promote these rights without discrimination of any kind.

To give binding force to the Declaration, work began on two covenants which would take the form of treaties. Governments would become parties to these treaties and special committees would be established to monitor states' compliance with their treaty commitments. Once the notion of governments having to accept limitations on the exercise of state power began to bite, the pace of events changed. Negotiations on the draft treaties took a further 18 years.

The initial result of the debates that took place within the UN between 1948 and 1952 was that an even clearer distinction was made between one set of rights, Civil and Political Rights, and the other set, Economic, Social and Cultural Rights. The first set comprised those rights that were seen as guaranteeing freedom from fear; the second set dealt with freedom from want. The ultimate result was two covenants to complete the international Bill of Rights: the International Covenant on Civil and Political Rights (ICCPR), and the International Covenant on Economic, Social and Cultural Rights (ICESCR).

Both sets of rights were held to be interrelated. ICCPR, for example, states 'the ideal of free human beings enjoying civil and political freedom and freedom from fear and want can only be achieved if conditions are created whereby everyone may enjoy his civil and political rights, as well as his economic, social and cultural rights'. However, argument about which of these two sets of rights had priority and whether one could be achieved at the expense of the other was to take up vast stretches of the highly politicized landscape across which the battle for universal human rights was to be waged for most of the rest of the century.

The second divisive issue that emerged once work began on drafting the two covenants concerned the doctrine of 'internal affairs of states'.

Many governments, but most notably the Soviet Union at the time, were concerned about any arrangements that would violate Article 2.7 of the UN Charter. This says that the UN is not to 'intervene in matters which are essentially within the domestic jurisdiction of any state'. How, then, was the UN to deal with the question of human rights violations in specific countries?

" *freedom from fear and want* "

The dispute surfaced over the means of dealing with human rights violations reported under the two international covenants. The Commission on Human Rights finally decided, by a vote of seven to six with one abstention, that a permanent Human Rights Committee should be established to receive complaints of human rights violations. But these could be submitted only by other states. Significantly, there was a far larger majority against considering complaints by non-governmental organizations (NGOs) or grievances brought by individual citizens. Eventually agreement was reached on an Optional Protocol to ICCPR, whereby states could unilaterally decide that the Human Rights Committee could hear complaints brought to it by that state's citizens. Equally, a state would remain free to decide unilaterally not to open that possibility to its citizens. To this day, the majority have not ratified this Optional Protocol.

© Jasper Young/Panos

Entry into force

The two covenants and the Optional Protocol were finally adopted by the UN General Assembly in 1966. Before they could become effective by 'entering into force' they had to be ratified by a minimum of 35 states. It took a full 10 years before 'critical mass' was achieved. ICESCR entered into force on 3 January 1976. ICCPR entered into force on 23 March of the same year.

Kurdish refugees flee after the 1991 failed uprising.
The UN set up a 'safe-zone' to protect the Kurds in Northern Iraq.

The debates of those first three decades established the fundamental political and legal framework within which the UN as an inter-governmental body was to address the deeply disturbing issue of human rights protection. All the elements for which it was later to be criticized were present.

The UN as a whole simply could not manage to elevate human rights above the divisions of the Cold War. Exactly the opposite. One side got locked into arguing for the supremacy of civil and political rights; the other insisted on the primacy of economic, social and cultural rights. Both approaches to human rights became propaganda weaponry in Cold War exchanges inside and outside the UN. Later both blocs used human rights as a bargaining chip.

Even without this poisoned atmosphere, it was clear that the ambitions of the drafters of the Universal Declaration were being watered down in practice. Governments were not at all keen to have their own practices scrutinized – and certainly not to be laid open to complaints brought forward by their own people.

This led to legalistic and diplomatic preoccupation with procedures. In the eyes of many governments – and also in the view of officials and others who were trying to push governments forward – this was necessary to enable sensitive discussions to take place in confidential sessions and to restrict indiscriminate access by individuals to even the limited complaints mechanisms. Without these restrictions, ran the argument, governments could not be expected even to embark on the deeply embarrassing and explosive process of discussing how they ought to be treating their citizens.

"*human rights as a bargaining chip*"

GLENCORE
INTERNATIONAL AG

We, at GLENCORE, are proud to be associated with the commemoration of the Fiftieth Anniversary of the United Nations.

As a leading international commodity trading company with a presence in more than 40 countries, GLENCORE trades in a wide range of goods including agricultural products such as cereals, soya, sugar, rice and cotton – all of which are essential commodities in today's world.

However, our activities are not just limited to the distribution, forwarding and dispatch of goods. GLENCORE provides credit to farmers in South America, Africa and the Commonwealth of Independent States, thus enabling many of them to grow their own crops. In addition, GLENCORE, by arranging barter trades, ensures that countries experiencing a lack of liquidity obtain essential goods.

With many countries heavily dependent upon the export of commodities, GLENCORE has a vital role to play in the economic and social development of the countries in which it operates.

Baarerstrasse 37, P.O Box 4562, CH-6304 Zug. Switzerland.
Tel: (042) 227722. Telefax: (042) 210791. Telex: 865272.

Global reform

It was difficult to counsel patience to the starving and to the relatives of those held in prison camps, police barracks and tiger cages. But the vast undertaking was only beginning, nothing less than the global reform of the behaviour of nation states.

The advances were slow, but cumulative. Once the international Bill of Rights had entered into force, a range of other more detailed laws could be elaborated. The pace of negotiation increased markedly. By the beginning of the 1990s a total of 67 international human rights instruments existed.

The scope of the subject matter, by any standards, is impressive:
■ The Right of Self-Determination ■ Prevention of Discrimination ■ War Crimes and Crimes Against Humanity, including Genocide ■ Slavery, Servitude and Forced Labour ■ Torture, Detention and Imprisonment ■ Nationality, Statelessness, Asylum and Refugees ■ Freedom of Information ■ Freedom of Association ■ Employment Policy ■ Political Rights of Women ■ Rights of the Family, Children and Youth ■ Social Welfare, Progress and Development.

At the centre of the UN's human rights work, almost from the very inception of the organization, has been the Commission on Human Rights. It is to the Commission that the UN Secretary-General refers the thousands of communications that arrive annually from individuals and organizations all over the world alleging human rights violations.

Once it had been determined, that the Commission should consist solely of representatives of governments, decisions appeared to emerge as a result of what many observers saw as a deep-seated conflict of interest. For many years, despite the key role assigned to it, the Commission considered that it had 'no power to take any action in regard to any complaints concerning human rights'. Efforts to change this view throughout the first two decades of its existence were successfully countered by those who invoked 'intervention in the domestic affairs of states'.

The UN's battery of international law has given it the status of international mediator.
UN peacekeepers remove ballot boxes from polling stations during Cambodia's UN-supervised elections in 1993.   © Jon Spaull/Panos

Consistent patterns

In 1965, once the Commission was enlarged in response to the increasing growth of the membership of the UN itself, new trends were discernible. Newly independent countries were keen to bring issues to do with colonialism and self-determination, racism and apartheid, and underdevelopment into the Commission's deliberations. This eventually led to the adoption of what is now known as the '1503 Procedure', a reference to Resolution 1503 of ECOSOC in 1970 authorizing the Commission on Human Rights to investigate 'communications, together with the replies of governments, if any, which appear to reveal a consistent pattern of gross violations of human rights'.

The year after the 1503 Procedure was introduced, ECOSOC adopted Resolution 1235 which gave birth to the practice of setting up special investigations by rapporteurs and working groups focusing on individual countries.

In 1980 the Commission established the Working Group on Enforced and Involuntary Disappearances. This was

"*the fear of publicity*"

To process the flood of petitions, letters, affidavits and reports, the Commission set up a sorting system run by a Sub-Commission on the Prevention of Discrimination and the Protection of Minorities. 'Appropriate' communications would be passed on to the Commission and the Commission in turn could refer its findings to ECOSOC. The screws were ever so slowly starting to tighten.

Significantly, the great fear seems to have been of publicity. Essential to the working of the 1503 Procedure was strict confidentiality. Even the names of the countries discussed by the Commission were to remain a secret. Everyone's lips remained sealed for a further 8 years. It was not until 1978 that the chair of the Commission began the practice of naming the countries that had been considered. Remarkably, this, in itself, was deemed to constitute such an embarrassment for the governments named that the diplomatic efforts within the UN system to prevent a country even getting on the list for consideration became noticeably more intense.

to be the first of what are now known as the 'theme mechanisms'. Others deal with torture and with summary and arbitrary executions as well as other widespread problems. Individuals or groups working under these theme mechanisms are invited to act independent of governments, but under the aegis of the UN, to examine an issue, receive information from governmental and non-governmental sources, and report to the Commission. These reports have the great advantage of being publicly available and are often regarded as some of the most authoritative and comprehensive material available on the abuse under investigation.

One in four people lives in absolute poverty.

MACEDONIA THRACE BANK S.A.

Macedonia Thrace Bank is proud to offer its support to the United Nations on this historic occasion. Situated in the Balkan peninsula, which is passing through turbulent times, the Bank's headquarters are in Thessaloniki, a historical capital in Macedonia since the Byzantine era.

Fifty years after its creation, the principles and goals of the UN re-emerge as a framework for stability, cooperation and development as we approach the third millenium.

The invitation to the international business community reflects the increasing awareness of the key role that corporate leaders can play in contributing to the economic, environmental, social, educational and cultural advancement of the modern world.

As a financial institution for development, managing private capital and producing social wealth, Macedonia Thrace Bank plays its part in the social and economic development of the country.

The Bank's strategy includes the creation of Balkan-integrated banking networks as well as the introduction of entrepreneurial mechanisms and institutions to assist in the development of the emerging Balkan market.

Greece may play a special role in this direction as an intermediary with the European Union. These efforts will contribute prosperity to the region and successful integration into the world economy.

In line with our cultural commitments, we finance projects highlighting the Byzantine tradition, which formed the common background of Greek and Balkan history and was a basic component of Western

Andreas Ch. Boumis
Chairman of the Board and C.E.O.

civilization. These projects encourage deeper understanding among people.

The Bank has been active in the establishment of a Balkan Centre for the professional training of staff within the banking and financial services industry.

Serving private and public interests for over 15 years, Macedonia Thrace Bank fully support the aims and objectives of the UN sharing in its vision of hope for the future.

Administration
5, Ionos Dragoumi str.
GR-546 25 Thessaloniki, Tel.:031/542.213, 542.313

Treasury International Division
61 Athinas str.
Ethnikis Antistasis Sq.
GR-105 52 Athens, Tel.:01/52.38.164

Intense lobbying

But, ask many people, what use are these investigations? Abuses are documented, but are they stopped? Although much of the decisive deliberation of the Commission and Sub-Commission takes place behind closed doors, it is well known that intense lobbying takes place. Countries strive to stay off the agenda, doling out assurances that they are putting their own houses in order. Others, failing to stay off the agenda, work into the small hours negotiating a change of wording so that abuses in the country are 'noted' rather than 'deplored'. But the price they pay for the semantic changes may well be a pledge to ensure that the issues are satisfactorily addressed at home. The pressure is discreet, but it is real.

On the other hand, it is not governments alone who are the actors on the UN human rights stage. From the very beginning, a significant role has been played by NGOs. The very first draft of the UN Charter included only a passing reference to human rights and it was thanks in part to the representatives of the NGOs that the 1945 UN Conference on International Organization in San Francisco was effectively lobbied to secure much more positive and extensive references to human rights in the Charter.

Over the years, it has been the burgeoning community of NGOs that has created a sustained context of high expectations and trenchant criticism which the UN human rights bodies could not ignore. This has been an essential, and often highly astute, counterbalance to the political horse-trading that has at times threatened to wreck the credibility of the inter-governmental discussions in UN meetings.

These actors came together for two weeks in June 1993 at the UN World Conference on Human Rights. Held in Vienna, it was the largest gathering on this issue ever assembled. Convened in the optimistic aftermath of the end of the Cold War and the emergence of democratic governments in a number of countries in Eastern Europe and elsewhere, it was attended by 171 governments and well over 1,000 NGOs.

The result, on the official level, was the Vienna Declaration and Programme of Action: 93 separate clauses painstakingly negotiated into the small hours of the last day of the conference.

In the end, the delegates reached agreement on formulae that could be adopted by consensus – making the Declaration the most thoroughly endorsed governmental statement on human rights ever made. Some positions restated the original objectives of the 1948 Universal Declaration. Others extended the human rights vision further.

"governments are not the only actors on the UN human rights stage"

The defence of civil and political rights is essential to protect voices raised on behalf of the world's poor.

© Marc Schlossman/Panos

Universal and indivisible

Fears that the Vienna Conference would 'turn the clock back on human rights' did not materialize. The universality of human rights was reaffirmed. The final Declaration states that 'the universal nature of these rights is beyond question. All human rights are universal, indivisible, interdependent and interrelated.' The entire spectrum of human rights was therefore endorsed without division. Human rights were reaffirmed as including civil and political rights and the broader range of economic, social and cultural rights, together with the Right to Development. This full conception recognized, in the words of the final Declaration, that 'the human person is the central subject of development'.

The UN General Assembly took immediate decisions on aspects of the Vienna Declaration. Of long-term significance was its decision in December 1993 to request the Commission on Human Rights to consider proposals and draw up a plan for a UN Decade for Human Rights Education.

That same month, the General Assembly decided to create the long-delayed senior post of UN High Commissioner for Human Rights.

A major question still hangs over the outcome of the Vienna Declaration, one that will affect the future credibility of the UN as it becomes increasingly energetic in human rights protection. It is the question of resources.

The UN Centre for Human Rights, which operates from the Palais des Nations in Geneva, has always been hampered by lack of resources. Understaffed and utterly overworked, its ability to store and retrieve human rights information has, at times, been far inferior to that of some of the human rights NGOs. The Commission's Special Rapporteurs, responsible for the high-profile, key investigations in sensitive situations, are recruited to work voluntarily – usually with minimal support services. All in all, a relatively tiny centre is now required to service a total of more than 60 UN bodies or officers. Following the Vienna Conference, both NGOs and governments adopted decisions calling for increased resources to be devoted to its vital work. The extent to which this is done will be one measure by which to gauge governments' commitment to the rhetoric of human rights.

Beyond government

There is one international institution whose powers transcend those of governments and whose decision-making is determined not by government representatives but by individuals. That is, of course, the International Court of Justice.

The Court is provided for in Chapter 14 of the UN Charter. This specifies that every member of the UN undertakes to comply with the decisions of the Court that affect it and that a failure on the part of any state to comply may be referred to the UN Security Council to 'decide upon measures to be taken to give effect to the judgement'. All members of the UN are automatically parties to the Statute of the International Court of Justice and other states are free to become a party to the Statute as well.

By the beginning of the 1990s there were 400 international treaties in force in which the International Court of Justice was specified as the jurisdictional body. In the period from its founding in 1946 until the end of 1992, the Court had delivered judgements in 41 disputes brought to it by states. It had delivered a further 21 advisory opinions.

Although the number of cases and opinions is relatively small, the influence of the Court is far greater since the effect of a judgement can set vital precedents or shape future interpretation of principles and treaties in the whole field of international law. So great is the implicit power of the Court that the decision by one nation to refer a case to it can greatly exercise the mind of any other government that would be affected by the decision. The vision of a world in which territorial conflict is resolved through reasoned argument, rather than by the sacrifice of civilians and combatants through war, lies at the heart of the case law of the Court. Many of its cases have concerned territorial and fishing rights at sea. However in the case of the border dispute between Burkina Faso and Mali in 1986, the Court was drawn into resolution of a conflict that had led to open hostilities on land. The Court directed continuance of a cease-fire, the withdrawal of troops from the affected area and 'the avoidance of actions tending to aggravate the dispute or prejudice its eventual resolution'. There were no

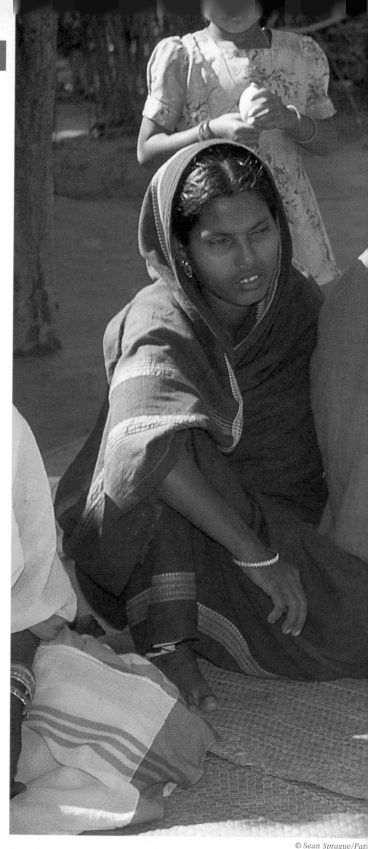

© Sean Sprague/Pan

further hostilities: the Court gave its ruling and the presidents of both countries indicated that they would comply with the judgement.

Anyone who longs for world federalism, or insists on the need for supra-national governance, would do well to examine the impressive record of the Court in bringing reason and peace to issues which, in times gone by, would have led to strident nationalistic posturing and loss of thousands upon thousands

Women's rights are a keystone of development.
A women's income-generating project in India.

of lives as armadas were launched and armies raised for battle.

Drawing on the quiet, but inspiring, example of the International Court of Justice, many victims of human rights violations have asked why their cases cannot be dealt with similarly and why human rights cases are almost always fated to be handled by essentially political bodies in which national interests so often conflict with the pursuit of justice.

COCOA PROCESSING CO

The Cocoa Processing Company (CPC) based in Tema, near Accra, is a wholly-owned subsidiary of the Ghana Cocoa Board, incorporated in November 1981 as a Limited Liability Company. However, cocoa processing in Ghana dates back to 1947 when Gill & Duffus of London, UK, established a milling plant in Takoradi which, in 1982, was taken over by the Ghana Cocoa Board.

At the time of its incorporation, CPC comprised four processing factories with its primary objective being to ensure effective coordination of operations. Two of the factories, then situated in Takoradi, have been divested leaving the other two, PORTEM Cocoa and PORTEM Confectionery in Tema, which were established in 1965.

Our achievements include Golden Tree Chocolates which have attained international distinction by winning local and foreign awards. In 1980, 1982 and 1989 Gold and Silver medals were awarded by the Monde Selection Competition of Brussels, Belgium, to PORTEM Confectionery for the best quality confectionery products. PORTEM Confectionery has also won Gold medals in International Trade Fairs held in Japan, Bulgaria, Cuba and the USA.

The manufacture and marketing of semi-finished cocoa and chocolate products is highly competitive and the Cocoa Processing Company has taken its place at the forefront of the industry, rising to meet the challenges set by international and local markets.

The throughput and output of beans are estimated below and we have the capacity to process a further 25,000 tonnes of cocoa beans. With this in mind, there are plans to construct an additional cocoa factory thereby increasing the total throughput to 50,000 tonnes. There is also potential to increase Chocolate to 5,000 metric tonnes, Pebbles to 1,000 metric tonnes, Instant Cocoa Powder to 2,009 metric tonnes and other confectionery products to 1,000 metric tonnes.

COCOA PROCESSING	TONNES
Beans	20,400
Liquor output	10,626
Packed liquor for sale	1,500
Liquor for pressing	15,126
Butter for sale	7,336
Cake for sale	7,790

CONFECTIONERY	TONNES
Chocolate	2,000
Couverture	200
Pebbles	300
Instant Cocoa Powder	1,200

For two consecutive years, 1992/93 and 1993/94, Cocoa Processing has proved to be profitable in its country of origin. The net profit on sales for 1992/93 was 14.9%, whilst in the financial years 1992/93 and 1993/94 the added value to the cocoa beans processed was 21.9% and 27.5% respectively. Ghana is therefore aiming to convert more raw cocoa beans into semi-finished and finished products thus adding value and increasing its foreign exchange earnings.

Enquiries to: The Managing Director, Cocoa Processing Company Limited,
Private Post Bag, Tema, Ghana. Tel: 233 221 2926/2624 or 6375
Fax: 233 221 6657 or 233 21 665076 Telex: 2082 COCOMAK

Pressing questions

The demand for effective and impartial international human rights protection is clearly not going to go away. Human rights lie at the heart of some of the most pressing questions confronting humanity today. Systematic political repression in many countries has not only blocked the development of public debate, democratic reforms and civil rights, but has claimed an appalling toll of victims.

In country after country, the threat of political arrest, detention without trial, torture, 'disappearance', the death penalty and other gross violations of human rights, such as extrajudicial executions, still hangs over dissenters and others across the political spectrum.

Those who stand up for human rights have been especially targeted. Human rights associations, individual activists, social and political campaigners, and members of the professions involved with human rights are all at risk from vicious attacks. They have been blown up in bombings, assassinated by death squads, abducted by security forces, and tortured and killed in police custody.

These violations can no longer be allowed to rage unchecked. Increasingly the UN is being drawn into anarchic situations marked by appalling human rights abuse. In many cases the anarchy itself is partly the product of those atrocities.

The UN provides food, water and medicine for millions of refugees around the world.
Rwanda refugees wait for food supplies.

© Liba Taylor/Panos

Indigenous peoples often have little redress against human rights abuses.

Human rights protection is rapidly becoming part of the UN strategy for peacekeeping and peace enforcement. The organization therefore needs to take account of the human rights dimension of the role that is being thrust upon it. In isolated cases individual soldiers operating under the UN flag have themselves violated international standards – and have been disciplined. As more and more governments commit forces to UN operations, it is essential that to guarantee the peace they be thoroughly trained in and adept at respecting human rights in the process. Similarly, close coordination between all UN bodies involved in human rights work must be present in peacekeeping and peace enforcement operations. The leading figure in ensuring this integration must be the new UN High Commissioner for Human Rights.

In the wake of the appalling carnage in Bosnia, the UN Security Council initiated proceedings that would lead to the prosecution of named individuals accused of war crimes and crimes against humanity in the conflict in former Yugoslavia.

The *ad hoc* tribunal which was set up was the first international body to try war criminals since the Nüremburg and Tokyo trials at the end of the Second World War. The legal technicalities involved are considerable, but if these can be overcome and proceedings successfully concluded, there are many who would regard this as an essential first step on the way to the creation of a permanent international court dealing with human rights.

In the face of the particularly hideous massacres in Rwanda in 1994, it was decided to extend the Yugoslav tribunal's remit to encompass Rwanda as well – grim proof of the need that many say exists for a permanent court. Creation of such a body would require a separate inter-governmental treaty. If, like the International Court of Justice, it had the power to impose binding judgements on countries and those acting in the service of the state, the bite of

international human rights and humanitarian law would be immeasurably strengthened.

Meanwhile, the world remains awash with millions upon millions of refugees and internally displaced people. Most are fleeing the most basic violations of human rights – desperate to escape death at the hands of the state and its agents. For years, the Office of the United Nations High Commissioner for Refugees (UNHCR) has courageously and with great persistence worked to alleviate the plight of these teeming populations, scattered in camps and settlements around the world. But the solution is not to feed and house refugees – it is to turn off the tap of terror that drives these people from their lands.

> *"fifty years ago such an idea was only a dream"*

Finally, there remains the question of selectivity. From the very first steps taken in the 1960s to investigate situations in individual countries, the UN has suffered from the fact that its members decide what the organization will do on the basis of their own interests and foreign policy objectives. It was easy to reach agreement on the need to condemn white ruled South Africa. It has never been possible in the same way to tackle human rights violations committed by members of the Security Council. As the use of military force has been authorized by the UN in some countries with gross human rights records, but not in other comparable situations, the charge has been made, again and again, that the UN is selective in its approach to human rights. The truth is that the UN can only reflect the political morality of its members.

Ultimately, therefore, the future credibility of international law and of the UN human rights protection programmes will depend upon the commitment and values of national governments. Progress towards a world culture of human rights is slow, painfully slow. Fifty years ago such an idea was only a dream. Now it is an imperative.

The Politics of Peacekeeping

The UN's 16 peacekeeping operations cost $3.4 billion a year.
UN machinery in Cambodia where the UN supervised the 1993 election.

a question of member state commitment

© Sean Sutton

- *The concept of peace*
- *International security*
- *Conflict resolution*
- *Future possibilities*

'The aim of traditional diplomacy was often limited to a stable balance of power: whether the balance conformed to justice was of lesser concern. But peace envisaged by the UN Charter is a just peace: take that moral dimension away and we are back to the disorder and the injustice of power politics.'

Javier Pérez de Cuéllar, 1986

United Nations peacekeeping is an overwhelmingly military affair. According to the UN, there have been 35 peacekeeping operations between June 1948 and January 1995; exactly half of them are currently taking place. With the exception of former Yugoslavia, they were all in what is usually called the Third World – 11 peacekeeping operations in the Middle East, 11 in Africa, four in Central America, four in South East Asia/the Pacific, four in the Indian Subcontinent and one in Europe. Over 650,000 military personnel have served as 'blue helmets' since 1948. In November 1994, 74,625 military and civilian police personnel were serving in peacekeeping operations.[1]

The upsurge in UN peacekeeping operations can be measured in dollars. Since 1948 the UN has spent about $12.4 billion on peacekeeping, while the annual cost to the UN of the 16 current operations is $3.4 billion. Put in the context of global military expenditure, the figures are even more telling. The national military expenditures of the 185 member states of the UN amounted to $815 billion in 1991, a figure that equals the combined income of 49 per cent of the world's poor. Around 30 million people are employed in the armed forces of the UN member states and 1.5 million are working in military

FLYING INTO HONG KONG at night is unforgettable.

From 5,000 feet the densely packed communities are like living cells linked by moving ribbons of light. Few of the incoming passengers sit back and reflect that this city would slow to a snail's pace but for a network of arteries deep beneath its surface. Everyday, millions of people are moved by one of the world's most efficient urban transport systems - the MTR.

But the MTR is more than a transport system —

It is a key element in the concept of a thriving city, creating a public transport system which is second to none.

OUR VISION:

The MTR is part of Hong Kong's urban landscape carrying 2.4 million passengers each weekday on its 43.2 kilometre route and making the railway one of the most widely used in the world. The safety, efficiency and reliability of the system is legendary and MTR have been pleased to offer their expertise to urban planners of transportation systems around the world.

TO BE THE MOST

Behind the MTR's commitment to its passengers and staff lies a simple vision:

to be the most customer-orientated urban railway in the world. This is reflected in our management approach - 'customer service', 'respect for the individual' and 'on time & within budget'.

CUSTOMER-ORIENTATED

The MTR has pioneered new concepts of running a modern public utility.

The high degree of autonomy given by the government has allowed the corporation to adopt prudent commercial principles. Fare rises have remained below the rate of inflation since operations began in 1979 and the corporation continues to invest in the railway's safety and efficiency. Between 1995 and 2002, approximately US$1 billion will be invested in improving customer services and upgrading equipment.

URBAN RAILWAY

In addition, the corporation is investing vast resources into development. A line for the new airport will provide Hong Kong with the best city-to-airport railway link in the world. This massive undertaking is one of the biggest civil engineering projects of the 20th century with other new lines to follow as Hong Kong grows.

IN THE WORLD.

Effective urban transportation is vitally important.

The heartbeat of a city is movement. In the 21st century, cities must change radically. They can no longer afford unfettered use of motor cars. The Hong Kong MTR provides efficient, safe, environmentally-friendly and socially responsible transportation. It offers a vision of hope for those who live in tomorrow's cities.

The Mass Transit Railway Corporation

research and development.[2] In other words, the members of the UN choose to spend 215 times more on warkeeping than on peacekeeping and engage 440 times more soldiers and military researchers than blue helmets. Furthermore, UN peacekeepers have been deployed only in a fraction of all the wars – about 150, depending on definition – that have taken place since 1945. The upsurge in UN peacekeeping operations has happened since the mid-1980s. Of the 35 peacekeeping operations since 1948, 22 have been initiated since 1988.

The 13 peacekeeping operations undertaken before 1988 were classic in the sense that their mandates had to do with observing the behaviour of conflicting parties, monitoring cease-fires, controlling buffer zones and preventing resumption of hostilities. After mid-1988 – due to the changes in the then Soviet Union, the new political thinking of the Gorbachev era and the subsequent ending of the Cold War – new tasks were added and more new missions decided.

But UN practice still, too much, works on the premise that international security is predominantly a military affair, with little recognition of the idea of peace as a process which requires an 'army' of many and varied civilian professionals deployed over time to heal human beings and entire societies.

In summary, UN peacekeeping operations are characterized by:

- an orientation exclusively on wars in the Third World with the large majority of peacekeeping personnel contributed by Third World states themselves

- a narrow concept of peace – understood as putting an end to wars and moving towards a settlement, often negotiated by parties other than the peacekeeping operation personnel - such as the Secretary-General, various powerful countries and at *ad hoc* conferences

- a focus on direct violence but not structural violence

- a focus on cure rather than prevention

- 'selective security' – only a tiny fraction of the world's post-1945 wars have been dealt with by the UN Security Council

A UN peacekeeper wears a protective mask in Bosnia.
The blue helmets of the UN peacekeeping troops have become a familiar sight in the world's conflict zones.

- extremely small budgets in comparison with the world's military and arms export budgets

- an inclination towards military operations with an extremely small capacity for on-the-ground peacemaking and peacebuilding.

The shape of UN peacekeeping

Peacekeeping, the most visible of all UN activities, works under the remit of the UN Security Council which aims to implement peacekeeping resolutions that abide by the spirit of the Charter. The General Assembly also has certain responsibilities. Last, but not least, the Secretary-General is always deeply involved in setting up peacekeeping operations.

The UN Charter

Chapters 6 and 7 of the UN Charter spell out the basis for UN peacekeeping operations. Chapter 7 requires all members to contribute armed forces, assistance and facilities to the Security Council and allow free passage for UN troops, as well as stipulating that members shall hold 'immediately available national airforce contingents for combined international enforcement action'. These provisions, it states, should be carried out by the Security Council 'with the assistance of the Military Staff Committee'. Among other things it is clearly stated that this Committee shall be responsible under the Security Council for the strategic direction of any armed forces placed at the disposal of the Security Council.

However, member states have not made military forces – nor peacekeeping units – available on standby, while the Military Staff Committee has been prevented from doing any serious work by a widespread reluctance among countries to have their military personnel operating collectively under UN command and flag rather than under national command.

A reasonable interpretation of Chapter 7 is that collectively defending a UN member, repelling an aggressor or deterring a potential aggressor is quite compatible with the Charter. However, one must be sceptical about the legitimacy of military attack, counter-aggression, selective bombing – particularly of civilian targets – and punishment actions.

The Charter gives priority to the use of peaceful means and views military action as a last resort to be employed only when everything else has been tried and 'proved to be inadequate'. In fact, there is a quite good in-built theory of conflict-resolution in the Charter. Chapters 6 and 7 form a fairly

functional and efficient progressive scheme of action within the formulation of the overall goals of the Charter.

© *José Nicolas/Rex Features*

With a limited mandate to intervene militarily, the UN's job is to accompany aid convoys to UN 'safe havens'.
UN peacekeepers trudge through the snow in Bosnia.

Step aboard for a trip to the future

Kowloon-Canton Railway Corporation (KCRC) believes that the movement of people and goods is not only essential for economic development, it is vital for life itself.

Indeed, since our first train made its way to China in 1910, the organisation has continually looked to the future needs of Hong Kong.

Today KCRC plays an important role both in carrying freight and livestock to and from China. In addition, 40 million KCRC passengers cross the border to and from Shenzhen each year, whilst trains to Guangzhou take passengers directly to the capital of China's wealthiest province, providing a link to China's railway system further north.

Our Railway from the city to the border and our Light Rail system linking important towns in northwest Hong Kong carry over one million commuters daily.

But we must look ahead. A booming economy in Hong Kong and Southern China needs effective communications for continued growth. KCRC is committed to providing efficient, fast, comfortable and environmentally-friendly transport having already achieved measurable improvements in punctuality, comfort, information, convenience and safety.

"As an organisation that aims to become one of the leading transportation companies in the world, we appreciate the important role that transportation can play in enhancing social and economic development.

KCRC fully supports the work of the UN and share in its 'vision of hope' for the future."

Kevin O Hyde
Chairman
Kowloon-Canton Railway Corporation

The Security Council

The UN Security Council consists of five permanent members and 10 members elected for two-year periods by the UN General Assembly. Unlike the General Assembly, the Security Council is able to take decisions which are binding. There has to be unanimity among the five permanent members of the Security Council. A veto by any one of them can stop any decision – a right that all five have exercised at one time or another.[3]

A dispute can be brought to the attention of the Security Council by any country. The Council usually recommends a peaceful settlement, makes an investigation, asks the Secretary-General to provide his Good Offices and sends a representative to the conflict area. It passes resolutions on measures to be taken by itself and all UN members and urges the parties to undertake certain actions or refrain from certain actions, in order not to aggravate the situation further and to start the path towards a peaceful settlement. With a few exceptions, the Security Council initiates peacekeeping operations.

Critics of the UN have suggested reforming the system. Some of the remedies may be to limit the Security Council's veto power; change the division of labour between the Security Council, the Secretariat and the General Assembly; diffuse the power of the Council; and invite new members. Reformers propose moving in the direction of democratization and genuine universalism.[4]

The General Assembly

This is the UN's plenary body, the main deliberative forum in which each member state has one vote. Decisions on important questions related to peace and security, admission of new members and budgetary matters require a two-thirds majority. Otherwise, a simple majority is used.

Among its tasks are issues related to international peace, disarmament, dispute settlement (if not dealt with by the Security Council) and human rights. It initiates studies, promotes international cooperation, respect for international law, human rights, elects non-permanent members of the Security Council, approves the UN budget and elects the Secretary-General.

Of particular relevance for peacekeeping is the Uniting for Peace resolution of November 1950, which provided that the General Assembly would meet to recommend collective measures in situations where the Security Council was unable to deal with a breach of peace or act of aggression. It acknowledged that the Council should be handling the more coercive of the peacekeeping and enforcement tasks but made provisions for General Assembly action when a veto led to stalemate in the Council.

Many suggest that the General Assembly should be given more of a say in matters related to peacekeeping. Conflicts should be brought before the Assembly and discussed in what could be a much broader framework than the Security Council. The Assembly could arrange hearings between the parties involved and with military and conflict-resolution experts. This would provide the Security Council with background analyses and recommendations based on better informed discussions.

The Secretary-General

The provisions for the functions of Secretary-General are the only concessions made in the Charter to supra-nationality. They state that he/she may bring any important matter to the attention of the Security Council; that the Secretary-General and the Secretariat, which today employs some 11,000 people[5], shall not seek or receive instructions from any government and that no government shall seek to influence them.

The Charter's definition of the job is extremely complex and not without tension between different roles. The Secretary-General is the very emblem of the UN and its administrative top manager. In addition, he/she is entrusted with a variety of functions by the Security Council, the General Assembly and other bodies. He/she is 'equal parts diplomat and activist, conciliator and provocateur'.[6]

Most intimately connected with the settlement of disputes is the Secretary-General's role as a mediator, conducting preventive diplomacy and

A UN election supervisor in Haiti tries to calm a potential confrontation between police and the crowd.

© *Marc French/Panos*

offering his Good Offices. In recent years, the Secretary-General, either directly or through special envoys, has been substantially involved in dispute settlement in Afghanistan, Cambodia, Central America, Cyprus, East Timor, Falkland Islands/ Malvinas, Guyana-Venezuela, the hostage crisis in Lebanon, Iran-Iraq, Iraq-Kuwait, Libya, the Middle East, the Rainbow Warrior dispute between New Zealand and France, Somalia, Western Sahara and former Yugoslavia.[7]

As with peacekeeping, the Good Offices function of the Secretary-General is not mentioned in the Charter. This role as independent mediator reached its peak around the mid-1980s. In most, if not all, of the cases mentioned his presence has had a significant impact. Indeed, his three 'I's (integrity, independence and initiative) may be needed more now – when so many conflicts are internal – than ever before.

Handling conflicts and creating peace

Peace looks so simple. Peace is when nothing happens, when the children have gone to bed, when soldiers stop shooting, when the sun has set – or somebody rests in peace. But with the media increasingly focusing on war, news about peace breaking out somewhere has stopped being news. Thus, very few citizens around the world have any insights into what a peacekeeping operation is, how it works and what it is supposed to do and not be able to do. UN peacekeeping operations appear predominantly in the popular media only when there is a failure or when there are allegations of mismanagement.

But peace must also be seen as the absence of structural violence. Around 25 million people have been killed in wars since 1945, while millions of others are killed not by bullets, but die from lack of clean water, housing, health care, education, clothes and shelter.

Viewed this way, peacekeeping is a very difficult concept. Within this definition, UN peacekeeping is not peacekeeping but various types of conflict-management, mitigation and resolution which, if successful, can help peoples and societies to create and maintain peace.

For the past 61 years, the Kowloon Motor Bus Company (1933) Limited (KMB) has formed part of the Hong Kong success story and today it remains committed to playing a vital role as the story unfolds.

Furthermore, as the economies of Hong Kong and China become more and more integrated, KMB is seeking to widen its horizons and play a part in the development of public transport in the vast hinterland.

With an operating fleet of 2,700 buses using more than 300 routes and carrying 2.65 million passengers daily, KMB is the largest public transport operator in Hong Kong. As such it is a crucial part of a modern, highly efficient and inexpensive public transport system contributing greatly to Hong Kong's social and economic development.

KMB is commercially operated under government franchise. It receives no subsidy from public funds and has to survive on its ability to sell its service to the travelling public.

That KMB has consistently been able to operate at a profit (US$45 million in 1993) is a tribute to the Hong Kong way of doing things. It is also a reward for KMB's unstinting efforts to improve its service to meet the ever-rising expectations of the travelling public. Comfort, safety, reliability, efficiency, value for money, user friendliness, environmental protection – all are aspects to which KMB's management pays continuous attention.

This commitment to continuous improvement remains central to KMB's thinking. So is its firm belief in improving the quality of community life as a natural part of successful business practice.

The UN works tirelessly to promote the principles of people - centred sustainable development. KMB fully endorses this philosophy believing that the international business community can do much to contribute to this process.

KMB firmly commits itself to playing its part.

John C. C. Chan
Managing Director

The Kowloon Motor
Bus Co. (1933) Ltd.
No. 1, Po Lun Street,
Lai Chi Kok, Kowloon,
Hong Kong.
Tel: (852) 786 8888
Fax: (852) 745 0300
Tlx: 45800 KMBHK
Cable: BUSSES

Not peacekeeping but conflict-management

Traditionally, a UN peacekeeping operation has taken place when there was 'a peace to keep' or at least a cease-fire agreement. However, peacekeeping has, more often than not, been reduced to monitoring, observing and reporting.

Between 1945 and 1985 peacekeeping, in the majority of cases, seems to have been 'cease-fire keeping'. The recent transformation of peacekeeping into much more complex operations, together with the added ingredient of military enforcement, is something for which the UN is simply not equipped.

Prevention is better than cure

The world community knows that prevention is better than cure. However, in most cases, the international community lacks agreed procedures, institutions, skilled operators and training for conducting violence-preventive diplomacy. Rather than intervening in the early days of a conflict and thus seeking out a 'bigger peace for the buck', the UN has found itself embroiled in impossible missions in the wake of catastrophe. In all cases hostilities have preceded the setting up of a peacekeeping operation with the exception of the UN command in Macedonia, a part of the UN Protection Force in former Yugoslavia (UNPROFOR). Preventive deployment – which is much closer to peacekeeping in a literal sense – is virtually non-existent.

William J. Durch, who has made an impressive comparative analysis of 20 peacekeeping operations, found that his analysis confirmed the following hypotheses:

- peacekeeping requires local consent, and consent derives from local perceptions of the impartiality and moral authority of the peacekeepers' sponsoring organization

- peacekeeping requires the support of the Great Powers and the US in particular

- peacekeeping requires a prior alteration in the local parties' basic objectives, from winning everything to salvaging something. A frequent corollary is combat exhaustion or battlefield stalemate.[8]

In these three points we also find all the contradictions of UN peacekeeping. Not all countries and constituencies subscribe to the notion of the UN's impartiality. As Durch states: 'US support has been particularly crucial for peacekeeping in the past. In 45 years of peacekeeping operations, all that have gone forward have had US support, while others that were stillborn suffered a lack of such support.'

The fact that the Security Council is the *de facto* decision-maker on peacekeeping operations undermines the UN's neutrality in the eyes of a number of member states. Between 40 and 50 clear-cut international aggressions have taken place around the world since 1945. Only a few of them have been acted upon by the UN.

"*peacekeeping requires the support of the Great Powers*"

Enforcing the peace

The more that major actors fall back on what former Secretary-General Pérez de Cuéllar calls the 'disorder and injustice of power politics', the more likely it is that local consent will not be obtained. This ought to make the UN give up the idea of peace enforcement as part of peacekeeping operations.

Some observers find that Chapter 7 is the essential element of the UN Charter. For instance, Roberts and Kingsbury maintain that 'with the end of the Cold War in the late 1980s, it (the UN) was at last in a position to act more or less as its founders had intended, taking a decisive role in many crises, including the Gulf in 1991'.

The whole spirit of the Charter, however, makes Chapter 6 the central one and Chapter 7 function only as a last resort. Article 42 is extremely clear. The Security Council may take military action if it considers that measures not involving the use of armed force up to and provided in Article 41 'would be inadequate or have proved to be inadequate'. There is a clear sequential philosophy of conflict mitigation built into the Charter, which aims to limit the UN to conflict settlement – not punishment or power politics.

Peace enforcement is a contradiction in terms. If the UN has to employ force, against one participant in a conflict, it is likely to create increased resistance. This holds true for domestic conflicts in particular. Peace enforcement is, ultimately, an expression of power politics. It should be done only in accordance with Chapter 7, while recalling that the UN Charter states that the highest aim is to save 'succeeding generations from the scourge of war' and that 'armed force shall not be used, save in the common interest'.

Secretary-General Boutros Boutros-Ghali wrote a letter to the UN Security Council on 24 July 1994[9] in which he outlined three options for UN peacekeeping in the former Yugoslavia. The letter is indicative of the turning point that the UN has arrived at on its 50th anniversary.

- **Option I** is that the UN be given enough resources and political support to enable it to carry through the new, much more compre-

hensive peacekeeping operations it has attempted in recent years. This he finds unrealistic, given the member states' policies and attitudes.

- **Option II** is to conduct these missions in close cooperation with NATO, as in the case of Bosnia. He concludes that this causes a number of problems in terms of control, coordination, contradictions – and scepticism on the part of the Russian Federation – and that it cannot be recommended as a model for the future.

- **Option III** is that the UN authorizes missions carried out by *ad hoc* groups of countries that can draw on the necessary resources and have the experience and infrastructure.

Boutros-Ghali argues that member states will provide neither the political commitment and legitimacy nor the financial resources or personnel to make the UN what it ought to be. But it is an intellectual and political cul-de-sac to recommend UN authorization of military interventions by one or a few Security Council members. Unavoidably, the world organization will become co-responsible for policies and actions – in fields and situations of extreme unpredictability – over which it will have no practical control.

The UN issued UN registration cards for the 1993 Cambodia elections.
The crowd wave their cards on polling day.

© Sean Sutton

Therefore, when peace 'enforcement' is combined with a UN peacekeeping operation, it stands a fair chance of doing more harm than good. Who among those being bombed with UN authorization are likely to listen to the advice and mediation efforts of the Secretary-General or a UN peacekeeping force commander? In short, the UN, to survive, must be seen as an organization that attempts to soften the worst consequences of the world's brutality and disorder. The UN must be careful not to become part of the power politics it is helping to remedy.

On the First Anniversary Celebration of the SBMA 24 November 1993. Chairman Gordon, who was a member of President Ramos' Official Party during the latter's U.S. State Visit, is seen following the President.

Aerial shot of the Subic Bay Freeport forest in the former Naval Magazine Area.

Fifty years ago the Philippines became one of the first members of the United Nations. After four centuries of colonial rule, we were a newly-independent nation and except for our own city of Olongapo – at that time a US Navy base – the country was struggling to come to terms with its own identity.

But in 1991 two incidents occurred that shook the Olongapo community to its core. Mount Pinatubo erupted, killing 60 people and destroying the city. It was the biggest volcanic explosion in living memory. The same year, the US Navy was asked to leave Subic Naval Base in Olongapo, a base that they had occupied for 94 years. The lives of thousands of people were affected by the closure, the economic fabric of the city was endangered.

But the people of Olongapo, under the leadership of their Mayor (now Chairman), Richard Gordon, came together in the fight to have Subic Bay established as a freeport, a vision that Gordon had conceived in 1971. They were successful and on 24 November 1992, Subic Naval Base was handed over to civilian authorities. But whilst the port infrastructure had an estimated value of US$8 billion, it had cost the US government some US$178 million a year to run. The City did not have the resources or expertise to manage such a huge project.

Once again, the people of Olongapo heroically and patriotically played their part. They worked as volunteers to protect and preserve the baselands, rebuilding the confidence of the people and enhancing the country's image abroad. Graduates and professionals from around the world joined them, recognising the potential in Subic Bay Freeport.

At Subic Bay Metropolitan Authority (SBMA) we set about the task of attracting investment to the freeport, informing potential investors of the many advantages available – our strategic location in the Pacific Rim; our world class infrastructure; the ease of entry and business start-up; special tax incentives and a well-trained English-speaking labour force.

Throughout this time we had the unremitting support and cooperation of President Ramos who saw in our achievements a model for Philippine development for the 21st century. His vision of a new Philippines gave birth to an economic agenda for the nation and called for a commitment to growth and development in a democratic system regardless of political differences, party lines and traditional vested interests.

Today, the dream is being realised. We have 16,500 new jobs and 118 new companies with approved projects. More than 80 are already in operation with a further 51 locating in the Subic Bay Industrial Park. Many multinational corporations have established centres at Subic and investments now total over US$740 million.

Tourism continues to grow and in recognition of the fact that over four million people have visited the area since its inception, Subic was recently named Destination of the Year by the Philippines Department of Tourism.

But industrial development can pay a high price in terms of ecological devastation. By a careful selection of non-polluting industries, with the enforcement of environmental laws and by protecting the forest and waters of the bay, SBMA's concern for the environment is paramount.

We at Subic Bay actively seek to work with those companies and individuals who share our vision for the future. We believe that together we can create a remarkable new city in the heart of Asia, a city that will soar and transform the Philippines into the New Eagle of Asia.

The Security Council contradiction

The Security Council members are responsible for well over 80 per cent of the world's arms exports and a somewhat smaller percentage of world military expenditures.[10] There is hardly a conflict in which one or more of them has not been among the causal factors behind the outbreak of hostilities. There is a profound contradiction between member states being, on the one hand, actors with their own political interests and, on the other, neutral third party mediators.

The human dimension

Conflicts and wars are acted out by human beings. If truth is the first victim in wars, complex understanding is the second. What type of expertise does the UN usually rely on when dealing with a conflict? It seems to be predominantly diplomats and legal and human rights experts. It goes without saying that such expertise is vital but is it also sufficient? Politicians and diplomats often reduce the complexity of situations to such a level of simplicity that they fail to do justice to the full reality.

It is indicative of the general ignorance of conflict-resolution as both a science and an art that most mediators and negotiators say they find their own experience and education sufficient when facing such delicate situations.

In addition, when a peace agreement is signed, the victims of conflict have to learn to live with 'the other side'. Family A may find that Family B is moving in again next door, knowing that their own son has fought against the nation of B and was killed in the process. If a true peace is to survive it would be naive to believe that ordinary citizens can manage without community builders, social workers and psychologists. If we do not include the human dimension in the planning of peacekeeping, peace-making and peacebuilding, we are likely to see the traumas acted out at a later point.

Wars are fought according to political principles and a knowledge of tactics and strategy accumulated over centuries. The most sophisticated of all technology is applied in warmaking. At least one-third of all the world's research and development is devoted to military affairs.

Nothing comparable exists in the struggle for conflict-resolution and peace. For example, there are fewer than 2,000 academically trained peace and conflict researchers worldwide. After 50 years, the international community is still trying to come to grips with such self-evident elements as early warning and comprehensive conflict analyses. The Secretary-General's *Agenda for Peace* is presented as innovative for its integrated approach towards conflict-prevention and peacebuilding.

It is tacitly assumed in current peacekeeping operations that a linear sequence of measures is used. First come preventive measures, then if war breaks out the UN turns its hand to peacekeeping, peace-making and, finally, peacebuilding. The result of this approach is that if one of the steps turns out to be less than successful, the next will not take place. In fact, the three elements should work side by side. Peacebuilding can take place in the local community long before there is a signed agreement between national leaders. Indeed, serious local peacemaking efforts – 'peace from the ground up' – can serve as an important stimulus for peacemaking at higher levels.[11]

"*peace from the ground up*"

Looking to the future

The weakness of the UN is a reflection of both the structures of the international system and of the individual UN member states. Since the mid-1980s member states have requested services from the UN to an extent which is totally out of proportion to what they are willing to contribute, and is more or less systematically undermined by the actions of some of the members themselves – particularly the five permanent Security Council members. Consequently the UN has failed, more or less, to stick to its mandate. As a consequence, there is a growing clamour for the UN to be given more 'teeth'. However, the solution may lie elsewhere.

First, what is needed is a serious commitment of member states to the principle of the UN Charter and a willingness to contribute the necessary financial resources, the qualified soldiers, officers, police and civil affairs and other staff.

In the words of the first UN Secretary-General, Trygve Lie, in 1946: 'The UN is no stronger than the collective will of the nations that support it. Of itself it can do nothing. It is a machinery through which the nations can cooperate. It can be used and developed ... or it can be discarded and broken.'

If the 185 member states would each make available, on average, 1,200 peacekeeping-trained blue helmets on a standby basis, there would be 221,000 blue helmets worldwide; 46,000 civil police would be available to the UN if each member state made available 250. If each member state would contribute only 600 civilians trained in all kinds of peacebuilding activities and local conflict-resolution, the UN would have at its disposal around 110,000 qualified peacebuilders. If all relevant non-governmental organizations (NGOs) worldwide trained their own people for such tasks – doctors, human rights monitors, peace activists, journalists, psychologists, engineers, social workers, peace researchers, economists and community developers – many thousands more could be added.

UN peacekeepers guarding the airport in Somalia's capital, Mogadishu.

© Crispin Hughes/Panos

For more than 20 years Xenel Industries has had the privilege and honour of being at the forefront of private sector involvement in the development of industries and infrastructure in Saudi Arabia. In determining and meeting the needs of government ministries, agencies and the private sector, Xenel has formed commercial and technical alliances with leading international companies and organizations whose long-term commitment to Saudi Arabia has provided contributions of lasting benefit to the community and to the Kingdom.

In 1995 the company had the pride and satisfaction of seeing its greatest international coalition come to fruition in the form of the financial closure of the Hub River Power Plant Project in Pakistan. At a value of US$1.7 billion the project, a 1,292 MW oil-fired power plant set up under the build-own-operate concept, is being financed on a limited recourse basis and is one of the largest private power plants under construction in South Asia. On its completion, it will supply 13% of Pakistan's electricity capacity and, in addition to paving the way for the realization of future private investments, will be a major component in facilitating the country's economic development.

An undertaking of this unique nature, magnitude and awesome complexity required the wholehearted cooperation, support and encouragement of innumerable individuals, organizations, institutions and governments that span the entire globe and that have drawn upon the talents of most of the known disciplines and professions. The Hub experience, therefore, represents the combined supreme effort of people of almost every race, creed and religion - a United Nations in microcosm - and has provided a further means of fostering greater understanding between them.

As a member of the international business community, Xenel Industries salutes the United Nations on its 50th Anniversary as it strives to achieve higher standards of sustainable development and peace throughout the world, and is honoured to pay tribute and join in the commemoration.

Mohamed A. Alireza
Chairman of the Board of Directors

Ⅹ XENEL INDUSTRIES LTD

Xenel Industries Limited
P.O. Box 2824 Jeddah 21461, Kingdom of Saudi Arabia.
TEL: (02) 643 7619   **FAX:** (02) 643 8405

The resources needed for these contributions are small compared to the benefits they would make for the common good. They would cost only a fraction of the present 'warkeeping' expenditures. In the long run, these preventive measures would benefit the entire international community. They could reduce the growth in refugees and displaced people, spare cities from meaningless destruction and prevent potential economic growth from being retarded.

The second solution lies in reducing the arms trade. Thirdly, it lies in much better coordination of UN-related actors. Fourth, the solution lies in a more comprehensive philosophy and understanding about conflicts. The UN needs a strategy for functionally integrated peacekeeping, peacemaking and peacebuilding that takes into account the human dimension and the building of peace not only from the top down but also from local leaders and communities upwards. Also, the UN must make systematic use of the accumulated experiences, evaluations and proposals of the thousands who have served in peacekeeping missions.

The solution also might lie in closer collaboration between the UN and NGOs working as 'white helmets' in all phases – conflict analysts, psychologists, social workers, human rights experts, community developers, economists, peace activists in general and women in particular – in short, all those who can do what the UN needs to do better or cannot do alone.

The UN is trapped in the structural contradictions of the international system. It cannot maintain impartiality – which is essential when trying to mediate. If government structures cannot be changed that quickly, the escape route may have to be the community of networks, NGOs, grassroots movements and individual expertise which are the seeds of an emerging transnational culture. Such a civilian capability for preventive diplomacy and peacebuilding is under way in the UN Volunteers programme (UNV) in cooperation with the UN Development Programme (UNDP), the UN Department of Humanitarian Affairs (DHA) and other bodies.

The solution lies in reviewing the role of violence in human affairs. Violence is what we fall back on when nothing else works. Violence, unfortunately, is equated with statesmanship and leadership with power. However, in reality, violence is all too often a consequence of frustration, lack of foresight and powerlessness. The UN Charter is truly visionary in that it does emphasize a non-violent handling of conflicts.

The UN is not – and should not be – a military organization. It is not equipped for that. The UN is a world organization devoted, first and foremost, to settling disputes with a minimum of violence. If governments and politicians change their thinking and look to the common global good, they will discover that the Charter is a document of great potential.

> **"*the solution lies in reviewing the role of violence in human affairs*"**

The UN's humanitarian efforts extend in crises to the protection of countless people driven from their homes by war.

© Jasper Young/Panos

Endnotes

1   Figures from the UN Department of Public Information, May and July 1994.

2   UN Development Programme (UNDP), *Human Development Report 1994*, Oxford University Press 1994, pp.47-48.

3   See *United Nations: Divided World*, Adam Roberts and Benedict Kingsbury, Clarendon Press, London 1993.

4   Some suggestions are presented in *A United Nations of the Future – What 'We the Peoples' and Governments Can Do to Help the UN Help Ourselves*, The Transnational Foundation for Peace and Future Research (TFF), Lund 1991.

5   UN document A/49/527, *Human Resources Management: composition of the Secretariat.*

6   The expression is borrowed from *Basic Facts about the United Nations*, Department of Public Information, New York 1992.

7   For an excellent analysis of these cases, see Javier Pérez de Cuéllar, *The Role of the UN Secretary-General*, and Thomas M. Franck and Georg Nolte, *The Good Offices Function of the UN Secretary-General*, both in Roberts and Kingsbury, op. cit., pp.125-183.

8   William J. Durch, *The Evolution of UN Peacekeeping: Case Studies and Comparative Analysis*, MacMillan, London 1993.

9   Boutros Boutros-Ghali, UN document of 24 July 1994. The letter states that the UN ought to pull out of former Yugoslavia whether or not the parties accept the so-called Contact Group's 'peace plan'. His letter appeared the same week as the Bosnian Serbs were to decide on the Plan which, paradoxically enough, argues for a major role of the UN in protecting and administering Sarajevo, various corridors and towns.

10   See UNDP *Human Development Report 1994*, op. cit., p.55.

11   For an analysis of such possibilities in the case of Croatia, see Kerstin Schultz (1994) *Building Peace from the Ground Up – About People and the UN in a War Zone in Croatia*, The Transnational Foundation, Vegagatan 25, Lund, Sweden.

This is an abridged and edited version of *The UN and the Keeping of the Peace. A Conflict-Resolution Perspective* (1995), The Transnational Foundation for Peace and Future Research, Lund, Sweden.

The destructive power unleashed by the atomic bomb, and later the hydrogen bomb, led to calls in the UN for the outlawing of weapons of mass destruction.
A mushroom cloud forms over a small, uninhabited island in the Pacific after the explosion of an experimental atomic bomb.

Disarmament ~ *making peace*

- Global arms control
- Nuclear-free zones
- New technologies
- Emerging conflicts

© *Sygma*

*I*n the shadow of the Second World War, the Allied nations in the newly-formed United Nations set themselves one major goal: to end the scourge of war. With this ambitious end in mind, arms control was given top billing. The first resolution of the 1946 General Assembly called for the setting up of a UN Arms Control and Disarmament Commission.

At the outset, the UN drew a line between weapons of mass destruction which it wanted to outlaw and conventional weapons which it sought to control. The memory of Hiroshima and Nagasaki was fresh in the minds of the Allied powers, while the experience of Hitler's march to power and the massive conventional forces needed to defeat the belligerent dictator caused the UN to set its sights on attaining a balance of conventional armed forces. To clarify this distinction the UN divided the Arms Control and Disarmament Commission into two sections: the UN Atomic Energy Commission and the Commission for Conventional Weapons.

This trend was broken, however, by two factors: the onset of the Cold War and the explosion of the first hydrogen bomb. The underground test at Eniwetok Atoll, a US-controlled island in the Pacific, dug a crater 60 metres deep and two kilometres long where the island of Engulab had once been. The explosion – the equivalent of 14 million tons of TNT explosives – left the atom bomb far behind and raised the tempo of demands in the UN for total disarmament.[1]

By 1959, the General Assembly – with its growing non-aligned membership – had staked out its new position with a sweeping resolution calling for

RAILWAYS AND DEVELOPMENT

Railways are a key factor in the economic development of a country providing an environmentally - friendly method of transport as well as a safe and economical way of travelling.

George E. Petsos
President, Hellenic
Railways Organization

With over 12,000 employees and with a network of 2,500 kilometres, Hellenic Railways carries nearly 12 million passengers a year. And through the help of the Cohesion Fund, the European Community's Support Frame, together with public funding, the Organization is modernizing, increasing and upgrading its service.

We are concentrating our efforts on operational efficiency in order to make ourselves competitive, not just in Greece, but also on the European continent. The recent turbulence in the region has underlined the urgent need for an alternative rail route between Greece and Italy through the port of Igoumenitsa, to bring Greece out of isolation at the end of the Balkan Peninsula.

Hellenic Railways is pleased to be able to contribute to the country's integrated transport system. As we step into the 21st century, our aim is to provide a modern and efficient railway system to enable our passengers to travel further, faster and in more comfort.

Hellenic Railways Organization
1-3 Karolou, Athens 104 37
Tel. 5240646-8, 5241710; fax 5242119

'General and Complete Disarmament'. The new goal was a global ban on weapons of mass destruction and the cutting back of conventional forces to levels sufficient for internal policing and rotation in UN forces. The campaign for disarmament became one of the UN's major preoccupations.

Treaties galore

Ironically, however, the UN's new tone was also an expression of its impotence in the face of the Cold War deadlock that had emerged between the two superpower camps. During the succeeding decades, the UN's burgeoning Third World membership used the UN as a forum for expressing growing anger at the superpowers' nuclear hold, while the superpowers themselves used it as an arena for scoring propaganda points. But the UN General Assembly did manage to push through a number of nuclear treaties designed to temper the superpowers' flourishing nuclear weapons programmes. These carried varying degrees of weight. All the treaties dealt with nuclear testing and nuclear-free zones and were useful to the extent that they put certain areas off-limits for nuclear activity. However, many of these forbidden zones were not of great importance to nuclear states. The first such treaty, the 1959 Antarctica Treaty, kept the vast wastelands of Antarctica free of military weapons. Four years later, the 1963 Limited Test Ban Treaty prohibited the testing of nuclear weapons in the atmosphere, in outer space and under water. The treaty merely succeeded in pushing nuclear testing – literally – underground.

The 1967 Outer Space Treaty prohibited the placing of weapons of mass destruction in outer space or on 'celestial bodies'. A more down-to-earth treaty was the 1972 Seabed Arms Control Treaty. It banned countries from putting nuclear weapons on the ocean floor more than 12 nautical miles (23 kilometres) from the coastline. The same year, 21 Latin American states signed the Treaty of Tlatelolco, which, in theory, transformed Latin America into the world's first nuclear weapons-free continent. When Brazil and Argentina renounced their nuclear

ambitions at the end of the Cold War, the treaty could finally be fully implemented.

The UN's most notable success was the Nuclear Non-Proliferation Treaty (NPT). Although the most substantial of the UN's nuclear treaties, it has predictably proved to be the most controversial. Approved in 1968, the NPT sanctions the possession of nuclear weapons in five countries – the Soviet Union, the US, the UK, France and China – and bans non-nuclear states from going nuclear. Instead, in what has been dubbed the 'nuclear bargain', the NPT promises non-nuclear states total freedom to develop and use nuclear energy for peaceful ends. The bargain has been especially contentious among Third World leaders who resent the perceived injustice of a treaty that endorses nuclear weapons among the world's most powerful nations, while outlawing them in the developing world.

Yet, since the treaty came into effect in 1970, the majority of the world's nations have signed up – either as a result of international pressure or trading off the disavowal of nuclear weapons for the wherewithal to develop peaceful nuclear industries. Only a handful of countries have refused to join. More damagingly, signatory countries have also been accused of pursuing clandestine nuclear weapons programmes in violation of their treaty commitments. Critics blame the consensus ethic of the treaty that has prevented the International Atomic Energy Agency (IAEA), the international body that acts as the inspectorate for the NPT, from flexing its muscles. Though IAEA has the power to demand inspections of suspect sites, it has in the past only investigated sites with advance approval by the inspected country. Yet, despite these evident drawbacks, there is a broad consensus that the treaty has been a useful instrument in establishing a norm of nuclear non-proliferation and lessening fears that runaway proliferation is unavoidable. Popular predictions in the late 1950s estimated that the following three decades would see the emergence of 25-30 nuclear powers. Instead, the number of nuclear powers is believed to be about a third of that.

" *broad consensus* "

The drive for complete disarmament

To illustrate its commitment to disarmament, the UN General Assembly declared the 1970s the First Disarmament Decade. When this had little effect – with the one exception of the landmark Biological Weapons Convention in 1972 – the 1980s became the Second Disarmament Decade. The UN-convened First Special Session on Disarmament in 1978 produced a final document, informally dubbed the UN's 'bible on disarmament', which laid the foundations for the UN's disarmament agenda and set up a number of institutions that some defence analysts argue could now be usefully resuscitated. Within the context of the Cold War, however, the UN's attempts at stealing the march on disarmament negotiations were doomed to failure. Despite back-up from a New York-based Disarmament Affairs Department and a Geneva-based UN Institute for Disarmament Research, the Conference on Disarmament, the 40-nation negotiating group set up by the 1978 Session, was too weak to come up with a single multilateral disarmament agreement until 1992 when it concluded negotiations on the Chemical Weapons Convention.

Bilateral is best

The loudly-proclaimed goal of complete disarmament – however unattainable – thus made a welcome diversion from the paralysis that dogged the UN during the Cold War. But it did have one benefit. By keeping the issue of disarmament – and, in particular, nuclear disarmament – at the forefront of the political and military agenda, it made it extremely awkward for the nuclear powers to abandon their search for arms control.

This search did finally yield some results. Bilateral talks between the US and the USSR culminated in a handful of nuclear-limitation treaties in the 1970s, including the Strategic Arms Limitation Treaty (SALT) in 1972 – although this treaty was aimed at freezing strategic arms rather than cutting them. It was not until Communism began to collapse at the end of the 1980s that the superpowers lost faith in the sacred canons of nuclear deterrence. The nuclear détente, when it eventually came, showed just how ineffective the UN had been in eradicating the nuclear threat. It took Soviet leader Mikhail Gorbachev's glasnost and the disintegration of the Communist empire to gradually dispel the distrust that had divided the two superpowers.

The decisive moment in reversing the Cold War's nuclear momentum came with Gorbachev's 1986

USSR President Mikhail Gorbachev and US President George Bush marked the end of the Cold War when they signed START, the first treaty in four decades to substantially cut nuclear weapons.

© Rex Features, London

agenda for nuclear disarmament. Though his argument for radical disarmament was dismissed as over-ambitious at the time, it injected the necessary boost into negotiations on strategic arms reductions. A year later, US President George Bush and Gorbachev started rolling back the shadows of the Cold War nuclear arsenal with a treaty eliminating all intermediate-range weapons.

In July 1991, the superpower leaders signed the Strategic Arms Reduction Treaty (START I) in Moscow. The treaty – which had taken just under

THE ZIMBABWE IRON AND STEEL COMPANY LIMITED

The Zimbabwe Iron and Steel Company Limited (Ziscosteel), established some 53 years ago, is the biggest integrated steel works north of the Limpopo and Zimbabwe's sole producer of steel for both domestic and export markets.

Based in Redcliff and with over 3,200 employees, Zisco plays a crucial role in Zimbabwe's economic development. The company has also forged permanent relations with countries in the Preferential Trade Area (PTA), providing aid for foundries and smaller steel works within the sub-region. With the assistance of UNIDO through its training programmes and financial contributions, Zisco's modernization programme is being implemented and is already showing results.

Whilst the company has, in the past, concentrated on Eastern and Central Africa and Asian and Far East markets, Zisco is looking forward to developing much stronger ties with the steel and iron industries within Southern African Development Co-ordination Conference (SADCC) and PTA countries.

We at Zisco believe that the winds of change, which have had an effect on so many parts of the globe, will yield further benefits and hopefully lead to a strengthening of the world body.

We wish to express our thanks and appreciation to the United Nations and its agencies for their achievements on behalf of the nations of the world over the past 50 years.

Dr. G.G. Masanga
Acting Chief Executive

THE ZIMBABWE IRON AND STEEL COMPANY LIMITED
Private Bag 2,
REDCLIFF, ZIMBABWE
Tel: 263 55 62425 Telex: ZW 70038 Telegram: ZISCOSTEEL

a decade to negotiate – marked the first time in over four decades that the world's nuclear weapons stockpile was to be substantially cut back in size. Under its terms, both superpowers agreed to limit themselves to 6,000 nuclear warheads and equalize their forces at 4,900 ballistic missile warheads. These reductions, however, were to a large extent symbolic. The remaining warheads could still unleash a nuclear Armageddon if deployed. Instead, START I was important as a gesture of newly-won trust that laid the necessary groundwork for halting the superpower nuclear arms race.

The reduction was speeded up by the abortive August 1991 coup in Moscow. The coup, which triggered the disintegration of the Soviet Union and quadrupled the number of former USSR countries with nuclear weapons on their soil, spurred fears in Washington that the collapse of central Communist command could leave nuclear weapons in the hands of unstable, and potentially hostile, regimes. Further talks finally culminated in START II. Signed in January 1993, START II calls for the halving of the number of nuclear warheads by 2003 and the elimination of all land-based missiles with multiple warheads. By any measure it was a remarkable agreement. Even the most sceptical observer was forced to admit that it signalled the end of the superpower nuclear arms race – for the foreseeable future. But problems remain. Even after these dramatic cutbacks, the number of warheads in the former foes' nuclear arsenals has merely been reduced to the levels of the early 1970s, when strategic arms talks first began in earnest. On top of this, the majority of the deactivated warheads have been dismantled rather than destroyed, prompting concerns that they could easily be reassembled, as well as fears that the resulting glut of fissile material could fall into hostile hands.

However, while the nuclear détente has virtually eliminated the threat of a superpower nuclear war, the post-Cold War era has swapped one nuclear threat for another. Although officially the 'nuclear club' still includes only the five permanent members of the UN Security Council, at least five other states are suspected of standing on the nuclear threshold, if they have not already crossed it. The threat of a nuclear war has now shifted to the developing world where there are fears that nuclear weapons could be used in a regional nuclear war or even a domestic political upheaval.

© Jasper Young/Panos

Children are the defenceless victims of modern warfare.
A young child is brought in for emergency treatment after a military raid.

The UN's answer and dilemmas

Since the end of the Cold War, the UN has stepped up its activity in the area of nuclear non-proliferation. The extension of the NPT has become the focus of its activity.[2] In his 1992 New Dimensions of Arms Regulation and Disarmament in the Post-Cold War World – or 'Agenda for Disarmament' – the UN Secretary-General, Boutros Boutros-Ghali, singled out the indefinite and unconditional extension of the NPT as a crucial step towards building a nuclear containment strategy. Its supporters argue that whatever the treaty's shortcomings it is the only nuclear-control regime in place.

Nuclear testing is another area where the UN has been flexing its muscles. In 1994, the Conference on Disarmament began formal negotiations on a Comprehensive Test Ban Treaty to replace the current Limited Test Ban Treaty. Support for the Comprehensive Test Ban Treaty is strong in the United States and Russia. In 1991-92, both countries announced moratoriums on nuclear testing until the mid-1990s. The UN has also been working hard on the chemical and biological weapons front. In 1993, the UN Conference on Disarmament in Geneva negotiated an international ban on production and stockpiling of chemical weapons. It has so far been ratified by 19 countries but requires ratification by 65 countries before it can go into effect. The Chemical Weapons Convention was modelled on the 1972 UN Biological Weapons Convention, which imposed a blanket ban on biological weapons. The Gulf War's exposure of preparations to use biological weapons was, however, evidence that the Biological Weapons Convention was not infallible. It has prompted demands that the Convention's verification measures be strengthened at the Fourth Biological Weapons Convention Review Conference in 1996.

Another thorny issue that the UN looks likely to have to grapple with is a ban on the production of weapons-grade plutonium and uranium. The end of the Cold War has left a glut of fissile materials removed from nuclear warheads and has removed the rationale for the endless recycling of plutonium. The 1970s dream of nuclear power as the energy source of the future has evaporated, and the bottom has fallen out of the uranium and plutonium market.

High military spenders in the developing world receive two-and-a-half times as much aid as other developing countries.

© *Kevin Weaver/Rex Features, London*

According to a study by the US-based Rand Corporation, by the year 2003 there will be enough weapons-grade plutonium to produce 87,000 nuclear weapons. But while the US has proposed an international convention banning the production of fissile materials for weapons purposes, the issue is pitting Washington against France, the UK and Japan, who fear a ban on fissile material could put at risk their huge investments in domestic plutonium. The UN Conference on Disarmament has recently established an *ad hoc* Committee on Fissile Materials to keep the pressure on governments.

Non-nuclear conflict

While the thawing of the Cold War and the resulting reversal in nuclear escalation have enabled Moscow and Washington to make drastic cutbacks in their weapons of mass destruction, it has opened a Pandora's box of potential conflicts as the old ideological allegiances have broken down. But fears that a rash of conflicts would spread across the globe have so far proved overly pessimistic. However, where the break-up of the Cold War status quo has resulted in conflict, the UN's attempts at containment have been hamstrung by its contradictory roles as both negotiator and peace enforcer.

At the same time, the end of the Cold War has precipitated a major slump in the world arms market. Ironically, however, this collapse – world arms exports in 1994 were half the 1984 total – could work against efforts to regulate the arms trade. It has left supplier countries jostling for a corner of the dwindling market and in no mood to talk about regulating the arms industry.

In contrast to its dynamic efforts to curtail the spread of weapons of mass destruction, the UN has so far been reluctant to set limits on the scale of conventional arms – the tinder of many of the world's conflicts. In this case its ability to act has been severely hampered by a mandate that enshrines self-defence as a fundamental right of states, and by the vested interest of supplier countries that see their arms industries as a vital cog in their economic wheel.

*H*ope for the future
lies in a balanced global development
based on the welfare of human beings.

*T*he Greek Power Corporation (PPC), established in 1950, has provided the country
with an extensive power network, thus contributing substantially to its development.
As a public utility responsible for the production, transport and distribution of
electricity, PPC is directly influenced by the course of international events in
an increasingly globalised economic and technological environment. The
very nature of its role and mission requires a commitment to a future based
on a balanced global development for the benefit of the people.
PPC believes that the United Nations, as an organization at the "centre" of
international events, is a forum where sovereign nations can work
together to find solutions to disputes and problems, promoting
sustainable, economic and social development.

Public Power Corporation of Greece

Department of Communication

The technology leap

The UN has also remained paralysed in the face of the global military spin-off of the technological boom. In South Africa, it was, ironically, a UN arms embargo on the apartheid regime that spurred the technologically-advanced country into working overtime to develop its own indigenous arms industry. Now the embargo has been lifted, South Africa could join the ever-growing list of supplier countries.

Southeast Asia has raced ahead in developing locally-produced arms. With some of the world's most dynamic economies, and huge spending on technology, Southeast Asian countries are increasingly able to maintain a modern defence industry. At the same time, Southeast Asia's arms imports are falling off. According to the Stockholm International Peace Research Institute, total imports of major arms by Asian nations in 1993 were $4,646 million, compared with $6,900 million in 1988. Despite the declining arms imports, the pace of the region's rising domestic defence spending has prompted fears that a slow-motion arms race is under way.

The newly established Regional Forum of the Association of South East Asian Nations (ASEAN), is the region's first attempt at a comprehensive regional security structure. But delegates at its first meeting in 1994 quickly became involved in a tug-of-war over the mineral and oil rich Spratly Islands in the South China Sea. In contrast, Europe has made some headway in securing a regional security framework under the umbrella of the North Atlantic Treaty Organization (NATO). Using confidence-building measures as the foundations of an arms reduction strategy, NATO and the former Warsaw Pact countries signed the Treaty on Conventional Armed Forces in Europe in 1990. This treaty, which sets limits on five major categories of 'large-scale offensive attack' conventional weapons, has ushered in a new era of military transparency in the region and has been touted as a model for a global arms trade control agreement. A second, complementary treaty, the Open Skies Treaty, which allows for observation flights over the territory of other signatory countries, has yet to go into effect.

Another initiative, the US-inspired Partnerships for Peace, has also helped broaden the security cordon in Europe. By bringing Eastern bloc countries into a closer arrangement with NATO, without yet giving them fully-fledged NATO membership, it has helped to alleviate their sense of isolation. But hopes that Partnerships for Peace would allay Russia's fears of a NATO alliance stretching to its borders proved short-lived, with Russia last year expressing anger at its perceived 'neo-isolation'.

Not only has Partnerships for Peace failed to 'square the circle' – in the words of US Ambassador to the UN Madeleine Albright – but it has also come under fire from peace lobbyists who claim that it has spawned a potentially dangerous by-product. The Cascade Programme, set up in tandem with the Partnerships for Peace initiative, enables NATO signatories, in the interests of 'inter-operability', to transfer to their new Eastern bloc partners military stock which exceeds their limit under the Treaty on Conventional Armed Forces in Europe. Peace lobbyists and defence analysts claim the off-loading of extra military stock could have a destabilizing effect in a region already fraught with tensions.

The transfer of military stock under the Cascade Programme is a reminder of the temptation of arms sales to countries that are watching their once-guaranteed arms markets dry up. Hopes were high among peace lobbyists after the Gulf War that arms exporting nations had learned a painful lesson. The five permanent members of the UN Security Council held their first-ever arms control meetings in 1991 and 1992 at which it was hoped they would agree on new restrictions on transfers of conventional weapons or, at the very least, a code of conduct. There were also discussions on making the Middle East a permanently nuclear-free zone. However, these talks appear to have lost momentum. Indeed, far from shrinking, arms exports to the region have been stepped up since the Gulf War.[3]

" *a slow-motion arms race* "

Under-powered arms controls

With countries unwilling to renounce their arms exports, there has been growing support for greater openness on the transfer of weapons. In the aftermath of the Gulf War, the UN resurrected an earlier plan for a UN Register on Arms Control. Put to the vote in 1991, 150 countries voted in favour and three abstained.

The register became operational in 1993, with some 80 states voluntarily providing data on the import and export of weapons in the preceding year. While the level of detail is left to the discretion of each country, the data can be cross-checked to build up an overall picture. The register is thus widely regarded as a promising first step towards transparency in the arms trade. But transparency and restraint are two different things. Among the major criticisms of the scheme are the fact that there are no punishments in place for non-compliance; the register covers only large-scale weapons and not small arms; it totally ignores the 'black market' in arms, and it does not look at home production, thus obscuring the huge military arsenals of the major arms producers.[4]

A further threat is the unchecked spread of missiles, particularly through dual-use equipment or technology that can be used to build up an indigenous missile production base. The biggest worry is that missiles can be loaded with nuclear, chemical or biological warheads. As a result, there are moves afoot to strengthen the Missile Technology Control Regime. The membership has already been expanded to 25 states and the Missile Technology Control Regime has adopted more stringent guidelines for exporting equipment and technology. But it remains an informal regime with guidelines self-imposed by member states and no system for punishing transgressors.

"*greater openness*"

The UN estimates there are 100 million mines in conflict zones around the world.
A mine awareness class in Mozambique.

© Liba Taylor/Panos

THE ROYAL COMMISSION FOR JUBAIL AND YANBU

In this year of important commemorations, Saudi Arabia is celebrating one of its own — the 20th anniversary of the founding of the Royal Commission of Jubail and Yanbu. Established in 1975, the Royal Commission was charged with developing, from scratch, two new industrial cities on opposite sides of the Kingdom — Jubail on the Gulf and Yanbu on the Red Sea. The new cities were envisioned as cornerstones of a diversified national economy and centres for human development and investment.

Today, Jubail and Yanbu are home to over 140 industrial facilities. Another 90 plants are in various stages of planning or construction. Together, the cities' industries can transport each year some 250 million tons of crude oil, refined petroleum, bulk petrochemicals, fertilizers, steel, and other products — plus a wide range of consumer goods — to domestic and export markets. Petrochemicals produced at Jubail and Yanbu account for five per cent of the world supply.

Jubail and Yanbu were also built for people, as their combined and growing population of over 100,000 attests. People are drawn to the communities by their attractive housing, modern public facilities, and abundant parks and landscaping. Numerous recreational facilities complement the cities' waterfront locations and offer plenty of possibilities for leisure.

Job and business opportunities also abound, thanks to the solid foundation of industries and infrastructure already in place and growing. Most of the main industries at Jubail and Yanbu are joint ventures between Saudi

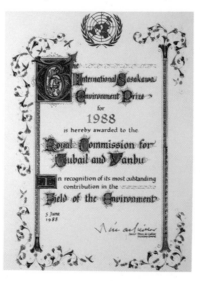

UNEP's Sasakawa Prize

firms and leading refining and petrochemical companies from Europe, America, and the Far East. Saudi Arabia encourages both large and small joint ventures with attractive investment incentives.

While promoting industrial productivity at Jubail and Yanbu, the Royal Commission is determined that the cities will also be models of environmental planning. From the beginning, it set high standards for pollution prevention and control. In 1988, the Royal Commission was honoured with the United Nations Environment Programme's Sasakawa Prize, the highest international environmental award, in recognition of its environmental policies and programmes.

Each in its own way, the Royal Commission and the United Nations are pursuing the goals of infrastructure development, economic growth, human enrichment, and environmental enhancement. We congratulate the United Nations on having achieved so much during its first five decades and wish it even greater success in making the world a better and more peaceful place to live.

Royal Commission for Jubail and Yanbu
P.O. Box 5964, Riyadh 11432, Saudi Arabia

Prospects for the future

The Cold War threat of a nuclear Apocalypse has given way to a cluster of smaller security threats. The superpowers' policy of arming client regimes resulted in proxy wars as far apart as Afghanistan and Angola, but at least had the advantage of providing a crude balance of power. Now the breakdown of the Cold War's ideological stand-off has left the world in a state of flux with the US, the sole superpower, no longer defending rigid 'principles'.

In this context, the traditional goals of arms control have become outdated. Instead, the UN has to become alert to the emerging threats of the post-Cold War era and shape its arms control agenda accordingly. One of the major threats derives from the unchecked diffusion of technology that is enabling countries to build up their own high-tech defence industries. On top of this, the spread of technology has been a major influence in the proliferation of nuclear states. At the same time, the controls on the world's stockpiles of nuclear warheads, fissile material and conventional weapons have slackened. The former Soviet bloc is the most glaring example of this. The winding down of the Communist armies has increased the threat of the spread of missile launching capabilities, seepage from stockpiles of nuclear warheads and fissile materials, and the proliferation of cheap conventional weapons on the market.

For many in the developing world, the proliferation of cheap arms has brought the security threat closer to home. Of the 82 armed conflicts between 1989 and 1992, only three were between states – the rest took place within the borders of states. The kindling of these wars is for the most part, however, not the tanks and heavy artillery of tracked arms shipments but the unregulated supply of small arms being hawked around the world. The ubiquitous AK47, better known by its nickname 'Kalashnikov', can be picked up for next to nothing in the world's arms bazaars. Around the developing world, these arms are being used by undemocratic regimes against their own people or by insurgent groups who have abandoned the democratic process and taken up arms.

The UN's juggling act

The break-up of the solid ice of the Cold War into dangerously drifting ice-floes has made the UN's job far harder. It is now being asked to deal with ethnic violence and rogue nationalism; develop the art of peace-keeping; turn its hand to becoming an on-the-ground arbitrator in conflicts, and contain the proliferation of both nuclear and conventional weapons. Weighed down with demands, the pillars on which the UN rested during the Cold War – the preservation of existing sovereignty and the right to self-defence – appear to be buckling. The creation of the Kurdish 'safe haven' in northern Iraq in the aftermath of the Gulf War, for instance, was the UN's first departure from its rigid defence of a country's sovereignty.[5]

The peacekeeping activities of the UN have forced governments to rethink some basic assumptions. Governments are increasingly having to face up to the thorny question of whether concerns other than the preservation of borders – in particular, the defence of basic human rights – can legitimize the use of force. This has thrown up a tricky contradiction: even as states are questioning the inviolability of sovereignty they continue to invoke it in defence of the arms industry. Fundamentally, the UN remains dogged by the dollar signs that pop into the eyes of the world's arms suppliers at the mention of the arms trade. Despite this, the UN does have a role to play. On the nuclear front, an indefinite extension of the NPT could be the bedrock of a strategy of containment. IAEA could also be strengthened to make full use of its right to carry out 'suspect site' special inspections and to help nuclear suppliers in the agency share intelligence.

"*the post-Cold War era*"

But the UN and IAEA both have their hands tied as multilateral bodies with competing interests and claims. The UN, while happy to deal with the less controversial issue of weapons of mass destruction, is less able to mobilize states in curbing conventional weapons transfers. The UN Register on Arms Control will help create a less suspicious atmosphere, but it lacks the teeth to contain arms flows and completely fails to address proliferation among producers. The UN's disarmament institutions have also been criticized for being under-funded, under-staffed and, in some cases, duplicating each other's work. Some private analysts' suggestions for reform have included increasing the financial contribution to the Centre for Disarmament Affairs in recognition of the key role it could play in circulating information, and combining the Conference on Disarmament in Geneva with the UN Disarmament Commission into one dynamic negotiating and agenda-setting body.[6] There is also a groundswell of opinion, from both within and outside the UN, in favour of broadening the scope of the UN's disarmament institutions to work towards global security – rather than limit their work to isolated disarmament agreements. Defence analysts see a future disarmament strategy as twin-track. The UN would work as monitor, manager and enforcer of a number of global arms agreements, while regional security structures would create the stability needed to build up a network of regional arms control agreements.

“*to work towards global security*”

The daily cost of Operation Desert Storm was about US$1 billion.
Two French Gazelle aircraft fly low over the desert during the Gulf War.

© ECPA

Under its Charter, the UN has led the quest for disarmament and deployed forces to keep the peace 'to save succeeding generations from the scourge of war'.

Balancing the equation

However, supply-side control is only one side of the equation. During the Cold War, aid was often used as a way of strengthening strategic alliances and consequently went hand-in-hand with military transfers. Until 1986, bilateral donors on average gave five times as much aid per capita to high military spenders than to low military spenders. In 1992 this figure had dropped, but high military spenders were still receiving two-and-a-half times as much aid. Broken down by individual countries, these sums appear even more stark.

This runaway military spending – often at the cost of social spending – has had horrendous consequences in the developing world. It is no coincidence that the highest military spenders in relation to their Gross National Product (GNP), in Africa for instance, are now seeing violent upheavals within their borders. The link has prompted growing pressure on arms exporting nations to stop using aid to curry favour with arms clients and to explore the relationship between development and disarmament. One approach that is increasingly being mooted would be to link defence spending to aid in the same way as donor countries tie aid to human rights and – in the 1990s buzzword – 'good governance'.

In the long run, the spread of weapons – conventional and otherwise – will be dictated by demand. Supplier countries are unlikely to adopt stringent rules on exports and, even if they do, determined arms dealers, whether governments or black marketeers, can always find a way to side-step them. While arms control regimes are a necessary factor in helping to slow the stream of arms, it is only when the world starts addressing the causes of conflict that it has any chance of diminishing the scourge of war.

Endnotes

1   The force of the first atomic bomb test, Trinity, that took place in the New Mexico desert in July 1945, was the equivalent of 19,300 tons of TNT chemical explosive. See *Nuclear Explosions and Earthquakes: The Parted Veil.* Bruce A. Bolt, 1976.

2   *Disarmament: A Periodical Review by the United Nations: Strengthening the NPT.* Vol.16, No.2, 1993.

3   According to the SIPRI Yearbook 1994, imports to the Middle East dipped in 1991 after the Gulf War from US$6,909 million in 1990 to US$4,350 million in 1991, then started climbing again to US$5,515 million in 1993.

4   *Moving Towards Transparency: An Evaluation of the United Nations Register of Conventional Arms.* BASIC Report 93.6, 1993.

5   The *'safe haven'* was set up in support of Resolution 688 with the full backing of the UN Security Council.

6   *The UN's Role in Disarmament: Retrospect and Prospect.* John Simpson. Contemporary Security Policy. Vol.15, No.1, 1994, p.66.

AL-MUHALAB CONTRACTING & TRADING CO.

We are all familiar with the text enshrined in the UN Charter that all human beings 'should practice tolerance and live together in peace with one another as good neighbours'.

With the many changes taking place around the world, these ideals can only be achieved on the basis of a new pattern of global cooperation between government, business and society. We believe that only in this way can advances be made for the development and future of all humankind.

The Al-Muhalab Contracting & Trading Co. believes that business has an important role to play in this regard, recognizing that we must all share in the decisions that affect our lives. It cannot be done in isolation. We must all work together for a better world society.

Mohamed Abdul Ghani Al Ghani
Chairman

AL-MUHALAB CONTRACTING & TRADING CO.

P.O. Box: 3245 - SAFAT - 13033. KUWAIT.

TEL: 4762272 - 4741338
FAX: 4762262

People-Centred Development

When the Charter of the UN was drafted, priority was assigned not only to the eradication of war, but to the root causes of conflict. The goal was "to promote social progress and better standards of life in larger freedom."

From its very first days, dealing with the mass of refugees in war-torn Europe, the UN has set about this work, enlarging it as the years went by and de-colonization gathered speed, to encompass the need to aid in the development of newborn nations that numbered more than 100.

Over five decades this work has grown in magnitude touching every aspect of human life, from health to reproduction, feeding the hungry to establishing labour conventions, from scientific discovery to the preservation of the heritage of humanity.

In the early years of the UN, the burden of this enormous effort was shouldered solely by government bodies and the specialized agencies of the UN. Today, a legion of independent voluntary bodies, known as non-governmental organizations, (NGOs) are playing an increasingly important role in supplying their own expertise and enthusiasm.

As international consciousness of planetary issues deepens the role of such citizens' groups is destined to grow, providing additional momentum to global efforts to achieve the high ideals of the UN Charter.

The Social & Economic

Watering a tree nursery in Burkina Faso.
Since the Earth Summit in Rio de Janeiro in 1992, the focus has been on development that does not drain the earth's resources.

Connection ~ *the development agencies*

- *Battle against poverty*
- *New strategies*
- *Environmental protection*
- *Achievements and constraints*

© *Jeremy Hartley/Panos*

When the United Nations was created nearly 50 years ago, its original mandate gave equal billing to the prevention of war and to the battle against poverty.

Armed with this mandate, the UN has achieved some resounding successes in the social and economic fields. It has spearheaded child survival, population stabilization, disease control, environmental protection and development assistance. But despite these achievements the world still faces a development crisis. The crisis has been aggravated by rising poverty, a sky-rocketing Third World external debt, declining commodity prices, increasing protectionist barriers, a widening gap between rich and poor nations, and the depletion of the world's natural resources. Social and economic crises, in turn, have threatened the political stability of many countries.

The UN, its agencies and its sister institutions, the World Bank and the International Monetary Fund (IMF), have to share both the successes and the failures of global, social and economic development over the last 50 years. In the post-Cold War era, however, the UN has found it increasingly difficult to fulfil its economic mandate, primarily because of rising military conflicts, humanitarian emergencies, a shortage of resources and a diversion of funds from development to peacekeeping.

The new challenges facing the UN have resulted in fresh thinking on development strategies for the next 50 years. The two new concepts currently under discussion are 'preventive development' and 'curative development'.

 the Telecommunications Organization of Greece, provides 53.3 phones per 100 inhabitants supplying automatic dialling and semi-automatic facilities to over 220 countries and 80 countries respectively. In addition, satellite communication via INTELSAT-EUTELSAT-INMAPSAT links OTE with the rest of the world.

The company is well prepared strategically and financially, priding itself on the high quality of its employees and its management. OTE is therefore not only uniquely positioned to maximise returns in the domestic market but is well placed to explore new opportunities in the Balkans and Eastern Europe.

Over the past four years, OTE's revenue and net profits have grown at a compound rate of 51.2%, 35.8%, 42.3% and 63.5% and it is envisaged that this growth is likely to continue. Further, OTE plans to offer 25% of its shares to the stock market in order to achieve its ambitious five-year Development Programme and the expansion of the new service HELLASCOM-HELLASPAC-HELLASTEL.

By the year 2000, OTE expects to attract domestic and international capital investments which are likely to exceed $4.5 billion, enabling the organization to build the best possible telecommunications infrastructure in the region.

OTE HELLENIC TELECOMMUNICATIONS ORGANIZATION S.A.

ΟΡΓΑΝΙΣΜΟΣ ΤΗΛΕΠΙΚΟΙΝΩΝΙΩΝ ΤΗΣ ΕΛΛΑΔΟΣ A.E.

Based on the theory that all – or most – of the world's conflicts are caused primarily by economic problems, the UN wants to root out the causes of civil wars. The philosophy behind the thinking is that it is far better to take pre-conflict preventive action than to prescribe post-war curative treatment.

UN Secretary-General Boutros Boutros-Ghali says the objectives of peace and development are inseparable. There can be no lasting development without peace; and there can be no real peace without development. In his new 'Agenda for Development' released in 1994, the Secretary-General admits it is time for the UN to revert to its original mandate giving equal priority to social and economic development and to peace and security.

The inequities

The work of the UN agencies has been hindered not only by declining funds but also by an international economic system riddled with inequities. Since the creation of the UN in 1945, the collective wealth of nations has multiplied more than sevenfold, from three trillion dollars to $22 trillion. But the significant increase in wealth has not resulted in global prosperity, primarily because the world's riches continue to be inequitably distributed between developing and industrial nations.

The inequity is not just in distribution but also in factors of production. The world's technological resources and capital continue to be the monopoly of a few rich nations. As a result, the UN is also engaged in the formidable task of trying to bridge the widening gap between rich and poor, both in terms of peoples and nations.

The poorer nations argue that most of the world's social and economic problems are caused not by a shortage of resources but by over-consumption. Currently, about 24 per cent of the world's population which lives in the richer North consumes an estimated 75 to 85 per cent of the world's depleting resources.

The world's ecological destruction is triggered mostly by affluence and its by-products: industrial waste and consumer-generated garbage, and pollution of the air and water by industry, automobiles and agricultural chemicals. Currently, industrial nations generate about 90 per cent of the world's hazardous wastes, emit 74 per cent of atmosphere-warming carbon dioxide and produce almost 100 per cent of ozone-damaging chlorofluorocarbons (CFCs). But the developing nations are also to blame for increasing global environmental degradation – shrinking forests, eroding soil, over-grazed pastures and overcrowded cities, caused mostly by pressures of poverty. All of these problems have been caused by lop-sided development triggered by over-consumption of the world's finite resources.

At the historic UN Conference on Environment and Development (UNCED), also known as the 'Earth Summit', in Rio de Janeiro in June 1992, more than 100 political leaders pledged to carry home a new message: sustainable development. No development model is worth pursuing unless resources are used in ways that do not over-exploit the carrying and productive capacity of the earth and do not incur ecological debts that future generations have to repay.

"an international system riddled with inequities"

The successes

While some of the UN's failures may be in politics and peacekeeping, its significant achievements are primarily in the field of social and economic development.

If there were no UN, the international community might still be fighting smallpox and most of the world's workers might have no right to collective bargaining. There might be no safety standards on air and sea travel, while artists, composers and authors might have no protection for their creative works. The UN has been in the forefront of curbing acid rain, containing nuclear accidents, protecting oceans, preventing overfishing, reducing traffic in illegal waste and safeguarding endangered species.

In 1974, only five per cent of children in developing countries were immunized against polio, tetanus, measles, whooping cough, diphtheria and tuberculosis. Today, as a result of efforts by the UN Children's Fund (UNICEF) and the World Health Organization (WHO), there is an 80 per cent immunization rate, saving the lives of more than three million children annually.

Poverty is causing deforestation and soil erosion as people are forced to clear land for farming.
Ethiopia's bald hills, stripped of topsoil, played a part in the devastating famine in 1984 that killed half a million people.

The constraints

But the UN's successes in economic and social development are being thwarted by a lack of funds. The UN Development Programme (UNDP), the largest single source of development and technical assistance, is the prime example of a UN agency which raises only about one billion dollars annually from the international community. The amount is infinitesimal compared with the estimated nearly $800 billion the world spends every year on the military – about 800 times more than the amount it provides to a single UN development agency.

In 1970, the UN General Assembly set a target of 0.7 per cent of Gross National Product (GNP) as Official Development Assistance (ODA) from industrial countries to developing countries. The target was reaffirmed unanimously by all of the political leaders attending the Earth Summit in Brazil in June 1992.

But over a 24-year period, only four of the 24 industrial nations – Denmark, the Netherlands, Norway and Sweden – have fulfilled their commitments to the world's developing nations.

Since all of the UN's resources for development activities come from voluntary contributions from member states, the obligation to provide funds is essentially moral, not legal. A proposal to fund development activities through assessed contributions from member states has already generated strong opposition from Western nations.

The flow of resources from industrial countries both to the UN and to developing nations has been progressively dwindling for political and economic reasons. The biggest loser is Africa – a continent once considered politically significant primarily because of Soviet-US proxy wars in that region.

The sharp decline in development assistance is also attributed to the recent global economic recession forcing donors to cut back on aid. Japan, the world's largest aid donor, is holding its official development assistance to its lowest level ever at $10 billion for 1994-95.

The US Agency for International Development (USAID) has completely restructured its foreign aid programme by cutting from 108 to 50 the number of countries receiving US assistance. There has also been a significant downturn in multilateral development assistance, according to the latest figures released by the UN. The decline in aid is expected to continue into the late 1990s and perhaps into the next century.

The significance of the cuts lies in the fact that development assistance is shrinking at a time when developing nations are desperately in need of an increase, not a decrease, in aid because of growing poverty, rising debts and new trade barriers against their industrial exports.

In 1982, the World Bank estimated Third World debt at $732 billion. By 1994, it had shot up to more than $1.6 trillion, $305 billion of which is owed by African countries that do not have the capacity even to meet their annual interest payments. A UN report released in late 1994 says that more than a decade of complex strategies has failed to alleviate the international debt crisis which continues to plague over 65 developing and transitional economies.

The UN says poverty and inequality appear to be worsening throughout the world. Poverty and destitution do not appear to have been reduced, either in terms of the numbers of people affected or in terms of severity.

Currently about 1.1 billion people, out of a world total of some 5.4 billion, live either on low incomes or on no incomes at all. The greatest number of poor people are in Asia, but in Africa half the population falls below an accepted poverty line. While poverty is most commonly measured by income, it is also a matter of consumption and is reflected in such indicators as nutrition, life expectancy, child mortality, literacy, illness and education. There is wide agreement that the best way to reduce poverty is to ensure that people have opportunities for productive and remunerative employment to support themselves and their families.

A Half Century of Bringing the World Together.

From the daring promise of Dumbarton Oaks to the
solid reality of five decades spent serving the world's
citizens, the United Nations has held to the belief that
together we can create and sustain a better world.

Entergy Power Group, which is helping bring about
that better world through the development of electric
power infrastructure projects, salutes the United
Nations on its 50th Anniversary and is proud to be a part
of the commemoration.

ENTERGY

Entergy Power Group/Three Financial Centre/900 S. Shackleford Rd., Suite 210/Little Rock, AR 72211

The UN's development thrust

The responsibility for helping Third World nations achieve their development goals lies with UN agencies, most of whom have a physical presence in these countries. Leading the pack is UNDP, which has been in existence for 30 years. The New York-based agency is trying to meet four major objectives: poverty elimination, job creation, environmental regeneration and the advancement of women.

The agency spends about one billion dollars annually, mostly on technical assistance and training, as well as the supply of equipment and technology to developing nations. UNDP also hires an army of experts to advise governments on national development strategies. UNDP's new development strategy – and its emphasis on 'sustainable human development' and 'human security' – is viewed by some Third World countries as an intrusion into a sovereign nation's right to choose its own development model.

The intellectual flagship of UNDP is its annual *Human Development Report* with its innovative, but occasionally controversial, ideas aimed at helping countries learn from the failures of others. The authors of the report say that it is political will, not finance, that determines whether national budgets and foreign aid go for education and health, or for arms, corruption and hidden subsidies for the wealthy.

UNDP points out that the UN can no longer acquiesce in the 'deafening silence' that accompanies the current development crisis. It is therefore time for the UN to reclaim its original mandate on the economic and social front. UNDP has also stressed that people should be at the centre of development and that human security should take precedence over military security.

The UN's 'one earth' agency

In a pollution-ridden world increasingly conscious of its environment, the UN Environment Programme (UNEP) is saddled with the task of ensuring that the air is clean, the forests and eco-systems are safe and that human health and the quality of life are protected from environmental degradation.

Established in 1972, UNEP's two major landmarks are the UN Conference on the Human Environment in Stockholm in 1972 and the 1992 Earth Summit in Rio de Janeiro.

The Stockholm Conference took an important step forward in the concept of 'global commons' when it declared that 'States have the responsibility to ensure that activities within their jurisdiction or control do not cause damage to the environment of other States or of areas beyond the limits of national jurisdiction'. This concept was further strengthened when, in 1982, the General Assembly adopted a Convention on the Law of the Sea after more than a decade of negotiations.

The Stockholm Conference also reinforced the need for gathering and sharing information about the global environment. As a result, UNEP set up the International Information System on the Environment (INFOTERRA), which promotes the exchange of environmental information between national news agencies. At the same time, it also established the Global Environment Monitoring System (GEMS), linking hundreds of national and international organizations thirsting for knowledge about the environment. A third contribution by UNEP was the creation of an International Register of Potentially Toxic Chemicals (IRPTC). The register, maintained by UNEP, provides information on the chemical make-up of toxic products, their use, storage and disposal, and regulations applied to them in different countries.

If the Stockholm Conference was the first significant warning about the dangers of a deteriorating environment, the 1992 Earth Summit in Rio de Janeiro was a major turning point in environmental history because it agreed on an elaborate plan of action to prevent the ecological degradation of a future world.

The Summit adopted a blueprint for action called Agenda 21. This comprises 40 chapters which provide guidelines and recommendations to resolve problems in all major areas affecting the relationship between the environment and economic development. The follow-up to the Earth Summit resulted in three major agreements: a Convention on Climate

Change, a Convention on the Protection of Biological Diversity and a Convention to Combat Desertification.

But UNEP has a long hard battle ahead in a world where most countries pay only lip-service to the cause of the environment. The Nairobi-based agency can succeed only if its member states generate the necessary political will to support its environmental cause at a time when, according to the World Conservation Monitoring Organization, around 6,000 of the world's 1.7 million species are under threat of extinction.

The health of nations

WHO is credited with leading a 13-year global effort to wipe out smallpox from the face of the earth. The eradication of smallpox – the first disease ever to be completely rooted out – is among the greatest public health achievements of all time. But WHO's claim to fame does not lie only in a single remarkable achievement.

WHO establishes norms in a variety of fields, including food and pharmaceuticals, sets standards in international nomenclature and helps classify diseases. The agency also generates and transfers around the world current information on health matters. In emergency situations WHO enforces regulations to prevent the spread of disease across borders.

Since prevention is its keyword, WHO leads a global immunization campaign against six communicable diseases afflicting children: diphtheria, measles, poliomyelitis, tetanus, tuberculosis and whooping cough. WHO has also saved seven million children from river blindness and rescued millions of others from dracunculiasis and tropical diseases.

© WWF/ICCE 1988

"countries pay only lip-service to the environment"

The world's rainforests are being cut down at a rate of 9,910 square miles every two months, an area the size of Belgium.

WHO's battle against AIDS has been described as one of its biggest endeavours in the 1990s. The joint programme – the first of its kind – involves six UN organizations based in New York, Geneva, Paris and Washington, DC.

The agency's ultimate goal, however, is reflected in its well-publicized slogan: 'Health for All by the Year 2000'. Explaining this, WHO says its goal does not mean that by the beginning of the next century disease and disability will no longer exist, or that doctors and nurses will be taking care of everybody. What it does mean is that resources for health will be accessible to everyone, with full community involvement.

FE ◁ ME ▷ SA

**Ferrocarriles Metropolitanos
Sociedad Anónima**

The city of Buenos Aires, Argentina, boasts a mega-system of trains which carries one million passengers daily, serving a population of more than 12 million people.

The concession of rail services to private operators which is now in its concluding stage, can be seen as a pilot experiment by the rest of the world.

This is one of the most revolutionary successes of the administration of President Carlos Saul Menem and his Minister of Finance, Domingo Felipe Cavallo, who set up a programme of economic change and government reform in 1989.

We are working for the people in an effort to improve the quality of life in this part of the globe.

With the United Nations, this is our vision of hope and expectation for the future.

The fight for workers' rights

The International Labour Organisation (ILO), which celebrated its 75th anniversary in 1994, is the only UN agency which sets international labour standards that member states pledge to enforce in their own countries. Every working person in this world has, at some point or other, benefited from the norms set by ILO through its 174 Conventions and 181 Recommendations adopted to date.

ILO is unique among world organizations in that employers' and workers' representatives have an equal voice with those of governments in shaping policies and programmes. ILO's labour standards cover a vast spectrum of issues – social, economic and political – in the workplace. These standards apply to any work environment, irrespective of whether it is a ramshackle factory in the backstreets of a Third World capital or a multi-billion dollar corporate office on Wall Street, New York.

The agency has been primarily responsible for the creation of a wide range of workers' rights, including collective bargaining, occupational safety and health, social security, the employment of women and children, the abolition of forced labour, the elimination of discrimination, the freedom of association and the right to trade unionism. It has supervisory functions to ensure that labour laws set out such principles and are enforced in practice. It also has a special procedure to investigate complaints of violations of the freedom of association.

The work of ILO has taken on an added importance because the world's active working population is increasing by 43 million people every year. The increase is particularly marked in developing countries at a time when unemployment and underemployment are at their highest levels.

As it moves into the 21st century, ILO needs to provide some intellectual and political leadership in the quest for solutions to the problems of job creation and poverty alleviation in the changing world context. But the agency is also caught in the middle of a controversial debate between rich and poor nations over the proposed introduction of a 'social clause' in international trade agreements. The developed nations say that goods produced either by child labour or in workplaces that do not have minimum labour standards and wages should be barred from the international market place.

'The defence of values is not a question of conceiving an arsenal of retaliatory measures to be used unilaterally by one country or a group of countries', ILO Director-General Hansenne has argued. 'What is required, in contrast, is a multilateral mechanism created to review systematically member states' efforts to offer their workers a share in the economic benefits resulting from the opening up of exterior markets.' The ILO, he says, seems naturally placed to contribute to the implementation of such a mechanism.

"standards apply to any work environment"

The world's cultural heritage

The UN Educational, Scientific and Cultural Organization (UNESCO) believes that since wars begin in the minds of men, it is in the minds of men that the defences of peace must be constructed. The idea for the Paris-based UN agency grew out of the ashes of two devastating wars. The founders who met in London believed that military conflicts could be prevented only through the spread of education and international cooperation.

Established in 1945, UNESCO continues to enjoy a privileged position within the world's intellectual community of academics, scientists and philosophers. The agency has provided assistance and know-how to develop and strengthen communications systems, establish news agencies and support an independent press.

In 1972, UNESCO adopted a convention to protect the world's cultural and natural heritage. The primary objective of the convention is to protect unique natural and cultural property against the ravages of time. The philosophy behind the convention is that certain natural and cultural properties, such as the Great Barrier Reef in Australia, Machu Picchu in Peru and the Great Wall of China, are 'world heritages' whose protection and conservation are the collective responsibility of the international community.

UNESCO works in support of press freedom, pluralism and independence. Affiliated to UNESCO is the International Programme for the Development of Communication (IPDC) which has successfully set up several national and regional news agencies. But UNESCO's highest single priority is 'a basic education for all' – a concept defined by the World Conference on Education for All held in Thailand in 1990. The programme aims to give everyone access to quality education that will lead to lifelong learning.

UNESCO, along with UNICEF and the UN Population Fund (UNFPA), is sponsoring an unprecedented education drive in which nine developing nations have pledged to universalize education and 'massively' reduce the illiteracy rate in their countries. The nine countries – Mexico, Brazil, Indonesia, China, India, Nigeria, Egypt, Bangladesh and Pakistan – have a combined population of 2.7 billion people and account for half the world's total.

© Sean Sprague/Panos

**Pollution, acid rain and deforestation are forcing the UN to focus its attention
on the environment.**
A Filipino boy plants a tree in Mindanao.

A WORLD
FULL OF
HOPE

It is all our responsibility to make
the world a better place to live in.
To care for the human and physical
environment.
To hand over to our children what we
have borrowed.

The right to food

The UN's Food and Agriculture Organization (FAO) has been leading the global campaign to eradicate two of the Third World's major problems: poverty and hunger.

FAO's basic mandate is to help alleviate poverty and hunger by promoting agricultural development, by improving nutrition and by ensuring food security. As the UN's largest autonomous agency with a professional staff of over 2,000, FAO offers direct development assistance, collects, analyses and disseminates information, provides policy and planning advice to governments and acts as an international debating forum on food and agricultural issues.

FAO has discouraged the use of pesticides by Third World farmers and encouraged biological control methods and natural predators, such as spiders and wasps, to stave off pests. The 400,000 Asian rice farmers who follow FAO guidelines have saved an estimated $10 million every year in reduced pesticide costs, while government bills for pesticide subsidies have declined by over $150 million annually. FAO has also used state-of-the-art technology to set up a Direct Information Access Network for Africa (DIANA). The network helps signal early warnings of food shortages caused by severe droughts in large parts of eastern and southern Africa.

The food crisis

The stark images of starving children standing naked pleading for food have been splashed across living rooms the world over. The World Food Programme (WFP) is one of the UN agencies responding to the crying pains of the hungry.

In 1993, the WFP provided direct food aid to more than 47 million people worldwide. 'This food aid is not charity', the WFP insists. 'It is a long-term investment in developing countries, so that one day there will be no more emaciated children, no more parents who have lost their children to hunger.'

With its headquarters in Rome, the WFP specializes in emergency aid, delivering food to refugees displaced by war and civil strife and to victims of droughts, earthquakes, storms and other disasters. Although it is being increasingly called upon to provide relief assistance, the WFP was originally set up not only to combat hunger but also to promote economic and social development. Since its inception, the WFP has provided more than five billion dollars in assistance to help developing nations increase their productivity.

"UN food aid is not charity"

With that objective, the WFP has built coastal dykes to protect farmland from salt intrusion, planted trees and created forest belts to prevent soil erosion and helped small farmers to adopt environmentally sound agricultural policies. The WFP stresses the integration of development and environment, generating employment and income and increasing access to food on a sustainable basis. The WFP claims it is now the largest source of grant assistance to developing countries, providing an average of more than $1.5 billion annually.

The agency has spent nearly $13 billion to provide a total of more than 40 million tons of food to combat hunger and promote economic and social development. 'Food aid has an intrinsic advantage over other forms of aid', says the WFP. 'No other form of assistance transfers such a large level of resources directly to the poor.'

The fall of Communism exposed an environmental disaster area in Eastern Europe and the former USSR.
A large chemical and toxic waste dump.

© Heidi Bradner/Panos

The agricultural burden

When the International Fund for Agricultural Development (IFAD) was established in 1977 it had a single-minded mission: to combat hunger and rural poverty in the low income food-deficit countries of the world. A UN agency which reaches out to people in remote parts of the world, IFAD provides assistance to the poorest of the world's poor: small farmers, landless poor, nomadic herdsmen and rural women. The Fund has developed a system of providing credit, often in very small amounts, to the poorest and most marginalized groups. The credit provided by IFAD has benefited over 230 million people in about 100 developing nations.

Since its primary interest is in the world's most poverty-stricken countries, IFAD has set up a Special Programme for Africa (SPA) which accounts for 36 of the world's 47 least developed countries. Targeting mostly small farmers, the Fund has been focusing on better utilization of water resources, soil conservation and the promotion of traditional drought-resistant crops. The Fund has spent more than $282 million, mostly in concessional low-interest loans, to finance these projects. The terms of the loans are more favourable than any offered by the best state-run and commercial banks in these countries.

The success stories cover not only Africa but also Asia, the Middle East and the Caribbean. In 1982, IFAD provided assistance to a project in north China under which 9,000 hectares of saline land were reclaimed and brought under irrigation and an additional 5,000 hectares of waste land were converted into forests and orchards. In the semi-arid deserts of Yemen, the IFAD-assisted Wadi Beihan Agricultural Development Project has virtually tripled the output of cereal, vegetable and citrus products.

"*the success stories*"

KENYA POSTS AND TELECOMMUNICATIONS CORPORATION

The United Nations has, since its inception, made a substantial contribution to both economic growth and social development and with the increasing globalization of the world economy, the telecommunications industry has an important part to play.

As we approach the 21st century, the world is closer than ever before to creating a planetary information network. However whilst technological advancements provide cheaper and ever more efficient telecommunication systems, it is a matter of concern that the gap continues to widen between urban and rural areas. It is in these areas that the improvement of telecommunications must be concentrated.

Kenya Posts and Telecommunications Corporation welcome the vision of hope of a global economy and a global information infrastructure. We recognize that although there are difficulties to overcome and challenges to be met, we hope that one day, that vision of hope will become a reality.

On behalf of the staff, management and customers of Kenya Posts and Telecommunications Corporation, I would like to extend our sincere congratulations to the United Nations on the occasion of the Fiftieth Anniversary.

S.K. CHEMAI Managing Director

The future goals

As it moves into its next 50 years, the UN has to pursue a new agenda for development, avoiding the mistakes of the past and gearing itself to meet the social and economic needs of the future.

Coordinating all of the UN's development activities in a single body may be one of the answers to the problems that continue to plague the UN. The single most important factor in its field activities, however, is funding.

The question that cries out for an answer is whether the UN really has the clout to set its own development agenda or whether the agenda is set by Western donors who hold the purse-strings. In the post-Cold War period, Western nations have been imposing new conditionalities and restrictions on development assistance. The UN is caught in the middle of a political shooting match between developed and developing nations.

During 1987-94, voluntary military cuts by both developed and developing nations are estimated to have saved about $935 billion. But no one has succeeded in tracking down this sizeable 'peace dividend'. The vanishing 'peace dividend' is one of the biggest mysteries of the post-Cold War era. UNDP has estimated that an annual reduction of three per cent in global defence spending during the period 1995-2000 could produce another saving of nearly $460 billion – money that could be diverted from the military to development.

In the late 1990s, the developing world will also continue to grapple with problems such as dumping, new tariff barriers, and social and environmental clauses in trade pacts barring Third World products from industrial nations. With the creation of the World Trade Organization (WTO) as a successor to the General Agreement on Tariffs and Trade (GATT), there is apprehension that the poorer developing nations stand to lose in the short run.

The positive results in new trade opportunities are far from commensurate with the additional obligations under new multilateral disciplines such as services, foreign investments and intellectual property rights. A study by the UN Conference on Trade and Development (UNCTAD) shows that short-term benefits will go mostly to industrial nations. The African countries alone are expected to suffer potential losses amounting to about $2.6 billion annually.

· · · · · · · · · · · · · · · · · ·

The right to development is a basic human right, with every nation having primary responsibility for its own development strategies. The UN's responsibility is to provide guidance, technical expertise and development assistance to help implement these strategies.

The UN's development agenda continues to cover a wide range of activities, including long-term social and economic development and post-crisis reconstruction and rehabilitation. If it is to succeed, it will also have to be able to deal effectively, and be given the resources needed for the job, with the full range of issues relating to population, the status of women, child survival, the environment, drug control, and housing and urban management. Nevertheless, at the same time that Secretary-General Boutros Boutros-Ghali argues that peace and development are inseparable, in reality during the post-Cold War era, the UN has been forced to spend as much money on peacekeeping as on social and economic development.

© *David Reed/Panos*

Governments are turning to prevention rather than cure in the fight against disease.
A helicopter sprays the breeding site of the oncho fly which causes river blindness.

The 1980s saw the springing up all over the world of small groups of grassroots activists.
Children celebrate Earth Day in the Philippines capital Manila with a street show.

Development ~ *a balance sheet*

- ■ *The momentum of change*
- ■ *Social reconstruction*
- ■ *Dangers and risks*
- ■ *The human dimension*

© Mark McEvoy/Panos

The 1980s were, in many ways, a decade of the people. All over the world, people were seized with an impatient urge to guide their political, economic and social destinies. The democratic transition in developing countries, the collapse of socialist regimes and the worldwide emergence of people's organizations – all were signs of a new bursting of the human spirit.

At first sight, this may appear too sanguine an interpretation. This was, after all, a decade that shattered many lives and many hopes – with mounting external debt, faltering economic growth, increasing unemployment, growing civil strife, rising ethnic tensions, threats to the environment and the persistence of abject poverty.

But amid these disturbing and painful trends is an unmistakable resurgence of human creativity. There are times in history when the human voice has spoken out with surprising force. These past few years have marked just such a watershed.

Now that the Cold War is over, the challenge is to rebuild societies around people's genuine needs. There is no good reason why the essential goals of human endeavour should not be achieved by the turn of the century. We have both the knowledge and the resources. But it does mean a different perspective, both domestically and internationally. It means cutting back on the military. It means winding down inefficient public enterprises and ensuring that government subsidies are actually aimed at the very poorest. It means emphasizing personal priorities and appropriate spending patterns. It means sound and judicious governance, involving people in decisions

VOLTA RIVER AUTHORITY

...producing energy for development

~In 1961, the Government of Ghana, in recognizing the strategic role that the supply of cheap electric power could play in the economic development of the nation, created the **Volta River Authority (VRA)**; the primary function being to generate electric power by developing the hydroelectric potential of the Volta River. It was also decided to construct and operate a transmission system for industrial, commercial and domestic use as well as for export in the West Africa sub-region.

The **VRA** is also responsible for the development of the world's largest artificial lake - the Volta Lake – as a source of fish and a means of transportation for the local inhabitants.

With the aid of the International Bank for Reconstruction and Development, the International Development Association, the World Food Programme of the Food and Agricultural Organization, together with other financial agencies and governments, **VRA** was able to construct the 912MW Akosombo and the 160MW Kpong Hydroelectric Power Stations. With the further assistance of these agencies, the building of a 300MW Thermal Generation Station is proposed for 1997.

The **VRA** currently provides electricity to Ghana's 10 administrative regions and, by pursuing a programme designed to ensure an adequate supply of power from additional hydro and thermal sources, it is planned that electricity will be available to all parts of the country by the year 2020.

Since December 1992, **VRA** has been supplying power to the neighbouring Republics of Togo and Benin and has been exchanging energy with its Ivorian counterpart, the Compagnie Ivoirienne d'Electricité. In addition, negotiations have almost been finalised to interconnect the transmission systems of Ghana and her northern neighbour, Burkina Faso.

Through the Union of Producers and Distributors of Electricity in Africa, the **VRA** is actively collaborating to achieve the ultimate goal of interconnecting the electrical system in Africa. These international power supply exchanges help to foster closer relations between Ghana and her sister African countries.

The **VRA** has sponsored the Kpong Farms Ltd. which trains farmers in modern agricultural practices; the Akosombo Hotels Ltd. offering modern facilities, thus encouraging tourism, and the Volta Lake Transport Company operating a water transportation system linking north and south Ghana. In addition, the **VRA** has set up a number of environmental programmes together with medical, social and welfare services for the lakeside communities.

As the **VRA** moves into the future determined to meet the power requirements of Ghana and help attain greater regional cooperation in the African continent, it will continue to need the assistance and encouragement of the international community.

It is universally recognized that the UN has improved the lives of millions of communities around the world. The **Volta River Authority** hopes that, by its own activities, it will generate sustainable improvements in the lives of the peoples of Ghana.

We salute the United Nations on the occasion of its 50th Anniversary.

VOLTA RIVER AUTHORITY P.O. Box M.77, ACCRA, GHANA
Phone: 664941/221124 Telex: 2022 VOLTA GH. Fax: 233-21 662610

which affect them and winning their acquiescence by demonstrating competence and fairness. Improved incomes are also important. There can be no sustained momentum over the years without a rise in income.

The world has already made a positive start. For the first time since the Second World War, global military expenditures are beginning to decline: between 1987 and 1990, they fell altogether by some $240 billion. Most of this reduction has been by the United States and the former Soviet Union. But the developing countries also cut expenditure, despite the fact that for many poor countries the ratio of military spending to social spending remains far too high.

Since the beginning of the 1990s, more than two million men and women have been demobilized, two-thirds of them in industrial countries and one-third in developing countries. Further demobilizations on a similar scale are expected in the next few years.

This represents considerable progress, but the nuclear threat is far from gone, and conventional weapons continue to take many lives. So greater emphasis must be placed not just on peacekeeping but on peacemaking and peacebuilding, demanding a new role for the UN.

As military threats have lessened, other dangers have surfaced. The world is entering a dangerous period: future conflicts may well be between groups of people rather than states.

All these changes highlight the urgent need to focus on human development, the concept defined in

© Liba Taylor/Panos

Over the last three decades, developing countries have made safe water available to 68 per cent of their people. A refugee drinks from a water tap in Lumasi camp in Tanzania.

the UN's first *Human Development Report* published by the UN Development Programme (UNDP) in 1990 as a process of widening the range of people's choices.

The balance sheet on human development

There have now been six editions of the annual *Human Development Report*. Together they enable us to draw a fairly accurate portrait of the progress of human society. Contrary to the often tormented images of emaciated children, economies over-whelmed by a tide of debt and mismanagement, and even the weather as a hostile force whose spite seems to worsen over time, the truth for most countries and most people is that life in the last 50 years has become more liveable and probably also more fulfilling.

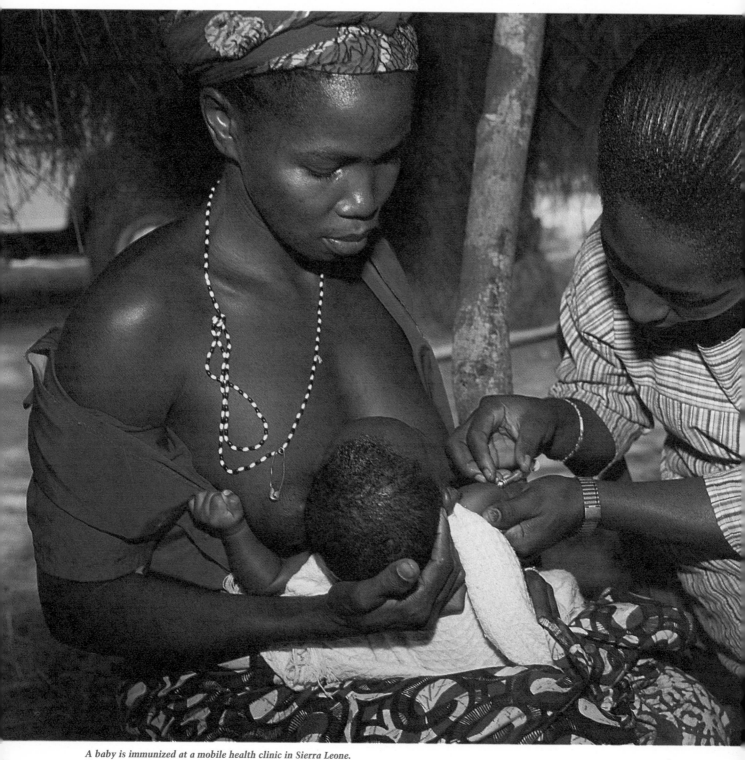

A baby is immunized at a mobile health clinic in Sierra Leone.
Despite a growing number of health clinics, each year 40 million newborn children are not properly immunized.

This balance sheet on human development begins optimistically, recording the remarkable steps taken by humanity in improving its condition in an historically very short span of time. But there is an immense job yet undone, and there are many complexities, economic, political and social, that have to be overcome to realize the planet's true potential. Only our world's selfish and often archaic institutions, habits and lifestyles keep the billions of people still struggling for a decent living from being able to live in security and comfort.

The essentials of progress over the last three decades are simply put.

On average:

- Life expectancy has increased from 46 years to 63.

- The mortality rate of children under five has been halved.

- Two-thirds of all one-year-olds are now immunized against major childhood diseases.

- Developing countries have made primary health care accessible to 72 per cent of their people and safe water available to 68 per cent, and per capita calorie supply as a percentage of requirements has increased from 90 per cent to 107 per cent.

- Adult literacy has risen from 46 per cent to 65 per cent,

© Jeremy Hartley/Panos

the number of children in primary school has increased sixfold and at secondary school eighteenfold.

- Although the South's average per capita income is only six per cent of the North's, its social progress has been so effective that its average life expectancy is now a remarkable 80 per cent of that of the rich industrialized world, and its average literacy rate a significant 66 per cent.

It is quite astonishing that this progress has been made despite inadequate resources, an often inhospitable international economic climate and, in many countries, not always the wisest or most responsive of governments. If this kind of momentum can be achieved in less than perfect conditions then it is not hard to imagine the further steps that can be made in a more democratic, socially aware and responsibly managed world.

"*progress has been made*"

The unmet needs are vast:

- 800 million people go to bed hungry every day.

- Nearly 900 million adults still cannot read or write.

- 1.5 billion people have no access to primary health care.

- 1.75 billion people are without safe water.

- 100 million people are completely homeless.

- A billion people eke out the barest existence in perpetual poverty.

- 40 million newborn children are not properly immunized. Fourteen million die every year before they reach the age of five and 150 million are malnourished. Twelve times as many women in the South die in pregnancy or childbirth as in the North.

LA PROTECTION IVOIRIENNE DE VIE

Côte d'Ivoire, formerly named the 'good people's coast' - with modern cities such as Abidjan, the commercial centre, and Yamoussoukro, the administrative capital - is the home of La Protection Ivoirienne de Vie, one of the country's leading insurance companies.

With the implementation of economic reforms and the promotion of private investment in Côte d'Ivoire, La Protection Ivoirienne de Vie has an important role in the challenges that lie ahead.

In the realization that insurance is essential to the growth of the economy, La Protection Ivoirienne de Vie is committed to playing its part.

La Protection Ivoirienne de Vie - a private corporation for the public good.

Tel: 225 22 17 50-1-2-3

There are also enormous differentials, even within those countries which are apparently 'making it'. In urban areas, in developing countries as a whole, there is double the access to safe water than there is in rural areas. Female literacy rates are only two-thirds those of men. And the better-off people often appropriate a major share of social subsidies.

Of all the disparities in human development, surely the most marked division is the North-South one, and there are also very significant differences among regions in the South.

The North

The industrialized countries provide for most of their inhabitants a relatively easy life. Almost everyone has access to clean water, sanitation, clothes and primary health care. Almost everyone can eat to their satisfaction.

Nevertheless, there are a number of industrialized countries where poverty is still very much in evidence despite the overall abundance in society at large.

"grave inequalities between men and women"

All over the industrialized countries unemployment in the last decade has worsened, seemingly becoming an intractable problem. It is substantially above the post-war norm, becoming increasingly chronic and long-term. Few countries put a large amount of resources into retraining the unemployed, despite the fact that in most societies there are a significant number of unfilled vacancies. Paradoxically, there are a number of cases where unemployment and unfilled vacancies have risen at the same time.

Even within the most prosperous of the industrialized countries there are often grave inequalities between men and women. In education, this is particularly apparent at college level and is very marked in scientific and technical subjects.

Educational disparities are replicated in the workplace. On average, roughly half as many women work in the labour force as men. Those women who do get jobs are significantly worse paid and are at much greater risk of unemployment. In all societies men play the dominant role in decision-making, whether it be in business or government. Even in those countries where women do enter parliament in large numbers – Sweden, Norway, Finland and Russia – women are no more than one-third of legislators.

All the advanced industrial societies are finding that, under the pressure of increased wealth, greater leisure time, more rapid communications and, for a significant minority, growing unemployment, their lifestyles are changing so fast as to precipitate a sea-change in cultural norms. The traditional post-industrial revolution Western nuclear family is under quite serious threat. Single parents now head an increasing number of homes. Many divorces are the consequence of the contemporary sense of individual freedom. But this freedom has a high price – individual trauma, the disruption of children's lives and family impoverishment. Crime and misbehaviour are rising as the signs of personal distress appear more manifest.

The South

Each of the Third World's continents has its own story. Asia, with 70 per cent of the world's population, has seen phenomenal progress economically, socially and politically over the last three decades. Life expectancy has increased from 46 to 64 years and the number of children in school has increased from 57 per cent to 71 per cent. Nevertheless, the differences between regions are so large that we can see the picture more clearly if we look at Southeast Asia and East Asia first and South Asia second.

Some countries in **East and Southeast Asia,** in particular, China, Singapore and Hong Kong, have achieved fairly rapid reductions in infant mortality – of around five per cent a year. Around 85 per cent of the region's children are immunized – a higher proportion than the average for the industrialized countries.

In several countries people can now expect to live beyond 70. At the same time contraceptive practice is commonplace – 66 per cent of all couples use it, compared with 70 per cent in the industrialized countries. Not surprisingly, population growth is much lower than the average for developing countries.

One important reason for this general state of improving well-being is the decision made years ago to redistribute land more equitably and to emphasize employment-intensive economic growth.

Now many of those countries, like the industrialized countries which they are close to emulating, are building future growth on the foundations of high levels of health and education and advanced, diversified production structures. South Korea, Singapore and Hong Kong are the three countries most advanced in this way. But Thailand and Malaysia are not far behind.

South Asia, while not exhibiting such spectacular success, has also made measurable progress over the past 30 years. Bangladesh has raised its average life expectancy from 40 to 53 years but, nevertheless, this is still 10 years lower than the average for developing countries. But immunization coverage of one-year-old children has shot up from one per cent to 60 per cent. In Sri Lanka it is now 89 per cent.

Economic growth over the last two decades has averaged only three per cent and high population growth has eaten into that. Gross National Product (GNP) per capita remains low, particularly in Nepal ($180) and Bangladesh ($170).

Inequality is severe throughout the region, between rich and poor, male and female, and different ethnic groups and religions. In the rural Punjab, landless families have an infant mortality rate 36 per cent higher than those of landowning families.

The greatest number of poor are concentrated in only two countries, Bangladesh and India. Only two-thirds of the people have access to basic health services and clean water; female life expectancy in particular is low.

Latin America and the Caribbean have been the site of impressive achievements in human development, despite the rather dramatic slow-down in the improvement in well-being during the difficult 1980s. Between 1960 and 1980 the under-five mortality rate dropped from 157 to 72 per 1,000 live births. Average life expectancy is now only seven years short of that in the industrialized countries. In Barbados, Costa Rica and Cuba people actually live longer than they do in the industrialized countries.

This region has the highest education levels of the developing world. Some countries, Argentina, Barbados, Guyana, Jamaica, Uruguay, Trinidad and Tobago, have literacy rates of over 95 per cent. With 40 scientists and technicians per 1,000 people, the region is well above the developing world average of 10.

The economic collapse of the 1980s resulted in an immense setback. In some countries child malnutrition and infant mortality started to rise again.

Moreover, in good times and in bad, the fruits of life in a number of countries are shared badly. The top one-fifth of the population in Brazil earns 26 times more than the bottom fifth. In Peru the bottom 40 per cent receive only 13 per cent of the national income. (In Morocco it is 21 per cent, in India 20 per cent and Indonesia 23 per cent.)

Two-thirds of the world's population live in rural areas, earning 25-50 per cent less than town dwellers.
A farmer builds a stone wall in Burkina Faso.

© Jeremy Hartley/Panos

VIETCOMBANK

BANK FOR FOREIGN TRADE OF VIET NAM
VIETCOMBANK

With more than 30 years of experience in international banking, an increasing relationship with the world banking and fiscal institutions together with a good customer base, Vietcombank is acknowledged as one of the leading banks in Vietnam. This is reflected in its major market share, the assignment by the Government to implement Governmental Aid Assistance and Loans, and the profile of its customers who are amongst the strongest industrial and commercial corporations in Vietnam. The Bank also enjoys strong trust and good credit from its correspondents and customers and is frequently requested by both domestic and international financial organizations to issue business guarantees.

Vietcombank's membership of the ABA (Asian Bankers Association) has created an opportunity for the Bank to be fully compatible with regional as well as international monetary activities. The Bank maintains a good and close relationship with foreign correspondents and the major international financial institutions including the World Bank, International Monetary Fund (IMF), Asian Development Bank (ADB) and the International Finance Corporation (IFC).

In line with the country's open door policy and on the basis of cooperation and mutual benefit, Vietcombank looks forward to working with international financial institutions and foreign correspondent banks throughout the world.

BANK'S PROFILE

47-49 Ly Thai To Street, Hanoi, S.R. Vietnam

Cables: VIETCOMBANK, Phone: 84-4-259859/265503

Telex: (0805) 411229/411504/411244 VCB

Fax: 84-8-269067/243180

Established 1963, authorized to deal with foreign currencies and all other international banking business.

Chairman & General Director: Nguyen Van De

Vice Chairman - First Dep. G.D : Nguyen Duy Lo

Other Dep. Gen. Directors: Tran Quoc Quynh, Ha Huy Sung, Vu Ngoc Gian, Bui The Uong

Branches: 17 throughout the country

Representatives: Paris, Stockholm

Subsidiaries: Vietnam Finance Co. Ltd, Hong Kong

Correspondents: over 700 Banks in over 85 countries

BANK FOR FOREIGN TRADE OF VIETNAM

Some countries, too, still have a long way to go, even to match the regional average. Only just over half Nicaragua's population has access to safe water, and in Bolivia, Haiti, El Salvador and Paraguay it is much less than half. Likewise, Bolivia, Paraguay and El Salvador have very low rates of school enrolment.

Latin America is one of the most urbanized parts of the developing world. Two-thirds of the population now live and work in the cities. Women are playing an increasing role in society – the proportion of women in the workforce has been growing steadily. A higher proportion of women than men have migrated from rural areas to towns and cities. Moreover, some 40 per cent of those new urban households are headed by women. Women, too, are increasingly educated. More girls than boys are in secondary schools, and female literacy is only five per cent less than that of men.

The revolution in oil prices has given many of the states of the **Middle East and North Africa** some of the developing world's fastest increases in income. At the same time there has been a remarkable improvement in human development. Life expectancy has jumped from 47 to 62 years, mortality rates for children under five have been reduced by almost two-thirds, access to health services is the highest in the developing world and access to safe water second only to Latin America. Nevertheless, there still remain 60 million adults who are illiterate and there are 40 million people living below the poverty line.

The potential of women remains largely unrecognized. Male-female disparities are the widest in the world. Female literacy is a mere 39 per cent, and only 15 per cent of the official labour force are women.

The countries that have oil have shot far ahead of those without. GNP per capita varies from $480 in Sudan to $15,770 in the United Arab Emirates. Even those oil-rich countries that now have reasonably good human development have index rankings that lag far behind other countries with a similar GNP.

Political instability and disproportionately high military expenditures threaten the region's future and could well thwart the chance of upgrading health and education in line with the region's wealth.

> "*for most of the 1980s economic growth was less than population growth*"

Inequities in the region have led to large numbers of migrant workers, both skilled and unskilled, leaving the poorer Arab countries for the richer. While their remittances are an important source of hard currency for their home country, the migrants drain their homeland of much-needed skills and vitality.

For all its setbacks **Sub-Saharan Africa** has taken important strides forward in its human development. Since 1960 infant mortality rates have fallen by 37 per cent and life expectancy has increased from 40 to 52 years. Adult literacy has increased by two-thirds.

For most of the 1980s economic growth was less than population growth, although there are now signs that the trend is reversing.

Women are increasingly joining the ranks of the world's paid workforce.
A woman welding in Niger.

© Ron Giling/Panos

More than half the population has no access to public health services; two-thirds lack safe water; 18 million people suffer from sleeping sickness; malaria kills hundreds of thousands of children every year; AIDS is spreading fast, devastating many families, and in the poorest countries a quarter or more of the children die before the age of five.

The economic catastrophe of the 1980s, the result of bad economic management, debt, drought and war, has pushed unemployment up to the 100 million mark, four times what it was a decade ago. Real wages have fallen by almost a third.

Women, disproportionately, bear the brunt of work in the fields, and girls are much less well educated than boys. So rare are the opportunities at home that many migrate, often hopelessly, to look for work in the overcrowded cities.

War, ethnic unrest, border conflicts and the attempt to end racial domination have created large numbers of refugees (six million) and disabled (50 million). Altogether, including those made homeless by natural disasters and difficult socio-economic conditions, there are 35 million displaced people.

"*refugees are fleeing war, ethnic unrest and border conflict*"

IN CASABLANCA, A SLIVER OF BONE REVEALED A CHUNK OF HISTORY when Dr. Jean-Jacques Hublin unearthed a few fossilized skull fragments. Then Hublin and a team of IBM scientists fed this shattered 3-D jigsaw puzzle into a unique program called Visualization Data Explorer.™ The tiny pieces helped form an electronic reconstruction of our early ancestor, the first Homo Sapiens. This new IBM technology has turned time back 400,000 years, uncovering clues to the origins of mankind.

Solutions for a small planet™

Comparisons and contrasts

If we look at these criteria of progress in more detail the course of this argument becomes even more clear.

Overall life expectancy goes hand-in-hand with a country's income level. But there are enough exceptions to prove that if a country is intent on putting life before riches it can achieve a significant improvement even in modest circumstances.

Improvements in literacy rates have transformed the ability to read and write within a generation. This has given people access to knowledge not only for improving their own lives but also for shaping a more informed and shrewd opinion about the world outside.

Overall, the percentage of people living in absolute poverty has fallen, although not at a fast enough rate to diminish the total number of poor. But in Africa the percentage of poor has actually increased and now amounts to about half the total population.

Food, health, water, sanitation and education are the basic elements of human survival and fulfilment. Without these at a minimally satisfactory level, humankind does not fully progress. In most parts of the Third World there have been significant advances in the availability of all of these. Only in Africa has progress slipped back on a wide front.

Food production has made a quite noticeable advance. The daily supply of calories in the developing world increased from 90 per cent of total requirements in 1965 to 107 per cent in 1985. The dark lining in the silver cloud is that the countries that most needed to improve have increased food availability least. In the poorest countries the supply of calories increased from only 88 per cent to 90 per cent of total requirements. At least 16 African countries saw an actual decline.

During the 1980s a number of developing countries came close to providing primary health care for all – South Korea, Costa Rica, Jamaica, Tunisia and Jordan in particular. But most developing countries fall far short of this target.

Progress in improving water and sanitation has been much slower than in health. Yet for many countries a dollar spent on clean water and good sewers would produce a greater improvement in the quality of life than a dollar spent on doctors or hospitals.

Just as it seemed that modern science could short-cut many of the hazards of underdevelopment, an apparently new disease has torn many poor countries asunder, both in lives lost and broken and, cumulatively, in the loss of some of society's most educated and active members.

The HIV (human immunodeficiency virus) epidemic has infected around eight to 10 million adults and half of them are likely to develop AIDS sometime in the next decade. It is estimated that a further 15 million new cases of HIV infection will be added in the 1990s – more than half in the developing world, with a high proportion in eastern and central Africa and the likelihood of a rapid increase in infected people in India and Thailand. Apart from the loss of usually young life, the financial implications in terms of medical costs are staggering.

Educational improvement, by comparison, is a success story. By the end of the 1980s an impressive 80 per cent of all children of primary school age were enrolled. Several countries in the developing world were close to the goal of universal primary education. Even in Africa progress has been rapid: half the children now attend both primary and secondary school.

All this progress bodes well for the future economic opportunities of the South. With four times as many students in primary school and twice as many in secondary school as in the North, it is developing a competitive edge.

All these advances together strongly suggest that for most of the world's people life is steadily becoming more liveable. Unfortunately, population growth eats away at many improvements and means that a growing number of people, albeit a smaller percentage of the whole, continues to suffer from severe deprivation. Since 1960 the population of the developing world has doubled. In Africa, in particular, this phenomenal rate of increase shows little sign of abating. Elsewhere, however, the rate of growth is falling. For too many countries, the economic slow-down of the 1980s and the still high population growth meant they were caught in a sharp pincer movement.

The question for the developing countries, ever more pressing given the difficult economic environment they confront, is how to maximize the use of the resources they have. Above all, how to find productive employment for their ever-growing, albeit better educated, workforce. It is not just population growth that has pushed up the size of the labour force; it is partly the sharp increase in women seeking paid work, and also poorer families trying to increase the number of income earners in the family.

Lop-sided development

This review of the progress of the developing world, good as it is in terms of accomplishments for many countries, would have presented a more positive picture if so many countries did not succumb to such severe inequalities – between urban and rural areas, between men and women, and between rich and poor – both in income levels and in their access to public services.

For a start, two-thirds of the people live in rural areas. But in many countries they receive less than a quarter of the resources spent on education, health and sanitation, and they earn 25 per cent to 50 per cent less than those who live in the towns and cities. Political and economic power, particularly in the early stages of development, is concentrated in urban

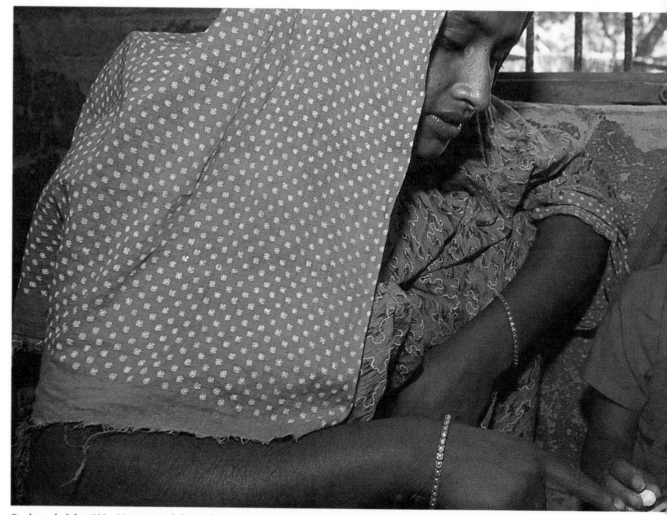

By the end of the 1980s, 80 per cent of the world's children were enrolled in primary school. A young girl learns to write in Dhaka, Bangladesh.

© Liba Taylor/Panos

areas. The consequence is a very lop-sided, often self-destructive, kind of development.

Male-female differentials are another source of severe inequality in many countries. During the 1960s, 1970s and 1980s women did share in the progress taking place in many developing societies, but in a number of important respects life did not improve for them as fast as it did for men.

Women, disproportionately, carry the burden of work. Throughout the Third World women are not, as widely perceived, merely mothers and housewives but are often a crucial contributor to the family's food supply. In Africa, in many cases, women are expected to produce or purchase nearly all the food eaten at home. Women typically work about 25 per cent more hours than men.

In many developing countries more girls than boys die young, the reverse of the situation in the industrialized countries. Girls get less to eat, receive less medical care and when pregnant do not receive the care and attention sufficient to minimize the maternal mortality rate. No other North-South gap is wider than the maternal mortality rate. In the industrialized countries it is often less than 10 per 100,000 live births. In some developing countries it is as high as 1,000.

Educational opportunities for women still lag behind those of men. In the developing world the female literacy rate is three-quarters that of males; in many countries the gap is more than that. However, slowly, the gap is beginning to narrow.

The social dividend of investing in women's education is immense. In Bangladesh child mortality is five times higher for children of mothers with no education than for those whose mothers have seven or more years of schooling. Better educated women also have much smaller families.

The income gap that most tears at the fabric of society is the one between rich and poor. Many developing countries have far more uneven income distribution than the United States, the most unequal of the industrialized countries.

Government social expenditure on public services, if carefully managed – as it was in Sri Lanka during the 1960s and 1970s – can do much to reduce such severe disparities. But there are many cases where free or subsidized services do not reach many of the poor. Such services are concentrated in the urban areas and information about them is more accessible to the better-educated who then manage to pre-empt the benefits.

Moreover, it is often overlooked that even free services have a cost. To get to a school or a clinic takes both time and, if it is a bus ride away, money. The very poor have neither.

Too often, in any event, government expenditures are not even targeted to reach the poor. In the Philippines in the early 1980s, annual subsidies to private hospitals catering to upper-income families exceeded the total resources appropriated to primary health care and mass health programmes, including malaria and schisto-somiasis eradication.

If one combines this review of urban-rural, male-female and rich-poor disparities, it is obvious that those most severely affected by inequality are poor, rural women. There are around one billion of them and their numbers are growing. Many are illiterate. Their incomes have not increased and in many countries have fallen. They receive no medical attention in child-bearing and their children are deprived of health care.

All this reminds us of the tremendous task still before us, despite the giant steps the world has taken over the past 30 years.

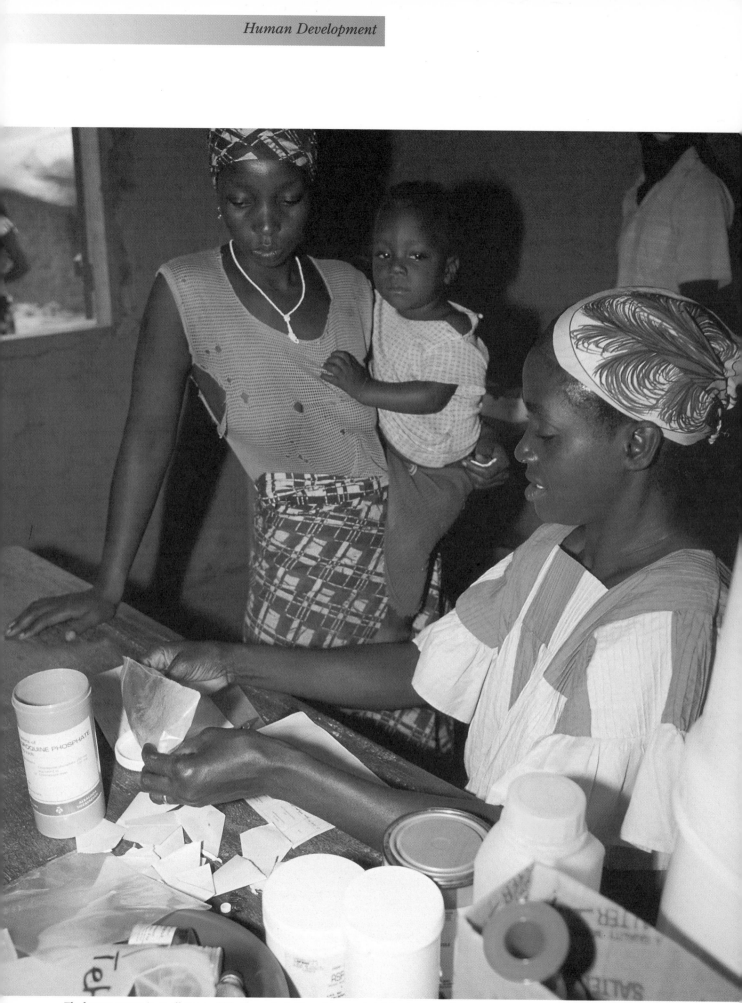

The human person is, at all stages of life, the central object of international development efforts.

© *Ron Giling/Panos*

Debt burdens and retrenchment

The opportunities realized during the 1960s and 1970s began to disappear in the 1980s, particularly in Africa and Latin America, rather less so in Asia. A growing mountain of debt compelled a large number of developing countries to take their foot off the economic and social accelerator. Indeed, for a number of them it meant going into reverse. In the 1990s, fortunately, recovery is under way.

The total external debt of developing countries multiplied thirteenfold over the past two decades, from $100 billion in 1970 to $1,350 billion in 1990. The debt is now so huge and new lending so small that the net flow is actually reversed – towards the richer countries. Between 1983 and 1989 rich-country creditors received a staggering $242 billion in net transfers.

The debt is highly concentrated. Over half is held by just 20 countries, with Brazil, Mexico and Argentina holding the most. Overall, the two continents that have suffered truly massive economic setbacks because of their debt burden are Latin America and Sub-Saharan Africa. The debt of Sub-Saharan Africa is 100 per cent of its GNP. In Latin America it is 50 per cent. Even today, after a decade of retrenchment and adjustment, only some of these countries are back to where they were 10 years ago.

It comes as no surprise to learn that between 1960 and 1989 the countries with the richest 20 per cent of the world population increased their share of global GNP from 70.2 per cent to 82.7 per cent, and the countries with the poorest 20 per cent of the world population saw their share fall from 2.3 per cent to 1.4 per cent. The absolute difference in per capita income between the top and the bottom increased from $1,864 to $15,149.

Wage earners have borne the brunt of the crisis. In Africa and Latin America wage cuts of a third to a half were not exceptional. In Latin America unemployment grew by six per cent a year and in Africa by 10 per cent. Rapid food price rises added to the squeeze. The removal of food subsidies, together with devaluation and decontrol, meant that food prices rose faster than other prices.

Governments felt forced to cut back on social services. Some, which started well by redirecting resources towards priority areas, were finally overwhelmed by the scale of the retrenchment they had to make. It was absolutely impossible to maintain social spending at the accustomed level.

"wage earners have borne the brunt of the crisis"

Even in a number of rich countries poverty has become more manifest. In the United States there has been a sharp rise in the number of homeless, and in London people are sleeping on the streets or in the parks in cardboard tents.

Tetra Laval: A Vision of Food Supply

A dedication to making more food available to more people.

IT IS A GREAT PLEASURE to take this opportunity to express Tetra Laval's support and alignment with the principles, objectives and activities of the UN. The most significant field of endeavour we have in common with the UN is food availability, our core business.

Food availability is also one of the world's most critical issues. Today, there are already over one billion hungry and undernourished people in the world. Tomorrow, there will unfortunately be many more. The UN Population Division has estimated that, between 1990 and 2025, the world's population will have grown from five billion to over eight billion people, increasing mostly in the Third World.

For greater global sustainability, the world needs to enhance the capacity of countries to participate in the global economy. This requires also that global poverty, hunger and over-population be addressed.

Another part of the solution lies in more food production, processing and packaging development in the future.

Companies within Tetra Laval are dedicated to making more food available to more people. For instance, when Tetra Pak, the largest of the four industrial groups within Tetra Laval, launched its first aseptic packaging system in 1961, fresh milk was able to reach people in remote countries for the first time. Last year, Tetra Pak provided packaging for over 40 billion litres of liquid food, including everything from milk, juice and water to soups and maple syrup. Because they are lightweight, compact, and do not require refrigeration, Tetra Pak packages have been used by the Red Cross and other similar organizations in disaster relief programmes.

Alfa Laval, Tetra Laval's second largest industry group, among many other things, has manufactured and installed numerous advanced purification systems to make drinking water safe and available to municipalities in countries all over the world. Alfa Laval products and systems perform key functions in the manufacture of food, pharmaceuticals, chemicals and energy. The company is also known for its environmental engineering products, such as waste water treatment equipment.

Alfa Laval Agri has been a provider of equipment and supplies to the world's dairy farms. Over the years, this organization has contributed significantly to raising the quality of milk in many parts of the world. This industry group's most recent development is an exciting new concept called 'farm dairies' – dairy farms, usually smaller ones, with a modest complement of processing and packaging equipment added and used to supply milk directly to nearby local markets.

Tetra Laval Food rounds off the industry group foursome and does everything that Tetra Pak does – processing, packaging, and distribution – but does it for solid and viscous foods instead of liquid foods.

Food availability is clearly the most prominent 'common thread' between the UN and Tetra Laval. Food supply is a common thread between families, nations and sustainable development. It links the present with the future. On a global scale, considering the current alarming levels of hunger in an exploding world population, food supply today and food supply tomorrow will continue to be one of humanity's most critical and pressing issues.

It is an issue to which our eyes must turn toward more and more, on which our hands must work harder and harder to solve, if we are to realize our 'vision of hope' for the future.

Göran Grosskoft
Chairman, Tetra Laval Group

Tetra Laval International AB
Landerigränden, S-221 86 Lund, Sweden
Tel: +46 46 36 10 00 Fax: +46 46 14 86 31

Costs and consequences

Economic growth has now resumed in most parts of the world, even in parts of Africa, and foreign exchange and debt problems are being improved. Nevertheless, the world has lately become more conscious of many of the costs of economic change and development. There is more crime than ever before, more drug and alcohol abuse, more deaths on the road and more pollution. There is also the breakdown of the extended family and, in the industrialized countries, even of the nuclear family. Modern warfare, ever more destructive as its technological capabilities increase, has created large numbers of refugees.

nuclear family could be even more devastating. The incidence of divorce is already very high in the industrialized countries and is rising. The number of single-parent families has risen precipitously in the South. Poor women in both North and South are most hurt. They are forced onto their own resources, having to work and care for children without much support. Yet they are often less qualified than men and have to take lower-paid jobs. We are witnessing the rapid feminization of poverty.

Human development, we can see from UNDP's detailed analysis, does not necessarily mean uniform

"*economic progress is not an uninterrupted push forward*"

The toll taken from the environment by unhindered economic growth has become more apparent by the year. Pollution is accelerating the extinction of species, spreading cancer, respiratory and diarrhoeal diseases, undermining public health in general, and perhaps foreclosing many opportunities for humankind in the future.

It is ironic that environmental degradation is usually caused by affluence in the North and by poverty in the South. But it would be quite unfair if global limits were imposed on the South's development in a manner that limited its potential. The world will have to find a way to share the same environmental space in an equitable manner.

Perhaps most uncertain, some would say ominous, for the future is the impact of development on family life. The extended family rarely survives modern day economic progress. The break-up of the

human progress. The infant mortality rate may fall but human confidence and security may diminish as other changes alter the bonds and bindings of traditional life. Economic progress itself is not a straightforward matter nor an uninterrupted push forward. Its uncertainties, upheavals and setbacks can create more misery than its momentum creates happiness. And the wide discrepancies between North and South and between regions within the South are also sources of potential tension.

If our goal is the betterment of human life we are compelled to work at many levels. Economic growth certainly, but at the same time ensuring a fair and reasonable distribution of its fruits. We also have to watch carefully and attentively for its harmful side-effects and pitfalls. Only if this is done can we be sure that humanity as a whole advances and development is not just for the benefit of a privileged minority.

This article presents a summary of the main findings of the Human Development Reports, 1990-94.

The Humanitarians

Millions of people fled the genocide in Rwanda, including one million who crossed into Zaire in one 48-hour period.
Food aid is handed out to displaced Rwandans inside the country.

a framework for preventive action

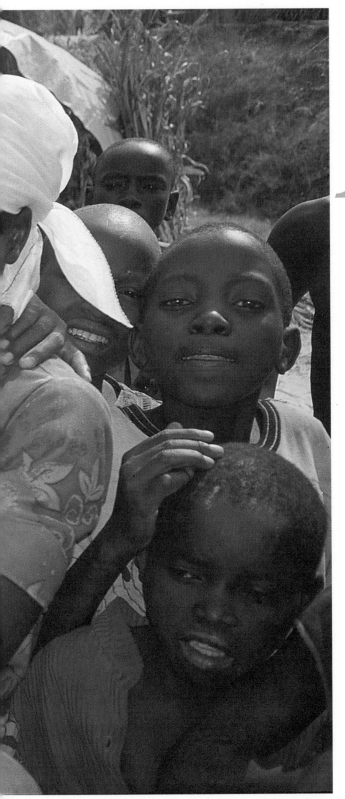

© Trevor Page/Panos

- A network of compassion
- Protecting refugees
- Disaster relief
- Contemporary challenges

Many millions of refugees, displaced people and famine victims throughout the world rely on the United Nations to survive. Indeed, during the past 50 years, the UN's humanitarian agencies have intervened sporadically to save the lives of victims of war and starvation and its efforts have had a discernible effect on the conscience of most governments. Still, the institutional structure, the level of coordination and the effectiveness of UN humanitarian operations fall far short of how many people would like to see the UN perform in humanitarian emergencies.

If anyone needs two terrifying examples to illustrate the inadequacy of the current approach to dealing with the world's humanitarian crises, they can be found in Bosnia and Rwanda. In the former, UN attempts to protect 'safe areas' call into question the very definition of 'safe'. And in the latter, the numbers alone tell the story: hundreds of thousands of civilians butchered in genocide and millions of people displaced, including some one million who crossed into Zaire in one 48-hour period.

But while these two examples are the ones attracting the most attention today, they are far from the only ones. In recent years, the international community has been confronted with one humanitarian crisis after another, in rapid, sometimes overlapping, succession. Crises in Africa, Asia, the Middle East, the Balkans and the former Soviet republics have strained the capacities of the UN almost to breaking point. Never in its history has the demand on the UN to intervene in humanitarian and refugee emergencies been higher.

OUR GOAL IS ELECTRICITY FOR ALL

*'We are committed to the total electrification of Zimbabwe
at world class standards and competitive prices.'*

Zimbabwe's energy requirements are projected to grow at about 6% a year. To meet this demand, ZESA has embarked on a multi-billion dollar programme that will see its generating capacity double by the year 2005.

The Authority is refurbishing 120MW of its old thermal power stations to improve the capacity for the next 10-15 years.

ZESA is planning to double the capacity of the 920MW Hwenge Power Station which currently provides over 55% of the country's energy requirements.

We are refurbishing and upgrading the 666MW hydro power station at Kariba South which has been in service since 1960.

New private sector initiatives are being encouraged. There are plans to develop a new thermal power station at the Sengwa Coalfield near Lake Kariba, and a series of mini-hydro electric schemes in the country's eastern district.

Construction has already started on interconnectors to South Africa and Mozambique which will put Zimbabwe at the centre of the evolving Southern Africa Power Grid by 1995.

Zimbabwe's tariffs are among the lowest in the world. ZESA plans to keep it that way.

*In the spirit of progress and cooperation, we wish to salute the
United Nations on its 50th Anniversary.*

Zimbabwe Electricity Supply Authority (ZESA)
25 Samora Machel Avenue
Po. Box 377
Harare
ZIMBABWE
Tel: 263 4 739081
Fax: 263 4 739854
Telex: 24323 ZESCOM ZW

History and evolution of the UN response

Organized international concern for people displaced by war and famine dates back to the aftermath of the First World War, when governments were confronted with massive numbers of stateless people devastated by the war and the break-up of multi-ethnic empires, mainly in Europe and the Middle East. In response, Western governments established the post of High Commissioner for Refugees and named Fridtjof Nansen, who proved to be a highly innovative and successful advocate for refugees. Again, after the Second World War, when millions of displaced people wandered throughout Europe and Asia, the scope of assistance operations reached a large scale, principally through the United Nations Relief and Rehabilitation Agency (UNRRA) and the International Refugee Organization (IRO).

The Cold War era

The contemporary UN approach to refugee problems emerged fully with the establishment of the Office of the United Nations High Commissioner for Refugees (UNHCR) in 1951. Initially, UNHCR experienced difficulty defining an independent role and implementing its goals. For most of the 1950s, the refugee problem assumed an almost exclusively East-West dimension. The UN created two new agencies: the UN Relief and Works Agency for Palestine Refugees in the Near East and the UN Korean Reconstruction Agency, exclusively to handle the humanitarian emergencies and massive refugee populations located in strategic conflict areas in the Middle East and Korea. It was not until the 1956 Hungarian Revolution that UNHCR was given the opportunity to demonstrate that it was the only UN agency capable of coordinating both international refugee relief and the collection of funds for emergency material assistance.

Decolonization and newly independent states

By the late 1950s, the UN faced further political problems arising not only from the Cold War and the East-West nature of refugee flows but also from anti-colonial insurgency and post-independence civil strife and warfare in Africa and Asia. In Africa, there were at least two distinct categories of humanitarian disasters and displacements: refugees from territories under French and Portuguese colonial administration (and later from Rhodesia and South Africa) and refugees produced by internal strife, political instability, ethnic conflict and repression in several countries that had already gained independence, such as Rwanda, Burundi, Nigeria and Sudan. By the end of the decade, there were over one million refugees in Africa.

African governments mounted impressive efforts on behalf of refugees from neighbouring countries, but these governments often lacked the infrastructure, resources or technical ability to deal with the emergencies they faced. Consequently, the patterns of international assistance changed radically from the mid-1960s onwards. In every year from 1967 to 1973, post-colonial African countries received more than 50 per cent of all UN refugee aid. Until 1971, UNHCR assistance in Africa was primarily targeted towards the development of rural resettlement zones for refugees. From 1972 onwards, UNHCR's African expenditure increased significantly to cover repatriation programmes in Africa and the needs of urban refugees, especially from southern Africa.

From this expansion in the 1960s, the UN embarked on ambitious assistance programmes in a number of humanitarian emergencies around the world. The first in Bangladesh occurred as a consequence of the 1971 war between West Pakistan and secessionist East Pakistan and the subsequent flight of 10 million East Bengalis to India. In response, the UN Secretary-General set up a separate international relief apparatus under a special coordination organization. As head of this organization, Sadruddin Aga Khan coordinated the work of all the UN agencies involved – including the World Health Organization (WHO), the World Food Programme (WFP) and the UN Children's Fund (UNICEF), among others – and mobilized UN assistance totalling $185 million. The success of the Bangladesh operation spurred the UN to launch similar system-wide relief efforts the following year in southern Sudan to repatriate and reintegrate over 200,000 refugees and to assist hundreds of thousands of displaced people. In 1974, the UN set up the UN Humanitarian Assistance Programme for Cyprus to assist 164,000 Greek Cypriots from the North and 34,000 Turkish Cypriots from the South.

Never-ending humanitarian crises

From the mid-1970s until the 1990s, the UN had to cope with a growing number of complex humanitarian emergencies and increasing numbers of refugees and displaced people. In the 1970s, political and civil unrest in Latin America resulted in

The UN estimates there are over 50 million refugees and displaced people in the world.
A Somali refugee camp in Kenya.

widespread political repression and huge refugee movements. The Latin American crises spawned a worldwide diaspora, as the exiles were resettled in 44 different countries with the assistance of UNHCR. On the other side of the world, over 1.5 million refugees fled Vietnam, Laos and Cambodia. In order to rescue the Indochinese refugees, the UN organized the largest overseas resettlement programme since the Second World War. In 1979, famine and the mass exodus of Khmer people following the Vietnamese ouster of the Khmer Rouge regime in Phnom Penh dominated the UN's attention. From 1979 to 1982, the UN mounted a three-pronged emergency relief programme: inside Cambodia, along the Thai-Cambodian border and operating refugee camps inside Thailand.

As the Cold War intensified during the 1980s, internal wars in Afghanistan, Central America, the Horn of Africa and southern Africa became protracted and debilitating affairs. These conflicts perpetuated endemic violence and caused massive physical destruction, which, in turn, generated large waves of refugees.

© Howard Davies/Panos

Consequently, over the past two decades there has been an alarming increase of refugees in the world. The total rose from 2.8 million in 1976, to 8.2 million in 1980, to over 20 million in 1995. In the same period UNHCR's expenditure rose from approximately $100 million to nearly $1.5 billion.

The relief network

During the past 50 years not only has the UN's global humanitarian reach extended dramatically but so too has the number of agencies involved in carrying out relief efforts. They include UNHCR, whose mandate it is to protect and assist refugees worldwide; the WFP, which coordinates food aid to victims of conflict, and UNICEF, which provides relief aid to women and children who comprise the majority of civilian victims in conflicts today.

The international community also relies on a vast network of non-governmental organizations (NGOs) to help in humanitarian

Ages

RRA9 DMB&B Respons

of wisdom

is communicated

from one person

to another;

from one generation

to the next.

The communication

is never

ours,

but belongs to

humanity.

It is our

ambition to help

the communicators

of the world.

Of all

ages.

Telenor International AS, Postboks 6701 St. Olavs Plass, N-0130 Oslo, Norway

emergencies. The network ranges from large international agencies to small outfits working in one particular country. Increasingly, NGOs are playing a vital role in emergency relief because of their ability to reach sources of funds, rouse public opinion and provide large numbers of technical staff willing to work under harsh conditions. As the implementing partners for the UN, NGOs shoulder much of the burden of delivering food and providing shelter, water, sanitation and health care to refugees.

UNHCR now has a staff of about 4,000 in over 100 countries and an annual expenditure of approximately $1.5 billion. Its work in protecting and assisting refugees is done with three durable solutions in mind: voluntary repatriation, local integration, or third country resettlement.

The growth in numbers and the complexity of refugee flows in recent years, however, has presented enormous challenges to UNHCR to plan, manage and fund its worldwide network of protection and relief programmes. Recently, UNHCR has improved its overall emergency relief preparedness and response mechanisms by bolstering its standby capacity in emergency staffing, relief supplies, needs assessment and emergency programme implementation. Five Preparedness and Response Officers and attendant regional emergency response teams have been established. Stockpiles of commodities for use in emergencies have been amassed and a roster of standby technical experts and relief workers for deployment in relief situations has been established.

Despite improvements in its emergency preparedness, UNHCR is chronically underfunded and understaffed. Although the number of refugees it serves has doubled in the last decade, funding levels for basic care and maintenance have remained at a virtual standstill.

In responding to humanitarian emergencies, UNHCR collaborates closely with other UN agencies – primarily the WFP and UNICEF – as well as a number of NGOs. In most recent emergency operations, the WFP has been a principal source of food aid. Originally conceived in 1961, it is today recognized as the world's coordinating body for emergency food aid. Although food aid for development remains a major part of its mandate, the expenditures representing emergency food aid have steadily increased in recent years.

Originally founded in 1946 to provide assistance to child victims of warfare, UNICEF now devotes a steadily increasing proportion of its efforts and resources in channelling relief and supplemental aid to women and children in emergency relief situations in Asia and Africa. The great majority of people in any humanitarian emergency are women and children, whose special needs are not always understood or are neglected in the provision of basic relief. Over the years, UNICEF has built up its rapid response capacities and its capability to respond quickly in most emergencies has been praised in several quarters. Not only has it been designated a lead agency in past emergencies but it was also instrumental in establishing 'days of tranquillity' in El Salvador and Lebanon in order to vaccinate children in these conflict areas.

Not all humanitarian crises, however, are covered by UNHCR, UNICEF or other UN agencies. Because a wide variety of people, including refugees, internally displaced people and victims of war, drought and famine, are likely to be affected in such situations, a number of agencies will necessarily be involved in response. In major emergencies, where there are sometimes hundreds of aid agencies working, effective coordination is essential to ensure that responsibilities and roles are clearly assigned and gaps in the relief response are covered.

"days of tranquillity"

The post-Cold War humanitarian challenge

While explosions of political and ethnic violence, persecution and massacres have produced humanitarian crises and large-scale movements of refugees throughout history, there are many new and unique features to the contemporary humanitarian emergencies. The scale, frequency and suddenness of contemporary humanitarian emergencies have exerted enormous pressures on international response capacities.

Complex emergencies

Present-day humanitarian crises are complex emergencies, combining political instability, ethnic tensions, armed conflict, economic collapse and the disintegration of civil society. They involve not only refugees but also internally displaced people, as well as victims of war, famine and drought. With modern powerful weaponry accessible even to the very poorest country, civil war can quickly devastate its infrastructure while population density means that a single conflict can cause millions of people to suddenly flee. In conflict situations, refugee movements frequently spill over borders and aggravate existing problems, such as environmental damage or severe food shortages. Humanitarian emergencies are seldom confined to single countries but often affect entire regions, such as central or west Africa or the Balkans. In recent years, few of these crises have been fully resolved. Consequently, resources from one crisis often have not been made available for use in the next.

Inside the borders

A critical weakness of the international humanitarian system is that at present there is no special international organization to protect and assist the world's 25 million internally displaced people. There is an inadequate body of international law to regulate their treatment by governments. While there is a clear mandate for the protection and provision of humanitarian assistance to refugees, internally displaced people are unprotected precisely because they do not become refugees but remain within the boundaries of their own countries.

Internal wars not only displace huge numbers of people but also prevent international aid from reaching people living in conflict areas. Although

a growing number of analysts and some governments and institutions are beginning to argue that there is a right to international intervention for humanitarian purposes, the international community is frequently

© *Rex Features, London*

Refugee crises are often full-blown before the world responds.
Hundreds of thousands of Kurds fled Iraq after the 1991 failed uprising before the UN created
'safe havens' in northern Iraq.

Italferr-sis. t.a.v., from design to implementation of a modern rail transport system.

Italferr-sis. t.a.v. S.p.A., is the consulting engineering subsidiary of the Italian State Railways (FS) founded in Rome in 1984. Shareholders are the Italian State Railways (94%) and Banca Nazionale delle Comunicazioni (6%). Share capital is 14,186 million Italian lire (US$ 8.87 million), fully paid up.

Italferr-sis. t.a.v. operates in the fields of high-speed and conventional railway systems, metros and other guided transport systems, and in complementary sectors.

Italferr-sis. t.a.v. offers a complete range of services covering all aspects of a modern railway system from management and personnel, finance and economics to operations, commercial matters, costs and tariffs, traffic control systems, lines and permanent way, signalling and telecommunications, electrification, motive power and rolling stock, ferry service, stations and marshalling yards, workshops and depot facilities, harbour-railway installations, intermodal terminals and management information systems.

ITALFERR-SIS. T.A.V. IN SUPPORT OF THE FIFTIETH ANNIVERSARY OF THE UN FULLY SHARES ITS VISION OF HOPE

GRUPPO FS

Italferr-sis. t.a.v. S.p.A.
Cinecittà Due - Via Vincenzo Lamaro, 13
00173 - Rome, Italy
Tel. +39 6 722.951 - Fax +39 6 722.952.1360

unable to assist or intervene and the ability of governments or international organizations to influence the behaviour of warring factions in such situations is limited. Former Yugoslavia is one such case. While the UN peacekeeping operation there has saved lives and salved the consciences of governments, it has also been accused of fostering ethnic cleansing by stimulating the forcible movement of unwanted populations. One of the principal lessons of the conflict in Bosnia is that the humanitarian mandate of UNHCR cannot be viewed as a satisfactory substitute for wider-ranging political solutions.

Repatriation and reintegration

UNHCR's more immediate short-term tasks include dealing with the consequences of refugee exoduses and determining when and how repatriation and reintegration is most appropriate. Even as new refugee crises emerge, there remain numerous long-standing refugee populations in the Third World –some dating back 10 years, some 20 or more years.

Although the international community is still dealing with immediate problems of handling sudden mass outflows of refugees and problems of reception in countries of asylum, there is much greater attention today on repatriation. Almost five million refugees have returned home since the beginning of the 1990s. If large numbers of refugees continue to repatriate at this rate, the focus of concern must inevitably shift from repatriation to more long-standing reintegration and development. It is becoming increasingly evident that in countries such as Afghanistan, Cambodia, Ethiopia, Mozambique and Rwanda one of the preconditions for successful returns is development aid and reintegration assistance aimed at alleviating poverty. Without careful reintegration and reconciliation, returning refugees will compete for scarce developmental resources which, in turn, may well result in fierce political and economic competition with local populations that did not flee.

Repatriation and reconstruction raise new and difficult questions for UN agencies. For how long should UNHCR seek to provide protection to returning refugees, particularly in situations of continuing conflict? Does the UN Human Rights Centre have the capacity to engage in human rights monitoring in countries of origin? How much and what kinds of assistance are required for returnees to re-establish themselves successfully? Should the international economic development agencies, such as the UN Development Programme (UNDP), provide refugee-targeted development assistance from the early stages of a repatriation? Should assistance be extended not only to returning refugees but also to needy local populations? Although answers to these questions have yet to be found, they are of critical importance if the UN is to respond effectively in the future.

Going beyond traditional humanitarian emergency assistance to facilitating reintegration of returnees into countries of origin requires the development of new or different competencies on the part of international agencies. A focus on reintegration will involve rethinking the roles and mandates of international organizations and NGOs, the shifting of their operational priorities from receiving countries to countries of return and closer cooperation between development, human rights and refugee agencies than has hitherto been the case.

"there are numerous long-standing refugee populations"

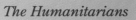

Neighbouring countries often shoulder much of the burden when refugees flee.
A food distribution point for Rwandan refugees in Zaire which is currently home to 857,000 refugees.

A framework for future action

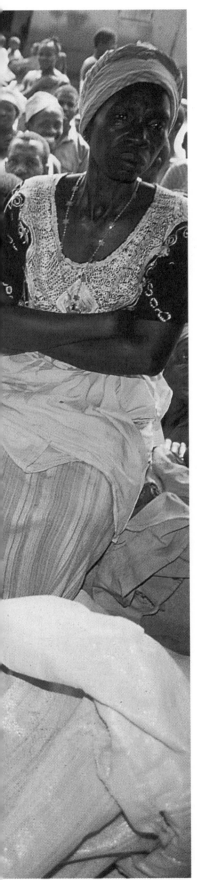

© Liba Taylor/Panos

The humanitarian emergencies of the post-Cold War era have highlighted the fact that combating the causes of internal conflicts and forced migration cannot proceed solely within the confines of international humanitarian organizations. There is a need for a better interface between the relief agencies and political and security operations on the one hand and emergency relief, development and human rights mechanisms on the other. A multidimensional strategy for humanitarian crises must involve practically the entire UN system, as well as regional organizations and NGOs, and requires enhancing these organizations' capacities to defuse, to deter and to mediate incipient crises before they need more serious and costly trans-sovereign intervention.

Early warning systems

Early information on impending crises is critical not only for possible preventive action but also for effective and timely humanitarian responses and for ensuring adequate preparedness. Establishing an effective monitoring body within the UN that would alert the Secretary-General, the UN Emergency Relief Coordinator and the Security Council to potential conflicts and humanitarian emergencies could provide an early warning mechanism.

For example, the capability and mandate of the UN Centre for Human Rights needs to be strengthened to enable it to monitor and collect accurate and up-to-date human rights information; to identify situations that have the potential to produce mass refugee flows and to bring these to the attention of the international community. The UN Commission on Human Rights could assign its Sub-Commission on Prevention of Discrimination and Protection of Minorities to monitor the treatment of ethnic and religious minorities and to alert the Secretary-General when action is needed. Similarly, the early warning capabilities, as well as inter-agency information swapping, in both UNHCR and UNDP should be bolstered.

Among the potentially most important new instruments added to the UN's capacities is the organization's ability to send UN fact-finding missions to defuse disputes and prevent major crises from expanding. Fact-finding missions are likely to play an important role in the early stages of conflict development and may prevent the misunderstandings that escalate conflict and result in more rigid positions. Observers in the field can also serve as a deterrent for those considering actions that cause forcible displacement. NGOs, such as Amnesty International or the Helsinki Watch groups, may in some instances be more successful than UN monitors in collecting information and bringing abuses of human and minority rights to the attention of the international community. However, it is not enough for monitors to be in place and for information about potential human rights abuses and refugee movements to be widely available – there must also be the political will to act.

Early warning programmes must be connected to decision-making and response strategies both in governments and in relief, development and human rights organizations. In many recent humanitarian crises, information about impending conflicts and mass migrations was well known in advance but there was no willingness to act on this information. In Burundi, Rwanda, Somalia and former Yugoslavia,

Connecting
people and places

As long as our world has existed, man has needed to communicate. Face to face, or across long distances.

Communication between peoples is the central pillar upon which community and understanding are based.

Post Denmark is one of the world's fastest and safest media for communication between people, businesses and nations.

A vital link in the chain of national and international relations irrespective of race, creed, generation and political belief.

Post Denmark is a modern, state-owned corporation run on business principles. Safe. Quick. Reliable connections. With a success rate that is measured by customer satisfaction.

The success of the United Nations is measured by the degree of popular involvement in creating understanding and progress in the world. A mission that deserves the respect of the world.

Across the globe, good neighbourliness comes from trust, contact and communication.

Good communication comes from trusted, reliable partners.

Post Denmark.

for example, international agencies and analysts had accurately predicted what would happen well before the disasters unfolded, but there existed no mechanisms and institutions for averting conflicts or for dealing effectively and rapidly with these crises at a time when they were still manageable. In December 1993, several months in advance of the massive bloodletting in Rwanda in 1994, the UN Special Rapporteur on Extra-Judicial, Summary and Arbitrary Executions reported to the UN Commission on Human Rights: 'Lessons should be drawn from the past and the cycle of violence which has drenched both Burundi and Rwanda in blood must be broken. To this end the impunity of the perpetrators of the massacres must be definitely brought to an end and preventive measures to avoid the recurrence of such tragedies must be designed.' The international community ignored this early warning and mass murder occurred on a gigantic scale. Even after genocide in Rwanda became widely known, the Western governments failed to support calls for a UN force for Rwanda while there was still time to curb the massacres.

"the cycle of violence must be broken"

Unless trigger mechanisms for prompt action are established and existing tools of diplomacy, human rights and conflict-resolution are reinforced, any measures that might be taken to prepare for future emergencies are likely to be of limited use. The value of such measures depends largely on the willingness of states and international organizations to take the necessary concerted preventive action.

The UN's vision of coordination

Making the system work better requires a more effective division of labour among the actors involved in responding to the humanitarian, political and security dimensions of internal conflicts. Over 20 years ago, in 1971, the UN General Assembly created the Office of the UN Disaster Relief Coordinator (UNDRO) which was to be the focal point within the UN system for mobilizing and coordinating relief assistance. In practice, UNDRO failed to provide the leadership required by its mandate. In order to fill this gap, the UN General Assembly, in December 1991, created the Office of Emergency Relief Coordinator, charged with providing a focal point for government, intergovernmental and NGO communication during UN emergency relief operations. In early 1992, Jan Eliasson, the Emergency Relief Coordinator, became the first Under-Secretary-General in the newly formed UN Department of Humanitarian Affairs (DHA) and was subsequently replaced by Peter Hansen in 1994.

The creation of DHA was an essential step in clarifying and assigning responsibilities to UN agencies in complex emergencies. This is particularly apparent in situations where mandates overlap or where no entity has a clear mandate to act; in making quick decisions on the best coordinating mechanisms to respond to humanitarian emergencies at the field level and in negotiating access for these agencies without waiting for a formal government request. Donor states influential in the creation of DHA envision the office gathering data, mobilizing resources, orchestrating field activities, negotiating a framework of action with political authorities and providing overall leadership to humanitarian aid efforts.

Unfortunately, the vision has so far not been realized. Lack of adequate staff in the field, a rapid succession of humanitarian crises in the post-Cold War period and incompletely established and largely untested mechanisms for inter-agency coordination have caught the department unprepared, leaving it unable to assume its intended leadership role in most recent emergencies. Perhaps the greatest difficulty

confronting DHA is that while every agency favours coordination in principle, few wish to be coordinated in practice. If DHA's presence is to lead to improvements in the response capacity of the UN, the significance of its coordinating role must be recognized by UNHCR and other agencies. The DHA must also be fully equipped both politically and financially to undertake effectively its assigned tasks.

Coordinating relief and development

Closer coordination between UNDP, UNHCR, UNICEF and other UN agencies is the key to dealing with refugees, returnees and the internally displaced. Cooperation between these agencies already takes place in joint UNHCR-UNDP projects aimed at assisting a variety of displaced groups in Central America, Mozambique and Cambodia. In recent years, in the Horn of Africa, UNHCR and UNDP have established joint management structures to create preventive zones and cross-mandate programmes to stabilize and prevent displacement.

Although there have been greater efforts at UNDP-UNHCR coordination in field operations, far more effective inter-agency planning, consultation and implementation are required. Institutional constraints inhibit closer cooperation between the two UN agencies. UNHCR is not a development agency. Although UNHCR can be a catalyst in initiating development-oriented assistance, UNDP is more suited to the task. Unfortunately, in most countries, a 'development gap' exists between short-term humanitarian relief assistance and long-term development. UNHCR-UNDP joint projects attempted to fill this gap in Central America, the Horn of Africa and Indochina where there are large returnee and displaced populations, but because these projects were small in size and limited in nature they have only partially filled the gap between immediate assistance and longer-term development. The task of the overall rehabilitation of these communities must be carried out by UNDP, or by other UN agencies, which can more appropriately deal with reconstruction and development. This requires a full transfer of responsibility from UNHCR to UNDP after the immediate emergency relief phase is over – again, an idea that UNDP consistently resists because it views itself as having a development, and not even a partially emergency, focus.

Finding the funds

Greater development assistance alone is not enough to create safe conditions for refugees; international cooperation must also ensure democratization and respect for human rights. The existing UN human rights machinery needs to be strengthened and applied more effectively to deal with refugees, returnees and the internally displaced – for it is integral to the success of UN peacemaking.

A UN food truck arrives in Upper Lofa, Liberia.

© Liba Taylor/Panos

In recent years, the UN human rights system has demonstrated its potential capabilities to respond quickly to a select number of human rights emergencies involving the internally displaced. For example, in 1992, in response to the situation in former Yugoslavia, it called an unprecedented meeting of the UN Commission on Human Rights and appointed a Special Rapporteur to investigate human rights abuses of minority populations and to make recommendations to the Security Council. Recently, international criminal tribunals for the former Yugoslavia and Rwanda, under Justice Richard Goldstone, have begun proceedings. In other instances, the UN human rights system has acted much too slowly. For example, it was not until after the genocide occurred in Rwanda that the UN

When disaster strikes, international efforts are mobilized across a broad front with special assistance to children at risk.

© *Jeremy Hartley/Panos*

Commission on Human Rights held a special session on Rwanda in June 1994 and appointed a Special Rapporteur to investigate the massacres there.

At the same time, the UN Centre for Human Rights, through its Advisory Services, has worked on a number of UN peacekeeping or peace-enforcement missions, providing significant technical assistance and cooperation to the UN human rights presence in the field, for example in El Salvador, Somalia and Cambodia. These actions underscore both the potentially key role of the UN human rights machinery and the growing involvement of the Security Council in humanitarian matters, and the recognition that the promotion and protection of the human rights of refugees, returnees and the internally displaced are an integral part of UN peacemaking.

If the UN hopes to respond more effectively to humanitarian crises, it must strengthen its capacity to monitor developments in human rights issues. The creation of the post of UN High Commissioner for Human Rights in late 1993 is an important initial step in this direction. However, a greater protection role in the field should be granted to UN human rights personnel. At present, the UN Centre for Human Rights has country expertise but no field presence. Despite widespread recognition of the need for more human rights monitors in civil war situations, the UN still has enormous political and financial difficulties placing adequate numbers of observers in such obvious places as Burundi and Rwanda. At a minimum, the Centre can strengthen its coverage in the field by the continued expansion of its advisory services and technical cooperation. In addition, by offering services such as training judges, strengthening electoral commissions, establishing ombudsmen, training prison staff and advising governments on constitutions and legislation regarding national minorities and human rights, the Centre is likely to be more successful in its activities and less threatening to governments than in more straightforward, fieldwork-oriented human rights monitoring.

There is much discussion about the creation of special human rights machinery for the internally displaced. At its 1993 session, the UN Commission on Human Rights reappointed the Special Representative on the Internally Displaced, Francis Deng, to monitor mass displacements of people, collect information on violations of their human rights and help sustain a positive dialogue toward achieving solutions with governments of the country of origin. But the Special Representative must be given proper political support and funding to carry out his tasks effectively. A General Assembly resolution confirming the role and mandate of the Special Representative is now required to institutionalize this office further. A significant first step towards trying to deal with the problem would be to designate a permanent representative for the internally displaced. This representative could undertake fact-finding missions, intercede with governments, embark on activities which strengthen institutions that sustain democracy and civil society, publish reports and bring violations to the attention of human rights bodies and the Security Council.

Recently, there have been attempts to create closer linkages between UNHCR and the human rights organs and activities of the UN system. In 1992, for example, the UN Centre for Human Rights and UNHCR drafted a memorandum of

"a greater protection role should be granted to UN human rights personnel"

THE
Polish Post

The traditions of the Polish Post can be traced to the 16th century when, during the reign of King Zygmunt August, the first regular postal service was set up linking the two cities of Kraków and Venice.

Since then the history of Polish Post has been one of considerable success. Throughout the fluctuations of Poland's history, the postal service has continued undeterred, connecting the remotest areas of the country to its biggest cities and enabling Polish people to communicate with one another wherever they may live.

With its modern post offices and wide range of facilities, Polish Post provides a first-class service to its individual customers and for Poland's many thriving businesses.

As a member of the United Nations Universal Postal Union and as one of the country's oldest and largest institutions, Polish Post aims to unite people around the world by providing an efficient and cost-effective postal system.

PL. MALACHOWSKIEGO 2 00-940 WARSZAWA, POLAND
Telephone: 48 22 26 90 10 Telefax: 48 22 26 61 56 Telex: 813001
Director General of The Polish Post - Grzegorz Szermanowicz

understanding so that human rights information collected by UNHCR could be forwarded to the Centre for Human Rights. At the end of 1992, UNHCR and the Centre established a joint working group to study mechanisms and approaches for enhanced and continuous collaboration. Such consultation should be strengthened to ensure that displacements emanating from human rights violations are brought to the attention of the UN Commission on Human Rights and that the work of the Centre's Advisory Services section adequately addresses human rights issues associated with refugee movements and internal displacements.

The need for preventive political action

In the post-Cold War era, there is an urgent need to re-examine UN humanitarian action and to understand better the possibilities and limitations of the UN system. While greater efforts at coordination are crucial, the challenge for the international community in the next decade will be to respond not only to the immediate humanitarian problems of growing numbers of human rights victims and displaced people but also to confront the conditions which lead to these crises. These are political tasks requiring a more active role from national policy-makers and a greater willingness to utilize fully the UN mechanisms on security, peacekeeping, peacemaking and human rights in anticipating as well as reacting effectively to humanitarian disasters around the world. Humanitarian aid must not be used as an excuse to hide the political decisions needed to avoid future humanitarian tragedies. Future stability and security depend on new approaches which will bring together conflict-resolution capacities, humanitarian relief agencies and human rights networks and observers.

UN peacekeeping forces are increasingly needed to protect humanitarian convoys in conflict zones.
An Italian UN soldier plays with children orphaned in war.   © Paul Smith/Panos

In Defence of Women and

A mother and child clinic in Ouagadougou, Burkina Faso.

Children ~ *a more unified command*

© Sean Sprague/Panos

■ *The rights of children*
■ *Women's empowerment*
■ *Preventing abuses*
■ *Global campaigns*

The work United Nations agencies do on behalf of children is their most unassailable, almost by definition. Even critics of the UN have tended to perceive the successes, chiefly of the UN Children's Fund (UNICEF), but also of the World Health Organization (WHO), the UN Population Fund (UNFPA) and others, as the most tangible signs that the world body can do good.

By contrast, the UN's work on behalf of women reflects the world body's more bureaucratic nature. The objectives of women's empowerment, elucidated in several UN General Assembly resolutions, are to be implemented by an alphabet soup of branches and agencies, including the UN Development Fund for Women (UNIFEM), the Commission on the Status of Women (CSW) and the International Research and Training Institute for the Advancement of Women (INSTRAW) – all in addition to a plethora of women's rights divisions in most wings of the UN. Thus far, the most vocal agency in the struggle for women's rights has been UNFPA, with its focus on women's empowerment as a prerequisite for population control. Perhaps it helps that UNFPA's focus on population presents the aspect of women's rights that is easiest to sell: the right of mothers to care for their children. UNICEF and the other agencies defending children's rights, of course, have the easier struggle, being able to focus wholeheartedly on society's most vulnerable – and yet still appreciated – subjects.

As with the UN's other lofty goals, the betterment of the lives of the world's women and children has often fallen prey to bureaucratization, inter-agency

CHANGE IS CONSTANT. CHANGE FOR THE BETTER IS A COMMITMENT.

With over three centuries of continuing service to the people of Canada, we understand the importance of a common goal.

As one of the oldest companies in the world, we know that longevity is based on the ability to change.

It is to that end that we celebrate the United Nations Fiftieth Anniversary and join them in their Vision of Hope.

A hope that all of us, in some small way, can look at our world a little differently and realize that its most valuable commodity is its people.

In this, our 325th year of operation, it's easy to dwell on the past, but at The Hudson's Bay Company, we'd rather celebrate the future.

THE HUDSON'S BAY COMPANY, 401 Bay Street, Toronto, Ontario, M5H 2Y4 CANADA.

bickering and North-South disputes. But at a time when the UN faces a growing clamour for change, the agencies working on behalf of women and children also offer an aura of competent idealism.

UNICEF and the rise of compassionate bureaucracies

The UN General Assembly created UNICEF – then the UN International Children's Emergency Fund – in 1946, to aid European children left sickly, malnourished, displaced, or injured in the aftermath of the Second World War. The organization sprang from a controversy over the UN Relief and Rehabilitation Administration (UNRRA), set up in 1943 by more than 40 countries – led by the US-Soviet-British alliance then in place during the Second World War – to provide aid for war-racked Europe. So an alternative agency to concentrate on the war-uprooted European child was born with the founding of UNICEF, and US businessman Maurice Pate became its first Executive Director.

UNICEF – like UNFPA – is one of the UN's 'fund' organizations: it was set up around a special fund, donated by various UN member states to the UN, as an executing agency. Unlike WHO and other UN agencies that are governed by independent assemblies of its member states and funded by their membership fees, UNICEF is part of the UN and funded by voluntary contributions from member states and, increasingly, the general public.

Within years of its founding, UNICEF had quickly established its reputation as the provider of essential food and medical aid for needy children. By 1950, with the 'emergency' in Europe drawing to a close and the agency cautiously expanding into China and elsewhere, UNICEF, like UNRRA before it, was deemed to be ready for shut-down. The Fund, however, had already garnered enough goodwill and support from developing nations and it was granted a stay of execution for three years. By 1953, the words 'international' and 'emergency' were dropped from UNICEF's formal name, ironically at the very moment that the agency began grappling more than ever with international emergencies.

In 1959, the UN General Assembly began its lengthy effort to formalize the concept of children's rights by adopting the Declaration of the Rights of the Child, which proclaimed that children should have the opportunity to develop; that they should be entitled to a name, a nationality, social security and education; and that they should be protected from neglect, cruelty and exploitation. By 1990, many of those rights were codified in the Convention on the Rights of the Child, a text which James Grant, former Executive Director of UNICEF, called a Magna Carta for children, and which by 1993 had been ratified by 154 countries. UNICEF is hopeful that all the world's countries will ratify the Convention by 1995, making it the first universally ratified human rights convention in history.[1]

> ❝*at a time when the UN faces a growing clamour for change*❞

UNICEF's greatest successes, however, have had more to do with its nuts-and-bolts work to ensure better health and living conditions for children in the developing world – its work as a bureaucracy of compassion – than its loftier rights campaigns. Even UN critics marvel that the Fund can take credit for annually saving the lives of some 400,000 infants under the age of five.[2]

UNICEF's success in its goal of providing health and nutrition for the young has made such a good impression that the agency can also boast of a profitable direct-sales branch unique among all UN agencies. UNICEF established a Greeting Card Operation in 1951, which easily became a top money-maker with its appealing line of multi-lingual, non-sectarian cards. The venture was later followed by other enterprises, such as collection boxes for youngsters celebrating Halloween in the United States, which contributed both to UNICEF's funds and to its lustre as the leading pro-child organization. By 1993, the direct sales unit of UNICEF was netting some $50 million annually while keeping UNICEF's name as a seal of good quality among UN branches.

UNICEF's appeal can also be traced to its community-based strategy, developed in 1976. In that approach, local workers are made to choose 'primary-level' workers in their communities to perform task-oriented techniques in health care, applied nutrition, provision of clean water, and sanitation and education.

That approach acquired more focus in 1982 when UNICEF, WHO, the World Bank and other officials developed a four-fold approach to grapple with child hunger and poor health called 'GOBI'. The GOBI approach stands for the four strategies to improve children's conditions that the agencies found most promising. 'G' stood for monitoring the growth of the youngest children; 'O' for practising oral rehydration therapy (ORT) to combat infant diarrhoea; 'B' for encouraging a return to breast-feeding; and 'I' for immunizing children from disease. The GOBI approach has become the centrepiece of UNICEF's efforts to pioneer a low-cost, primary-level approach to child health in the Third World.

Fourteen million children die every year before reaching the age of five.
A very sick child at an orphanage.

© J.C. Tordai/Panos

*"**UNICEF's successes have more to do with its nuts-and-bolts work than its loftier rights campaigns**"*

INTERNATIONAL
INVESTMENT WORLD Co. Inc. (U.S.A.)
GROUP OF COMPANIES
REGIST. OFFICE (USA) WILMINGTON, DELAWARE
INTERNATIONAL LOANS

The formation of the United Nations 50 years ago was one of the most important events of this century.

Created at a time when the nations of the world were in turmoil, the UN laid the foundations for a future based on the principles of justice, peace and freedom.

Twenty five centuries ago, Ancient Greece, the cradle of democracy and freedom, had a similar vision - to create a country where its citizens could live together in peace and harmony.

The International Investment Group of Companies, with its large network of offices, specializes in all aspects of finance, international trade and business, offering assistance to governments, banks, major corporations and individuals, sincerely contributing to the efforts for a better future for humanity.

We fully support the UN's belief that, by working as a global family, we can change things for the better and in the process change our world for the better.

President
Panagiotis A. Papadakis

USTERISTRASSE 23 - ZURICH 8001,
SWITZERLAND
Tel: 41-1-212 7323
Fax: 41-1-212 7328

Vice President
Alexandra P. Papadakis

Much of UNICEF's health work is and has been done in a sometimes uneasy collaboration with WHO, which has, perhaps inevitably, vied with UNICEF over which agency has the greater jurisdiction to ensure children's health. From the start, WHO and the Food and Agriculture Organization (FAO) doubted whether UNICEF should operate projects or merely draw in funds. It was felt that there should be a separate mechanism for planning programmes for children and safeguarding their interests.

Formally founded in 1948, WHO is a highly decentralized, regionally-divided organization whose basic mandate is 'the attainment by all people of the highest possible level of health'.

To achieve that goal, WHO embarked almost from its inception on a series of campaigns to eradicate diseases, particularly through child immunization. In the 1940s, it kicked off a programme to combat malaria as part of a broader campaign against tropical diseases. The organization also sought to bring six other communicable diseases under control: smallpox – which was declared eradicated in 1977 after a global WHO campaign – poliomyelitis, tuberculosis, cholera, worm infection and tropical diseases.

In many of these campaigns, WHO and UNICEF worked together on child immunization. Buoyed by their successes, the two agencies, at the 1978 International Conference on Primary Health Care in Alma-Ata, in the Soviet Union, pledged themselves to a goal of 'Health for All by the Year 2000'. The two organizations in subsequent years expanded their joint immunization programmes against malaria, diphtheria, whooping cough, tetanus, poliomyelitis and tuberculosis – all of which strike particularly at infants and children under the age of five in the developing world.

WHO and UNICEF racked up an impressive set of victories throughout the 1970s, culminating in their campaign to establish an international code governing the marketing of breast-milk substitutes. That campaign was one of many that pitted the agencies – particularly WHO – against industrialized nations. The agency, under Director-General Halvdan Mahler, accused developed countries of deliberately promoting the sale of infant formula as breast-milk

substitutes in developing countries 'where they were likely to be misused and produce severe infant health problems'.[3]

Medical experts contended that children in poorer nations would suffer malnutrition and die as infant formula sales to the Third World increased. Finally, the World Health Assembly, WHO's governing body, recommended a marketing code for infant formula in 1981. WHO charged industrialized nations' drug companies with 'drug imperialism' through the dumping of outdated products on the Third World and the withholding of low-cost generic drugs from those nations.[4]

Such stand-offs with the North often compromised WHO's effectiveness in garnering funds for child-oriented programmes; and, in fact, the organization remains short of funds for the ambitious global projects it undertakes, particularly those directed at developing nations. The trust fund for WHO's Global Programme on AIDS – very much a key concern in the industrialized world – is some $178 million at present, far outstripping the agency's resources for maternal-child health (MCH), the fight against river blindness or emergency aid.[5] In fact, WHO must accomplish its task of 'Health for All' for the 1994-95 biennium mostly from 'extra-budgetary' contributions from the rest of the UN system. Although current WHO Director-General Hiroshi Nakajima proposes to spend $1.84 billion during that period, the organization's assessed contributions of its members stands at only $872 million, less than half of its stated needs.[6]

Resource shortfalls are not as much of a problem for UNICEF, which has resourcefully used its various commemorative days and years – such as the annual Day of the African Child and the International Children's Day of Broadcasting – to prod members to fund its plethora of programmes. Its total income for 1993 was $866 million, including $170 million for emergency relief. This figure is a slight drop from 1992 (when UNICEF gained $938 million in contributions, $204 million of it for the emergency fund), reflecting an overall decline in government contributions. But the Fund remains uniquely well-equipped to weather any wave of government tightfistedness; its greeting-card and related concessions alone netted $107 million during the 1991-92 fiscal year.[7]

Risky business in the war zones

What is the money buying? Although UNICEF's focus remains on child health, improvements in sanitation and water and family-based services – spanning the gamut from advocacy of oral rehydration therapy to campaigns to promote breast-feeding at 'baby-friendly' hospitals – emergency relief takes a bigger chunk of UNICEF funds than ever. In 1993, $223 million went to emergency relief, more than a fourfold increase from the 1989 figure.[8]

In part, this shift reflects the UN's own move towards larger emergency operations: the rise in UNICEF relief runs parallel with the growth of UN peacekeeping operations. UNICEF has been expanding its programmes into some of the most high risk – and controversial – ventures it can undertake, often running up against the geopolitical concerns of its main donors in the US and Europe.

It is true that UNICEF remains in the public consciousness by maintaining a high profile in such recent conflicts as the wars in Somalia and Rwanda; but those successes followed years of soul-searching by the agency in which many donor countries worried about how much authority UNICEF ought to have in providing aid during wartime. The first major such operation – during the 1967-70 war in Biafra – sparked considerable debate over whether or not UNICEF's mandate to protect children in Biafra potentially interfered with Nigerian sovereignty. But UNICEF had more room to manoeuvre. Its founders had insisted that no child be seen as 'an enemy' and its original resolution stated that assistance be dispensed 'on the basis of need, without discrimination because of race, creed, nationality status or political belief'.[9]

Rather than shrink from the political challenge of defending children amid politically touchy crises, James Grant of the US took on an ever-expanding roster of civil conflicts. In the main countries assisted in 1993 – from Afghanistan to Angola, Sudan to Bosnia-Herzegovina – UNICEF pursued a wide range of tasks to protect children, including assisting mine-clearance projects and studying the effects of sanctions on Haitian and Iraqi children. That year, the agency also sponsored workshops on the concept of establishing 'zones of peace'

where fighting could cease so that children could be given essential supplies. In countries where conflicts were easing, such as Eritrea and Chad, UNICEF expanded its efforts to reunite families whose children had been abandoned in war. All this, of course, was in addition to its more traditional efforts to provide food and medicine to children in war zones.

Family planning has become a hot topic as the population of the developing world has doubled since 1960.

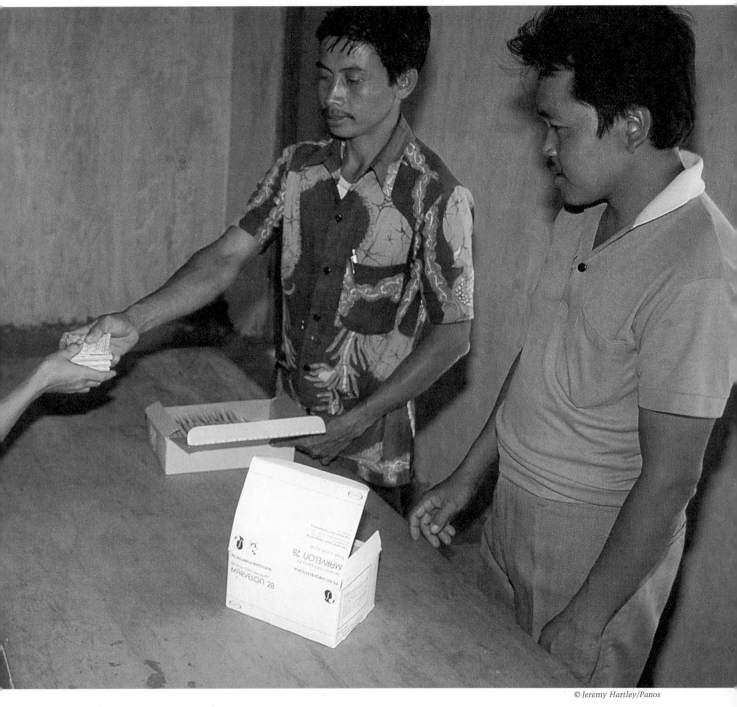

© Jeremy Hartley/Panos

"*an ever-expanding roster of civil conflicts*"

STCO

SHAHER TRADING COMPANY LIMITED

The Shaher Group is a privately-owned, multinational group with its corporate headquarters located in Sanaa, Republic of Yemen, and offices in Cairo, London, Berlin and Moscow.

The parent company, Shaher Trading Company Limited, was formed in 1962 to trade in essential commodities including sugar, wheat and wheat flour. Under the entrepreneurial leadership of its Chairman and Founder, Mr. Shaher Abdulhak, the organisation grew rapidly and diversified from a pure commodity trading company to a broad-based multinational group with trading and manufacturing interests in the Middle East and Europe.

Since the 1970s, the Shaher Group has invested heavily in Yemen, building the country's first five-star hotel and founding the International Bank of Yemen – the country's first privately-owned commercial bank. In the 1980s, the group expanded its Yemen investments into the manufacture of consumer goods whilst acting as agents for some of the world's largest companies including Xerox, Daimler Benz, KLM and General Electric.

In the mid 1970s, the Shaher Group diversified into Egypt with substantial investments in banking, soft drink bottling and glass container manufacturing. In 1994, the group entered into a joint venture with The Coca Cola Company to manufacture and distribute Coca Cola products throughout Egypt. This joint venture became the first privatisation of a publicly-owned enterprise in Egypt and is now the largest beverage operation in the Middle East.

P.O.Box 28 Ali Abdulmoghni Street SANAA (Y.A.R.)
Tel: 272968 / 272969   Telex: 2205 BASHAIR.Y.E.   Fax: 274112

Caring for mothers and other women

In marked contrast to the prospects for improving children's lives within the UN system, the efforts to promote women's rights still seem, to some, fledgling and diffuse. As with the ability of UN member states to unite behind the cause of children, some of the blame lies in the lack of political will of countries in the UN General Assembly to push for more effective women's agencies. But some lies with the organizations themselves, which have only recently found a common rallying point: the right of all women to exercise choice in family planning. That this focus revolves around the figure of the mother – only slightly less unimpeachable than that of the child – is probably no coincidence.

The role of women in family planning – which occupied the centre stage during the September 1994 International Conference on Population and Development (ICPD) in Cairo – was not even a marginal issue during the first UN-sponsored World Population Conference, staged in Bucharest in 1974, or the 1968 Tehran Conference on Human Rights, where 'birth spacing' was first adopted as a right. The main struggle during that era was to convince developing nations to implement national policies to control population growth to prevent future shortages of resources. Most of the newly independent nations countered that development, more than population control, was necessary to ensure that the world could support its entire population. The upshot of that dispute, along with the opposition of more traditional societies to the concept of family planning itself, was to make population planning more of a controversial

> "*efforts to promote women's rights still seem, to some, fledgling and diffuse*"

task than UNICEF or WHO were willing to handle. To take the pressure off UNICEF and WHO, which had included family planning programs in their work for decades, the UN Population Fund (UNFPA) had been launched in 1967. The funding of UNFPA was voluntary and therefore governments who opposed family planning could simply refuse to contribute to it. UNFPA, for its part, could still coordinate activities with its predecessors and thus be in a position to take on more controversies in defending family planning. Even the United States, under the Reagan and Bush presidencies, denied funding for the agency, and US funding was not restored until 1993.

The advocacy of women's rights by UNFPA initially focused strictly on maternal-child health, which still possessed the aura of unimpeachability associated with children's concerns. WHO designated maternal-child health as a top priority from its

A woman attends a business course at a women's college.
*Although women's education has increased, the female literacy
rate in the developing world is three-quarters that of men.*

© Howard J. Davies/Panos

inception in 1948, and it joined with UNICEF in building up projects throughout the developing world aimed primarily at providing supplies necessary for mothers to ensure the survival of their children. Over time – and with greater urgency following UNFPA's creation – the health of the mother herself became a cause of concern. Despite increasing objections from governments, the agency began to examine the dangers to the lives of mothers arising from unwanted or unintended pregnancies, publicizing, for example, estimates that half a million women die each year from pregnancy-related causes, and that some 60,000 die from unsafe abortions. Although UNFPA has never advocated abortion as a means of family planning – and indeed explicitly refused to do so at the International Conference on Population in Mexico City in 1984 – its efforts to ensure that any abortion is performed safely have rankled a wide range of critics. Likewise, the agency's focus on the health and well-being of mothers has been interpreted by some governments as a 'secularist' attempt to undermine traditionalist conceptions of the family.

As a consequence, UNFPA has become the unlikely standard-bearer for a variety of feminist concerns, and its recent emphasis that family planning cannot succeed without the empowerment of women seems a logical extension of its aims. The organization's image has been further cemented since Nafis Sadik, a female Pakistani doctor, replaced Rafael Salas of the Philippines to become one of the UN's few prominent Third World women in a top spot. Under Sadik, UNFPA has increasingly become associated with several

"*the health of the mother*"

INTERNATIONAL BUSINESS CENTER

As a pioneer of privatization in the region, Mexico very much symbolises the view that public sector challenges can be best resolved through private sector solutions.

Indeed, private capital participation at airports has increased dramatically in recent years and Grupo Hakim, one of Mexico's leading construction companies, is playing a key role in enlarging and expanding the Mexico City Airport.

Located in the new wing of the International Airport, the International Business Center offers a wide range of telecommunication and language facilities together with financial market information and computerized banking services.

In short, the International Business Center has been specifically designed to provide the most comprehensive range of business facilities available – as befits the new Mexico.

Please contact us for further information on (525) 726 0480

MEXICO   CITY   AIRPORT

women's rights goals: the education of girls in the developing world, a practice the agency contends is crucial to maintaining low birth rates; the provision of contraceptives and family planning information even to younger women, to discourage unwanted births; programmes to combat sexually-transmitted diseases and AIDS through education and the development of appropriate contraceptives; and a campaign against female genital mutilation, which

for women's empowerment – socially and economically as well as in the context of family planning choices – as the key to all future population policy.

For all the political importance of the Cairo process, UNFPA's nuts-and-bolts work still consists primarily of providing contraceptive services to developing countries. Other UN agencies – notably CSW, UNIFEM and INSTRAW – are entrusted with

> *"UNFPA's work consists primarily of providing contraceptive services to developing countries"*

UNFPA claims puts between 85 and 114 million women at risk.[10] The language the agency employs to defend these goals is often ground-breaking: in its most recent annual report on *The State of the World Population*, the agency argues in favour of women having access to their own line of credit and gaining security from domestic violence, genital mutilation and female infanticide.[11]

UNFPA's many campaigns to strengthen the position of women culminated in the 1994 ICPD in Cairo, where the organization's traditional mandate to use population programmes to further development took a back seat – rhetorically, at least – to a battle between traditionalists and secularists over the impact of some of the women's empowerment issues UNFPA proposed. The Cairo Conference's final document, produced after months of often furious invective from critics, managed to skirt controversies over 'non-traditional' (non-male headed or homosexual) families and the legality of abortion. The document nevertheless maintained firm support

implementing policies to advance women outside their maternal roles. CSW, which was established in 1946, has had its greatest success with the Convention on the Elimination of All Forms of Discrimination Against Women, adopted by the UN General Assembly in 1979. The Convention affirmed that discrimination against women should be eliminated in all public and private spheres and that the exploitation of prostitution should be suppressed. It also paved the way for future working groups examining the slavery of women, prostitution, female genital mutilation and other abuses.

But women had to wait for more than three decades before the UN member states actually developed agencies which both focused solely on women and possessed significant funding. In 1976, INSTRAW was set up to enhance women's role in development. Almost two decades later, the voluntarily funded agency, based in Santo Domingo, The Dominican Republic, still has to justify the reasons for its independent existence. Also established in 1976 was the UN Decade for Women, Equality, Development and Peace, one of the UN's many commemorative events, which actually succeeded in giving birth to a new organization. The beginning of the decade in 1976 provided an opportunity to set up a Voluntary Fund for the Decade for Women; by the end of the decade, in 1985, that fund had metamorphosed into UNIFEM, which works in tandem with the UN Development Programme (UNDP). UNIFEM continues to be relatively small compared with other agencies, relying on its trust fund and a largely government-supported income of some $11.9 million by 1993. But the agency, under former Director Sharon Capeling-Alakija, at least gained a toehold in the bureaucratic domain where funds are to be won, and has been able to start up several projects to empower women in the developing world.

"*women's causes*"

Beyond its work campaigning for women's social and economic rights, UNIFEM has joined various UN agencies and non-governmental organizations in opening ambitious programmes to provide credit for women in developing countries. The Fund has provided lines of credit to some 40 women's groups in Tanzania, more than 3,000 women in Colombia and nearly 2,000 in Bolivia.[12] It has also sought to promote technologies that take account of women's special needs, devising technical guidelines for sustainable development programmes that incorporate women-friendly approaches. However, UNIFEM remains similar to other UN bureaucracies in requiring a substantial budget and public interest before it can truly make an impact. As a result, the women's agencies are expending considerable energy gearing up for the 1995 Beijing Fourth World Conference on Women. The Beijing Conference, to be chaired by Gertrude Mongella of Tanzania, has already been preceded by UNIFEM-sponsored workshops. Indeed many staff at UNIFEM clearly hope that the atmosphere of the Cairo and Beijing conferences can revitalize women's causes in time to begin the UN's second half-century.

Forty million newborn children are still not properly immunized.
Medical care for a sick child in Liberia.

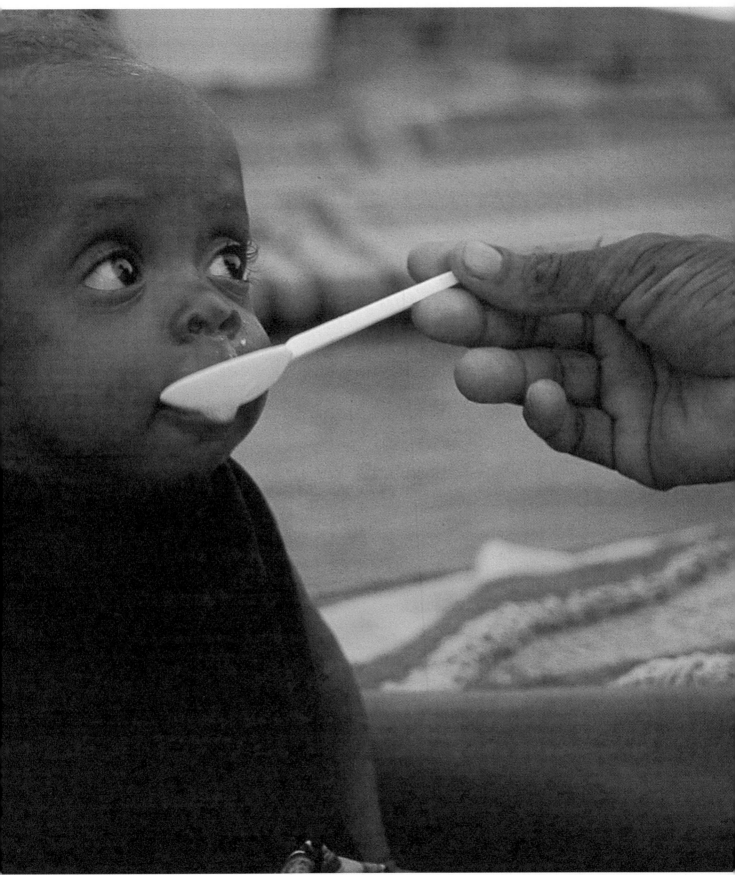

© Liba Taylor/Panos

Shaheen Business & Investment Group

The unfolding of the Middle East peace process will hopefully bring much needed economic development to the region.

Certainly with the Jordanian Government and the UN's financial agencies actively encouraging private sector investment, business has a vital role to play in the infrastructural development of the country.

These are also crucial times for the business community to demonstrate that it can be a social force now and for the future. By creating wealth and employment, industry and commerce is able to provide some of the basic tools for the betterment of humankind.

As a company with a wide range of trading interests, the Shaheen Business and Investment Group recognises that business has social, educational and environmental responsibilities in the communities in which it operates.

The Shaheen Business and Investment Group fully supports the aims of the United Nations in its efforts to promote a new agenda for social and economic development.

Tel: 696111
Fax: 688009
P.O. Box 93
Amman - Jordan

What next for women and children?

While the women's agencies prepare for Beijing, the UN as a whole can expect to receive all kinds of suggestions about how to reform itself. The cries for reform probably will do little to tamper with the perceived successes of UNICEF, UNFPA and WHO. Still, certain basic reforms affecting those organizations seem to be picking up momentum. Perhaps the main one is to make UN field offices more efficient by combining the various agencies' field work to allow for more joint programming. In recent years, agencies like UNICEF, FAO and UNDP have begun to share the same housing in the field. The

next logical step, in the view of some, is to place all the branches under a more unified command, perhaps by each nation's Resident Representative of UNDP.[13]

Related to that reform is the growing demand for better division of labour among agencies in development activities and emergency operations. Particularly as crises take up more of the UN agenda, there is a need to avoid overlapping responsibilities. Such cases include Somalia or Angola, where famine and war require the assistance of all the refugee-

© Betty Press/Panos

As a rash of internal conflicts spreads across the globe, emergency relief is often replacing development assistance.
Food aid for Rwandan refugees in Tanzania.

*For too long the role of women in the world's workforce has been
undervalued and unprotected.*

© Ron Giling/Panos

related, humanitarian, children's and women's rights, food and health branches of the UN.

In general, UNICEF and WHO will need to take on new challenges, ranging from new health hazards like AIDS to the consequences of modern structural adjustment policies. Agencies have yet to study the effects that AIDS is having in producing a generation of orphans in particularly hard-hit countries. The dislocation and potential collapse of national authority that has followed the implementation of structural adjustment, particularly in Sub-Saharan Africa, may prove just as damaging in the long run to providing sufficient care for children. However, both agencies seem well-equipped to tackle such topics in their efforts to defend children; after all, UNICEF was the first UN branch to point out the social drawbacks of structural adjustment.[14]

Although Beijing remains the largest matter on the agenda for women's agencies, UNFPA will also need to direct its post-Cairo authority towards generating projects that can empower women beyond its standard family planning paradigm. Having staked considerable energy on arguing that women's education and socio-economic advancement are crucial to effective population planning, UNFPA may now be uniquely positioned to propose programmes for women's credit, women's education and the broad range of related needs. It remains too early to see how ambitious an agenda for women the member governments of the UN will allow. Yet it is not inconceivable that, particularly if the built-in appeal of mothers can serve as a spark plug for the advancement of all women, projects to help women will one day be as unassailable as those for children.

Endnotes

1   UNICEF, *UNICEF Annual Report 1994* (New York: UNICEF, 1994), p.39.

2   Silvio Brucan, 'The United Nations as a World Authority', in Jeffrey Harrod and Nico Schrijver, ed., *The UN Under Attack* (Aldershot, UK: Gower, 1988), p.11.

3   Leon Gordenker, 'The World Health Organization: Sectoral Leader or Occasional Benefactor?' in Roger A. Coate, ed., *US Policy and the Future of the United Nations* (New York: Twentieth Century Fund, 1994), p.177.

4   Ibid.

5   Gordenker, p.176.

6   Gordenker, p.175.

7   *UNICEF Annual Report 1994*, p.99 and p.103.

8   *UNICEF Annual Report 1994*, p.100.

9   Black, p.272.

10 UNFPA, *The State of the World Population 1994* (New York: UNFPA, 1994), p.48.

11 UNFPA, p.49.

12 UNIFEM, *UNIFEM Annual Report 1994* (New York: UNIFEM, 1994), pp.14-15.

13 Erskine Childers and Brian Urquhart, *Renewing the United Nations System*, *Development Dialogue 1994:1* (Uppsala, Sweden: Dag Hammarskjold Foundation, 1994), p.91.

14 Childers, p.75.

A growing number of emergency relief operations means the UN and NGOs must increasingly work hand-in-hand.
Children at a feeding centre in Somalia washing their hands.

Perspective ~ *a necessary voice*

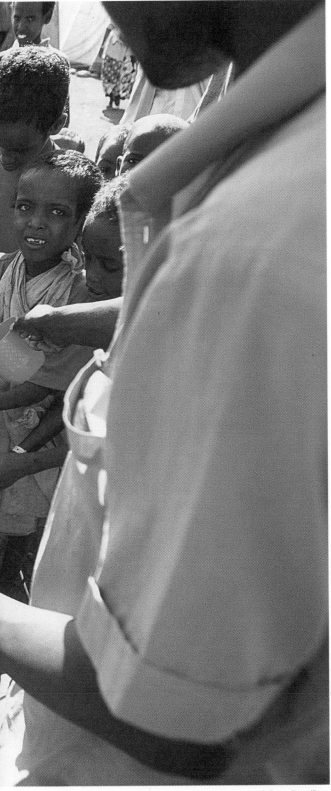

- Popular organization
- International mobilization
- Coalitions and constituencies
- An essential dimension

'When is an NGO not an NGO? When it is a UN agency.' This statement, made by some NGO representatives at the 1994 UN International Conference on Population and Development (ICPD) in Cairo, sums up the uneasy relationship between the UN and NGOs. The statement was in protest at the fact that some UN bodies had stalls at the NGO Forum being held parallel to the Cairo Conference.

The comment also demonstrates that while both the UN and NGOs agree that their relationship is ever-expanding, a lack of mutual trust and, in some cases, a lack of respect still remains. Some NGOs use every opportunity to criticize the UN system, especially regarding the body's peacekeeping efforts and the activities of the World Bank, while a few UN agencies in their turn have been sceptical about the effectiveness of non-governmental groups. In the *Human Development Report 1993* issued by the UN Development Programme (UNDP), for instance, the agency wondered whether NGOs have had as much success in tackling poverty as they claim. 'Nobody really knows', said the report. 'What seems clear is that even people helped by successful [NGO] projects still remain poor'.[1]

The report added that NGOs reached less than 20 per cent of the 1.3 billion people living in absolute poverty and urged NGOs to engage more constructively with governments to avoid being marginalized in national debates on development.

Few NGOs, however, believe that they will ever gain the influence on or access to governments that

© Betty Press/Panos

COMPANHIA ENERGÉTICA DE SÃO PAULO (CESP)

Companhia Energética de São Paulo (CESP), with its headquarters in the province of São Paulo, was set up in 1966 as a result of the merging of 11 electrical companies working within the region.

CESP, now one of Brazil's largest electrical companies, has a 20% share of a market that is rapidly expanding to remain in step with Brazil's technological development. Indeed, São Paulo, also known as 'the engine of Brazil', produces some 52% of Brazil's total industrial output.

Over the past 30 years CESP has concentrated on hydroelectric power and other renewable energy sources to feed the ever-growing demands of São Paulo's buoyant industrial sector.

But whilst CESP has hastened to keep pace with progress, the company remains aware of environmental considerations recognizing that the only real development is sustainable development. Consequently, the company is seeking out renewable energy sources and working on the reforestation of Brazil's valuable tropical forests.

Today CESP meets approximately 93% of the electricity demands of São Paulo's 8.9 million consumers, currently providing 351 watts per person. However, as the province of São Paulo continues to attract national and international investment, the demand for electricity will grow.

With this in mind, CESP welcomes investors with similar ideals and a commitment to join in the economic and social development of Brazil.

Al. Ministro Rocha de Azevedo, 25, São Paulo, SP 01410-900, Brazil
Tel. 55 - 11 284 3641.   Fax. 55 - 11 287 0871. Telex. 11 31004

"the Earth Summit was a landmark in the UN-NGO relationship"

they would like to have. And what weight do they carry within the UN system itself? 'NGOs have been a fundamental part of the UN machinery since the drafting of the UN Charter. But the early, informal rapport between the UN and NGOs has gradually evolved into a bureaucratic, inflexible relationship over the past decades', according to Ann Doherty of Action for Solidarity, Environment, Equality and Development (ASEED).[2] Doherty said, however, that the 1992 UN Conference on Environment and Development (UNCED) – or Earth Summit – in Rio de Janeiro, was a 'sharp break from this gradual erosion of access for NGOs'.

For its part, the UN believes that UN-NGO interactivity 'abounds at all levels'. According to a 1994 report by the UN Secretary-General, 'the contribution of NGOs has been significant in many areas of United Nations work'. The report said that the relationship had moved beyond the formal framework defined in the UN Charter and subsequent resolutions.

This view suggests the UN is at odds with Doherty's assessment. But it supports the belief that the Earth Summit was a landmark in the UN-NGO relationship.

'These institutions contributed to the shaping of the agenda, to the process of international mobilization around the concept of sustainable development, and to the building of the political commitments that made possible the adoption of the Rio Declaration, Agenda 21, the conventions on climate change and the protection of biodiversity,

and the statement of principles on forests', said the Secretary-General's report.[3]

In fact, Chapter 27 of Agenda 21 speaks of NGOs in positively glowing terms, noting their 'vital role' in participatory democracy and their 'experience, expertise and capacity' in evolving sound development.

However, in 1993, at the World Conference on Human Rights in Vienna, the 'bosom-buddiness' of Rio dissolved into recriminations and criticism as NGOs were barred from monitoring closed sessions of the drafting committee that would draw up the final document of the conference. Some charged that the 'erosion of access' had begun again.

Despite such feelings, NGOs continue to work closely with many UN programmes and agencies, such as the Office of the UN High Commissioner for Refugees (UNHCR), the World Food Programme (WFP), the UN Development Fund for Women (UNIFEM), the UN Environment Programme (UNEP), the World Health Organization (WHO), the UN Children's Fund (UNICEF), the UN Conference on Trade and Development (UNCTAD) with its UN Non-Governmental Liaison Service, the International Research and Training Institute for the Advancement of Women (INSTRAW) and UNDP. The one UN body that some NGOs love to hate is the World Bank, but it too has clear operational rules for collaboration with NGOs.

Overall, the UN-NGO relationship has come a long way, with still much scope for closer cooperation.

Looking back

From the very start, the founding members of the UN recognized that NGOs existed and had an important role to play in the economic and social life of people, both on a national and international level. Thus, when the founding members drew up the UN Charter, they included a specific article devoted to formulating relations between the UN and such groups.

Article 71 of the Charter reads: 'The Economic and Social Council [ECOSOC] may make suitable arrangements for consultation with non- governmental organizations which are concerned with matters within its competence. Such arrangements may be made with international organizations and, where appropriate, with national organizations after consultation with the Member of the United Nations concerned.'

The Charter was signed on 26 June 1945 and became effective on 24 October of the same year. At the time, many of the major NGOs of today (Amnesty International, Médecins Sans Frontières, World Vision International, Greenpeace) had not yet come into being, but there were enough active non-state organizations to merit the inclusion of an article devoted to the UN-NGO relationship.

A look at some of the organizations that predate the UN include, for example, Anti-Slavery International, founded in 1839; the Salvation Army, 1865; the American Red Cross, 1881; Wildlife Conservation International, 1897; the American Friends Service Committee (Quakers), 1917; Oeuvres Hospitalières Français de l'Ordre de Malte, 1927; Save the Children Federation, 1932; and the World Jewish Congress, formed in 1936 to fight Hitler's persecution of the Jews.

In the United States particularly, private voluntary organizations were many in number and quite influential. More than a hundred years before the signing of the UN Charter in San Francisco, the 19th-century French author and statesman Alexis de Tocqueville had noted that democracy in the new United States had been achieved partly because of the influence of voluntary organizations.

© Howard J. Davies/Panos

An NGO water project in Bardera, Somalia.

"TO REAFFIRM FAITH IN FUNDAMENTAL HUMAN RIGHTS, IN THE DIGNITY AND WORTH OF THE HUMAN PERSON."

Charter of the United Nations, 1945

SINCE 1988, REEBOK HAS HONORED YOUNG
HUMAN RIGHTS HEROES AROUND THE WORLD.

To receive a nomination package for
the Reebok Human Rights Award, contact:
Reebok Human Rights Program
Reebok International Ltd.
100 Technology Center Drive
Stoughton, MA 02072
USA
phone: (617) 341-5000
fax: (617) 297-4806

Reebok Human Rights Award

Indeed, Article 71 of the UN Charter was included as 'a result of pressure brought to bear ... by representatives of NGOs on the United States delegation'.[4] It had not been part of the original draft of the Charter. The NGOs had lobbied to be accorded consultation on political questions, and although they were given status only on economic and social issues, the article was still 'unprecedented in establishing formal relations between "interest groups" and an intergovernmental body'.[5] These interest groups included a wide range of organizations who called themselves (and still do) a variety of names such as private voluntary organizations, voluntary agencies, or citizens' groups. But partly because of the UN Charter, 'NGO' is a term that has become widely accepted among the public.

"interest groups"

The means of applying Article 71 were first defined in 1946 by ECOSOC in Resolution 3 (II), which 'provided for NGOs to be placed in consultative status with the Council and to hold consultations with the Secretariat'.

Both the UN and NGOs had a stake in co-operation following the Second World War. NGOs devoted to promoting peace and defending human rights saw the need to work with the new world body and its member states. In Caux, Switzerland, the Moral Re-Armament (MRA) movement played an important role in rebuilding relations between France and Germany after the war. This rapprochement helped to lead to the formation of the European Community.

In fact, just as the war gave rise to the UN, it also sparked the formation of other organizations, such as the Lutheran World Federation in 1947 and the World Council of Churches in 1948. Oxfam, currently one of the biggest international NGOs, was formed in 1942.

By the late 1940s there would be the international tension created by the Cold War, which also affected NGOs. 'For almost four decades, the international evolution of the non-governmental sector was dominated by rivalries between the super-powers and their satellites.'[6] But the UN too was dominated by such rivalries: in the 40 years after its formation, the veto was used some 400 times in the Security Council. Since the late 1980s, with the fall of the Berlin Wall, the democratization process in Eastern Europe and the break-up of the Soviet Union, the veto has rarely been used.

Meanwhile, the NGO situation has changed as well. Now, instead of an East-West divide, there are new challenges caused by ethnic conflicts and the growing tide of refugees in the world. A reflection of this is the fact that the Office of the UNHCR is one of the fastest growing UN agencies and the one that works most actively with NGOs. According to UNHCR information, NGOs carry out programmes on behalf of the agency to help refugees in many areas of the world. In 1993, there were more than 200 major NGOs working with UNHCR in the field.

The new challenges were highlighted in 1994 by at least one group of NGOs. At the 20th General Assembly of European Development NGOs held in April of that year, the main topic was the 'role, position and experience of NGOs on conflict, development and military intervention'. Among other issues, the conference examined the problems of NGO operations in war-torn countries such as the former Yugoslavia and Somalia, the need for post-conflict development and rehabilitation, and the role of the UN.

Apart from these concerns, another aspect of the post-Cold War situation is the emerging North-South division among NGOs along with increased competition for scarce funds. The North-South rift was in evidence during the 1993 UN World Conference on Human Rights in Vienna as well as during the 1994 ICPD in Cairo. A cartoon by the Indian satirist, Ajit Ninan, aptly captured the situation when it showed NGOs on a make-believe winners' podium at the end of the conference. Among

the 'first-place' finishers were smiling Northern
NGOs, while Southern NGOs had to settle for
third place. In Vienna, too, Southern organizations
accused those from developed countries of trying
to set the agenda.

Yet, neither rifts nor the international political
climate have prevented NGOs from working for
greater access to the UN. In addition, NGOs themselves realize that they need more coordination
among, and solidarity with, one another. Many have
come together to form networking and liaison groups
with one another as well as with governments.

According to the UN Secretary-General's 1994
report, NGOs' participation in the UN's decision-
making systems and operational activity has 'far
exceeded the original scope' of Article 71, primarily
because of the enormous growth in NGO activities.

Today there are thousands of NGOs in the world,
representing a myriad of concerns such as environmental protection, sustainable development, defence
of human rights, promotion and defence of women's
rights, children's welfare, family planning, poverty
alleviation, humanitarian assistance and other areas.
Some have grown out of a tradition of anti-govern-
ment activity, some from religious movements, from
weak government structures, from oppression or
from conflicts such as the Second World War and
the Vietnam War.

In Germany alone, there are an estimated 2,000
local and national NGOs working in development;
and according to the Organization for Economic
Cooperation and Development (OECD), northern
development NGOs collectively spend about $10
billion annually.[7] In 1993, the 12-country European
Community allocated some $830 million to various
NGO programmes, for emergency assistance, food
aid and projects to help refugees and displaced people.

It is not only in the North that NGOs have been
proliferating rapidly; many of the newer associations
have been created in developing countries. In the
South, the 'numbers of NGOs involved in development activities have increased spectacularly over the
last decade. In some countries, with a particularly
vibrant society, there are several tens of thousands of
NGOs and people's organizations', says the UN
Secretary-General's report.

© *Jeremy Hartley/Panos*

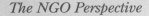

According to estimates by UNDP, the activities of both Northern and Southern NGOs reached some 250 million people in developing countries in 1993, more than double the number reached a decade before. Further expansion is being predicted as national and international events spur private citizens to take action.

'The activity of non-state actors has today become an essential dimension of public life at all levels and in all parts of the world. Examples abound to show the dramatic rise in people's capacity to organize among themselves and in the influence exerted by social movements in virtually all areas of concern to communities, large and small', says the Secretary-General's report.

" NGOs are an essential dimension of public life "

NGOs still reach less than 20% of the 1.3 billion people living in absolute poverty.
A feeding programme for malnourished children in a Somali refugee camp.

GHANA COMMERCIAL BANK LIMITED

Ghana Commercial Bank Limited (GCB) established over 40 years ago, is the largest commercial banking institution in Ghana with its Head Office located in Accra, Ghana, West Africa.

In addition to 136 branches throughout Ghana, GCB has a branch in London, and correspondents worldwide. The Bank offers a wide range of retail and merchant banking services and plans are in hand to explore new vistas of banking business.

In order to achieve greater efficiency and profitability, the Bank is being privatised and investors worldwide are being invited to become partners for growth. Like the eagle, we are determined to soar to bring greater development and progress to our country and be part of a world where peace, unity and brotherhood prevail.

We congratulate the UN on its 50th Anniversary and are proud to share in its vision of hope.

Mrs. Helen K. Lokko - *Managing Director*

HEAD OFFICE	LONDON OFFICE
PO Box 134	69 Cheapside
Accra, Ghana	London
	EC2P 2BB
Tel. (233 21) 664914	Tel. (171) 248 2384
(233 21) 663529	(171) 248 0191
Fax. (233 21) 662168	Fax. (171) 489 9058
Telex. 2034	Telex. 888597
COMBANK GH	GHBLDN G
Swift No.	
GHCBGHAC	

BANKING IN GHANA - THE CHOICE IS GCB

Consultative status

In 1945, there were only 41 NGOs in consultative status with ECOSOC; by 1993, that figure had risen to more than 1,500, according to UN figures.

The UN-NGO consultative arrangement is guided by ECOSOC Resolution 1296 of 23 May 1968 and covers various principles governing the relationship. The NGOs are divided into three categories. Category I includes the big international groups which are involved in activities relevant to the Council, which represent many people and have essential contributions to make in their economic and social life. Category II includes organizations which are internationally recognized for their competence within specific fields and Roster status may be granted to other groups which can make 'occasional and useful contributions' to the UN's work.

According to UN rules, Category I NGOs have the widest-ranging rights. They may place items on the provisional agenda of the Council and may propose items for the provisional agenda of subsidiary bodies. NGOs in both Categories I and II may have observers at the Council's public meetings and are entitled to submit written statements relevant to its work. They may also request to be heard by the Council. NGOs on the Roster may submit written statements. Some organizations that have consultative status include Amnesty International, Friends World Committee for Consultation, Human Rights Internet, the International Confederation of Free Trade Unions, the American Association of Retired Persons, International League for Human Rights, Muslim World League, Service, Justice and Peace in Latin America, World Young Women's Christian Association, the Pan-Pacific and South-East Asia Women's Association, and Eurostep (a network group of 22 major development NGOs from 15 countries).

The activities of about 200 NGOs with consultative status are coordinated by the Conference of Non-Governmental Organizations (CONGO), which meets every three years for a General Conference and to elect a president and board members. CONGO works mainly to improve relations between NGOs and the UN and since 1974 it has sponsored several NGO forums alongside UN conferences.

For its part, ECOSOC can suspend or withdraw consultative status from NGOs under certain conditions, including if the 'organization clearly abuses its consultative status by systematically engaging in unsubstantiated or politically-motivated acts against Member States of the United Nations'.

This issue emerged at the 1993 World Conference on Human Rights in Vienna, where the aspirations of the NGO community clashed with official decisions. The NGOs found themselves excluded from observing the vital drafting committee. Several were prevented from registering on the objection of governments and there was a running tussle about arrangements to discuss country-specific issues on the Conference premises.

'NGOs are divided into three categories'

NGOs in Vienna were outspoken in other areas as well. They resented being excluded from the main sessions of the drafting committee working on the final document of the conference and they charged that the UN had not invited some NGOs because of their country-specific work. In all, there were more than 2,000 NGOs represented in Vienna, with about 200 having consultative status.

In Cairo, there were a similar number of NGOs present, accounting for 10,000 representatives altogether, and the issue was also one of access both to national governments and to the UN as a whole. These complaints continued despite the fact that some UN officials and government ministers made a point of addressing the NGO Forum, which was opened by Egypt's first lady, Suzanne Mubarak. When the conference was over, many NGOs doubted that they had had any significant effect on the contents of the final programme of action.

NGOs had lobbied for several issues that were not attained. Meanwhile, many Southern NGOs felt frustrated for other reasons, saying that the UN conference focused on the 'Northern agenda of population control' and overlooked development. This had to wait until the World Summit for Social Development in Copenhagen in March 1995. The NGO Third World Network, for instance, said the issues that are important to developing countries, such as structural adjustment and debt-servicing problems, tended to be side-stepped during UN conferences. But the NGOs said they had learned many lessons from Rio, Vienna and Cairo, and planned to cooperate more closely and to speak with a united voice at future UN conferences.

Since Rio, many NGOs have been re-examining their roles and are now gearing up to influence reforms of the UN system. The UN is also reviewing its relationship with NGOs. In 1993, ECOSOC adopted a resolution calling for a 'general review' and update of current arrangements for consultation with NGOs.[8]

In July of the same year, another resolution was passed establishing an open-ended working group to carry out the review. Its first session, comprising six meetings, was held in New York from 20-23 June 1994, with 59 member states and more than

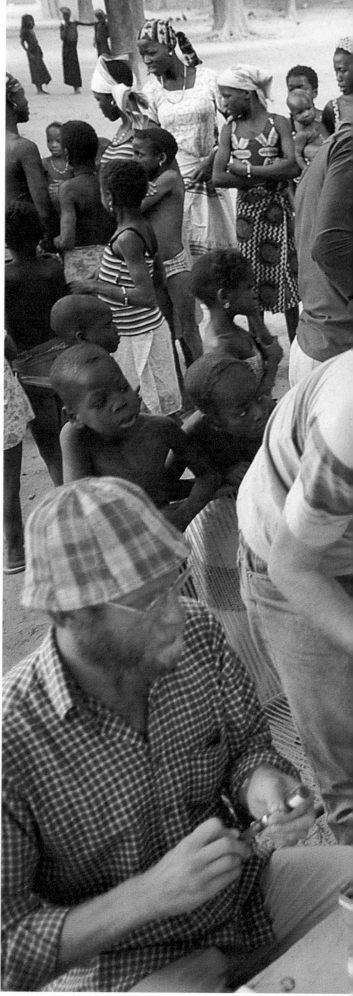

© Ron Giling/Panos

194

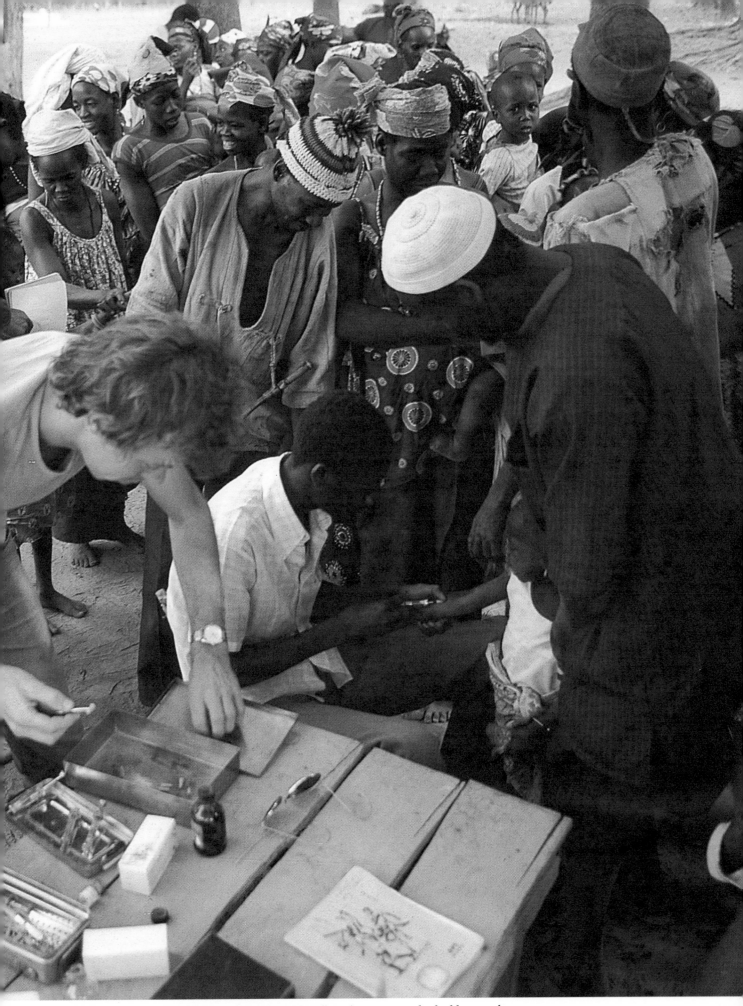

Only 10% of aid is spent on development assistance that affects the poorest people – health care and education, safe water and sanitation, and primary education.
An immunization programme in Mali.

A VISION OF HOPE

Union National Bank is deeply honoured to participate in *A Vision of Hope*, the commemorative publication celebrating the United Nations' 50th Anniversary. For us in the United Arab Emirates, the timing is particularly apt as we are soon to celebrate 25 years as a committed member of the United Nations, an organization whose humanitarian and environmental goals are shared by our President, His Highness Sheikh Zayed Bin Sultan Al Nahyan.

For any commercial organization, achieving corporate goals without any detrimental social or ecological factors is an ambitious objective. At Union National Bank we have managed to meet this challenge, continually improving our market share in the banking sector whilst embarking on public awareness campaigns which focus on crucial environmental and conservation issues.

In 1991 we launched the `Save the Dolphin' campaign which sought to avoid pollution in the Gulf waters. This highly successful campaign was followed by involvement with other projects such as the Arabian Leopard Trust, the Save the Turtle Campaign, the Gordon's Wildcat and the Islands Archaeological Trust.

This commitment to the community and the environment demonstrates our belief that as we move towards the 21st century the world community must strive to maintain the delicate balance that exists between progress and ecology. While we continue to play an active role in the development of our country as a leading bank in trade finance, project finance and consumer banking, this social responsibility is never neglected.

Strategically, the UAE plays an important role in trade and investment throughout the Middle East. It is the regional headquarters for many international corporations encouraged by the hospitable business and social climate, first-class infrastructure and thriving local economy.

As a leading UAE commercial bank and banker to some of the most prestigious private and public-sector companies, we convey a message of support from the UAE business community to the United Nations' global initiative of **'Uniting the People of the World for a Better Future'**.

Anwer Qayum Sher
Acting Chief Executive

Nahayan Bin Mabarak Al Nahayan
Chairman

UNION NATIONAL BANK

P.O.Box 3865, Abu Dhabi, United Arab Emirates. Tel. (971 2) 741600 - Fax. (971 2) 786080

60 NGOs present. The activity of the working group, chaired by Ambassador Jamsheed K.A. Marker of Pakistan, was to be the most important in this area since 1968.

The review

The 1994 working group meeting in New York focused on several issues. This included a review of the categories of status for NGOs, an examination of consultative arrangements and accreditation to UN world conferences, and a look at the 'problems and bottlenecks' that NGOs face under the current arrangements. Participants also considered the experience of the Commission on Sustainable Development in working with NGOs.

The task of the working group was essentially seen as coming at a crucial moment, as the contribution of NGOs is critical at a time when the world body itself is searching for a more focused role in development and peace.[9]

Both member states and NGOs stressed that Resolution 1296 needed updating to allow more NGOs to participate in UN activities while 'retaining a reasonable filter to exclude' organizations whose objectives were 'incompatible' with those of the UN Charter.[10]

While Resolution 1296 is widely regarded as being in need of updating, it remains a viable basis for consultations between the UN and NGOs. Any revision, NGOs believe, should result in strengthening this relationship rather than curtailing the existing participatory rights of those organizations in consultative status.

NGOs are also worried about the trend of asking them to form 'coalitions' and 'constituencies' and to speak through a chairperson. Some feel this practice could destroy the diversity of views.[11] However, many at the UN believe that this could lead to greater efficiency.

A key area of concern for both NGOs and member states is the small number of Southern NGOs participating in UN activities. Some NGOs believe that a certain percentage of NGOs taking part in UN conferences should come from the South, while others reject the idea of a quota.

Overall, however, there was broad agreement that the UN should take steps to improve communication with NGOs, by fully using electronic communications facilities to provide the organizations with complete and up-to-date information on UN activities.

"a key concern is the small number of Southern NGOs participating in UN activities"

The future: 'warp and woof'

The review by ECOSOC of arrangements for consultations with NGOs started 25 years after the adoption of Resolution 1296 in May 1968. It came when NGOs had become a 'vibrant, living link in the warp and woof of human society', as Ambassador Marker put it. Whatever the outcome of the review, NGOs seem set to continue being this link and the UN has recognized that fact. In 1994, several UN agencies and programmes expressed their desire and plans to work more closely with NGOs.

At the ICPD in Cairo in September of that year, the Executive Director of the UN Population Fund (UNFPA), Nafis Sadik, said the Fund hoped to work more widely with NGOs on national levels. She also stressed the role of NGOs in monitoring the actions of governments and charged them with the task of informing the public about the conference's programme of action.

At about the same time, Giorgio Giacomelli, Executive Director of the UN International Drug Control Programme (UNDCP), gave credit to NGOs for their assistance to the UNDCP and the 'international community at large' in developing policies and programmes to tackle the problem of drug abuse. Giacomelli expressed firm UNDCP support for the NGO World Forum on Drug Demand Reduction that took place in Bangkok from 12-17 December 1994. 'This will be a major event in the UN Decade Against Drug Abuse', he wrote in an editorial.[12]

With such recognition, there seems great hope for a long and fruitful relationship between the UN and NGOs in the future. But the partnership, if it can be called that, will probably never be a completely smooth one, because the UN is an intergovernmental body and NGOs are, after all, NON-governmental organizations.

"a long and fruitful relationship

Communities are increasingly learning to help themselves.
A self-help construction community centre in São Paolo, Brazil.

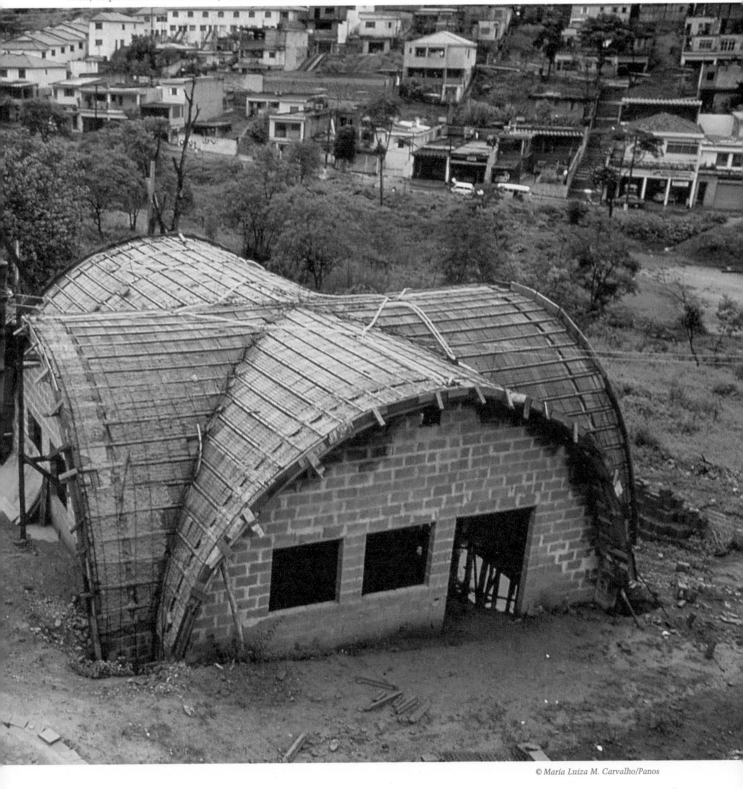

Women are often at the centre of grassroots self-help organizations.
The Mtaala Mpya women's group in Tanzania.

© *Susan Hackett/Panos*

Endnotes

1   *Human Development Report 1993*, United Nations Development Programme, New York, 1993.

2   *Terra Viva* newspaper, 25 June 1993, World Conference on Human Rights, Vienna, Austria, p.22.

3   *ECOSOC General Review of Arrangements for Consultations with Non-Governmental Organizations.* Report of the Secretary General, E/AC. 70/1994/5, 26 May 1994, p.13.

4   Ibid, p.11.

5   Ibid, p.11.

6   Ibid, p.12.

7   Ian Smillie and Henry Helmich, *Non-Governmental Organizations and Governments, Stakeholders for Development*, OECD, Paris 1993, p.14.

8   *Terra Viva* newspaper, 11 June 1993, World Conference on Human Rights. Vienna, Austria, p.13.

9   Ibid. p.13.

10 Jan Reynders, *Report on the ICPD and the concurrent NGO Forum for the Liaison Committee of Development NGOs to the European Communities*, p.8.

11 *Go Between*, 47, Aug/Sept. 1994. Geneva, p.16.

12 ECOSOC Report A/94/215 - E/1994/99, 5 July 1994, p.10.

SOLIDERE

As the United Nations celebrates its 50th Anniversary we in Lebanon have reason to be proud. As a charter member of the UN and a participant in the drafting of the charter, we are part of its noble history, encouraging understanding among nations and greater respect for human values.

We also have reason to be proud because, concurrent with these celebrations, Lebanon has embarked on a massive reconstruction programme that will transform it from a land devastated by war to one radiating confidence and optimism.

Solidere, the Lebanese Company for the Development and Reconstruction of Beirut Central District, a joint-stock corporation, has launched a project that will bring new life to the heart of the capital. The project will cover a surface area of 1.8 million square metres and add 4.69 million square metres of built-up space to the city's traditional centre and along a new waterfront.

Solidere is developing a quality urban setting attentive to social and environmental considerations and making use of the most up-to-date expertise in urban planning. Our plans call for the establishment of a financial and office complex commanding a superb view of the Mediterranean and the mountains of Lebanon. They also include the restoration of the historical core of the city centre - an urban settlement that predates the Roman temples that still grace the streets. In addition, they call for the establishment of hotels, public parks and commercial and recreational areas on the sea front, an archaeological park, public gardens, pedestrianized areas and tree-lined promenades to enlarge Beirut's famous coastal boulevard. Half of the built-up area is reserved for residential development where existing neighbourhoods will be extended to the waterfront.

We are enthusiastic and proud of the work we have embarked on. To us, the rebuilding of Lebanon is one symbol of the vision that is being celebrated this year: a strong sense of hope and the belief that we must do our share for a better world.

We are pleased to have been asked to participate in this tribute to the United Nations.

Nasser Chammaa
Chairman of the Board of Directors & Secretary General

89 Riyad El Solh Street,
Industry and
Labour Bank Building,
PO Box 119493,
Beirut, Lebanon.
Tel: **(01) 346881/3**
(01) 646128-35
Cellular 1 (212) 4783915
Fax: **(01) 646133**
Cellular 1 (212) 4783914

An Economic Perspective

Alongside the search for peace and social justice, the founders of the UN recognized the vital importance of a new global, financial and monetary infrastructure to protect the world from the economic turbulence that precipitated the great world wars in the first half of this century. Two entities, known as the 'Bretton Woods institutions' were created: the International Monetary Fund and the World Bank group.

The role of these institutions and their impact on the world economy must be seen in the light of the major changes in international financing that have occurred in the intervening years. Today both the International Monetary Fund and the World Bank are looked to, more and more, as the possible foundation stones for world financial order, to bring discipline and perspective to worldwide currency and investment transactions which have moved beyond the effective reach of even the richest governments.

A sound world economy is vital if the other institutions of the UN are to succeed in their mission. The business of the UN must include business, for without that we will live in a world fraught with poverty and unemployment and the social and political instability that they spawn.

To achieve these goals, the UN, as it enters its sixth decade of achievement, has embarked on an examination of its own structures and working methods in order to concentrate better its scarce resources on the tremendous range of tasks that urgently demand its attention.

Chapters

With the worldwide commodity glut, Africa alone has lost US$50 billion in reduced earnings since 1980.
A country like Kenya relies on its tea crops for much of its export earnings.

Capital ~ *the Bretton Woods institutions*

- *The global economy*
- *Monetary management*
- *Development policies*
- *Institutional reforms*

© *Jim Pickerell/IBRD*

The birth of the international financial institutions, known as the Bretton Woods institutions, in the 1940s was a direct response to the dismal experience of the 1920s and 1930s. The world had witnessed the Great Depression in the years following 1929. The global economy had gone through many traumas – from banking failures to monetary instability, trade protectionism and extraordinarily high levels of unemployment.

Many of those who surveyed the wreckage of the global economic system during the dreary days of the Second World War – especially Lord John Maynard Keynes, the dominant economic thinker of that time – came to a simple conclusion: the world's economic system needed some honest referees. The global system could not be left to the mercy of unilateral action by governments or to the unregulated workings of international markets. It needed multilateral institutions of economic governance which could lay down some agreed rules by which all nations would conduct their affairs. Thus emerged the International Monetary Fund (IMF), the International Bank for Reconstruction and Development (IBRD or the World Bank), and, at a later stage, the General Agreement on Tariffs and Trade (GATT).

The starting point was the United Nations Conference on Money and Finance held at Bretton Woods in the United States, in July 1944. At this conference Lord Keynes (representing the United Kingdom) and Harry White (a member of the US delegation) were the towering intellectual figures, setting the stage for a more orderly global economic transition after the Second World War.

THE ECONOMIC BANK

The Economic Bank with its headquarters in Sofia, Bulgaria, was founded in 1987 following the merger of several specialist departments of the Bulgarian National Bank.

Set up to finance large-scale projects and with some of the country's largest state-owned enterprises as customers, the bank is now the second largest commercial bank in the country.

As a member of The Bulgarian Association of Commercial Banks, whose aim is to improve and develop the banking system in the country, The Economic Bank is one of the most active and respected participants. The bank is also a founder member of 'Atanas Bourov', an organization involved in the education and training of bank officials within Bulgaria.

The Economic Bank recognizes that a well-structured financial sector is vital to the economic development of a country. Commercial banks, in particular, have a special role to play in this regard, promoting and assisting investment within the region.

We are proud to represent the business community of Bulgaria in *A Vision of Hope* and offer our congratulations to the UN on this historic occasion. It is only through their continuing efforts that progress can be made towards a world of peace, stability and wellbeing for humankind.

Head Office.
1000 SOFIA, 8 SLAVIANSKA STR.
TEL: (00359 2) 885526.
TELEX: 25001 ECBAN

INTERNATIONAL DEPARTMENT
1606 SOFIA, 12-A TUNDJA STR.
TEL: (00359 2) 522362. TELEX: 23910.
FAX:650541
SWIFT-COD ECOBBGSF

With memories of the Great Depression still fresh in their mind, the battle cry at the Bretton Woods conference was: 'Never Again!' Unemployment had been heavy – so the new objective was full employment. Trade and investment rules had broken down – so the new objective was to prevent beggar-my-neighbour policies. The international monetary system had collapsed – so the new objective was to maintain stable currencies with agreed procedures for adjustment. Unilateral national policies had created world economic chaos –so the basic idea was to fashion new institutions of global monetary and economic governance, with clear objectives and with changes in global policies engineered through a broad international consensus.

The structure emerging out of the Bretton Woods Conference was supposed to rest on four pillars of multilateralism:

- the IMF: to maintain global monetary stability, primarily through the mechanism of fixed but adjustable exchange rates.

- the IBRD: to reconstruct the war-torn economies of Europe and Japan and to stimulate the growth potential of the less developed regions in the Third World.

- the International Trade Organization (ITO): to stabilize international commodity prices and to manage a liberal trading regime.

- the UN: to maintain peace between nations as well as to encourage social and human development within nations.

While the first two pillars of this global economic system emerged in a fairly strong form, the other two pillars were shaky right from the start. The ITO, with its broader mandate, was never established. Instead, the GATT was set up in 1948 to police the world trading system, joined later, in 1964, by the UN Conference on Trade and Development (UNCTAD) which generated some pressure – largely unsuccessful – for commodity price stabilization. The UN system was never

given the role of a development agency that was originally envisioned. The UN development system never received adequate financing leading to an ineffective and inefficient role, and the alleged inefficiency of the UN led to a further erosion of its financial support.

An analysis of the five decades since the Second World War shows that the Bretton Woods institutions had a major influence on the global economic environment, particularly in the first 25 years. This influence has been on the wane in the last 25 years and the Bretton Woods institutions have been increasingly marginalized in global economic governance. Their influence on economic management in the developing world, however, remains quite significant.

In the first 25 years after the Second World War (1945-70), industrial countries grew nearly twice as rapidly as in any comparable period before or since. In Western European countries, national output increased by 4.4 per cent a year in the 1950s and 4.8 per cent in the 1960s. The corresponding annual growth rate in the US was 3.2 per cent and 4.3 per cent, and in Japan it was 9.5 per cent and 10.5 per cent respectively. Even the developing countries grew at a satisfactory rate during this period, normally five to six per cent a year. These healthy rates of growth in Gross National Product (GNP) bear a striking contrast to the rather pallid growth of recent decades.

Many factors contributed to the strong world growth performance in the first 25 years under the Bretton Woods institutions. Of course, the more liberal trading regime set up under the GATT rules helped considerably. The annual export growth rate in the 1950s and 1960s was nothing short of spectacular: 16.5 per cent in Japan, 12 per cent in West Germany and 5.3 per cent in the US. Such robust trade growth kept feeding rapid economic expansion.

The good economic performance during this period was also assisted to a great extent by global monetary stability established under the IMF rules.

Fixed exchange rates were established by all nations, which could be changed only in consultation with the IMF. Whether in rich or poor nations, the IMF rules had a major influence on domestic monetary policies.

In these first 25 years the spotlight was often on the IMF and the GATT. The task of reconstruction and development in Europe and Japan was taken over largely by the Marshall Plan, with the World Bank playing only a limited role in this effort. The Bank's influence grew significantly in the developing countries but this was a development of the last three decades, particularly after the addition of a new soft loan affiliate in the shape of the International Development Association (IDA) in 1960 to provide concessional finance to low-income developing countries.

There were several reasons for the relative success of the Bretton Woods institutions in the first 25 years of their existence. The world economy was run by a relatively small number of countries which enjoyed overwhelming influence in the weighted voting structures of these institutions. The US emerged after the Second World War with a national output which was about 50 per cent of the world output, so it was in a position to lay down the global rules of the game and keep the management of the Bretton Woods institutions firmly in line. At the same time, a good deal of growth was possible as the closed economies of pre-war and war days were opened up to global competition, and as new technologies developed during the war were applied to civilian industries.

These favourable trends disappeared in the 1970s and 1980s. The collapse of the influence of the Bretton Woods institutions started in dramatic fashion in 1971 with a decision by the US to abandon the regime of pegged but adjustable exchange rates and to opt instead for a floating rate for the dollar. The world entered a new era of exchange rate instability. The stable monetary regime introduced through the IMF was no more.

Many other global developments began to undermine the influence of the Bretton Woods institutions during this period. There was an increase in the number of international players with economic influence on the global scene – for instance, the Organization of Petroleum Exporting Countries (OPEC), Japan, West Germany, the developing world – yet the management and voting structures were too slow and too rigid to respond to such shifts in global economic power. The US share of global output fell from 50 per cent to 20 per cent, yet its desire to control Bretton Woods institutions showed

no comparable decline. At this stage, direction of global economic policies started shifting into the hands of the Group of Seven industrial nations

(G-7), often bypassing the framework of the Bretton Woods institutions.

There has been a dramatic marginalization of the Bretton Woods institutions in global economic governance in the past two decades. By now, these institutions police only the developing world. They have practically no role in the industrial nations or in the global economy as a whole. It is important to understand what was the original vision for these institutions and how the present reality contrasts with that vision before considering some proposals for their orderly reform. The Bretton Woods institutions constituted a remarkable initiative on behalf of mankind. They need to be reformed rather than allowed to die.

© Michael Harvey/Panos

A hydroelectric plant.
Large-scale infrastructure projects have on occasion pitted local communities against government in developing countries.

*T*he aims and objectives of an electricity utility corporation should be to combine science, technology and the preservation of nature with economic development and improvement in the quality of life.

Edenor, formed on 1 September 1992, following the privatization of Argentina's electricity sector and responsible for the distribution of electricity throughout northern Argentina, is committed to these objectives.

We believe that our activities should contribute directly to the development of society's potential and, consequently, we have embarked on a substantial programme of expansion and improvement, having committed to invest $80 million every year for the next five years.

For Argentina's economic growth to be sustained, a modern approach to electric power generation, transmission and distribution is the key. **Edenor** is proud to play its part in this process.

Edenor – not just aiding Argentina's development but investing in it.

Francisco Fernando Ponasso
CHAIRMAN

**Av. de Mayo 701, Piso 20 - (1084) Buenos Aires - Argentina
Tel: (54.1) 334-0797/0798 Fax: (54.1) 348-2123**

The International Monetary Fund

The IMF in its present form is merely a pale shadow of Keynes' original vision.

Keynes proposed a Fund equal to one-half of world imports, so that it could exercise a major influence on the global monetary system. In practice, the IMF today controls liquidity equal to two per cent of world imports. It is too insignificant to exercise much global monetary discipline at a time when speculative private capital movements of over one trillion dollars cross international borders every 24 hours.

Keynes envisioned the IMF as a world central bank, issuing its own reserve currency (the bancors) and creating sufficient international reserves whenever and wherever needed. By now, Special Drawing Rights (SDRs) constitute only three per cent of global liquidity. The world economy is dollar-dominated. For the world monetary system, the actions of the heads of the US Federal Reserve Board and the German Bundesbank are far more important than the actions of the Managing Director of the IMF – a long distance from the original Keynesian vision.

Keynes regarded balance of payment surpluses as a vice and deficits as a virtue, since deficits sustained global effective demand and generated more employment. This led him to advocate a penal interest rate of one per cent a month on outstanding trade surpluses. The situation today is exactly the reverse: deficit nations, particularly those in the developing world without a reserve currency of their own, come under tremendous pressure for real adjustment. There is no symmetry by way of corresponding adjustment pressures on the surplus nations.

In the Keynesian vision there would be no persistent debt problem, as surpluses would be used by the IMF to finance deficits. No separate International Debt Refinancing Facility was needed. Nor would the poor nations be obliged to provide a reverse transfer of resources to the rich nations (as they are doing now) to earn their legitimate requirement of growing international reserves: these reserves would have been provided by the international currency issued by the Fund. But an automatic mechanism for meeting the liquidity requirements of developing countries has been replaced in practice by punitive measures for dealing with debt problems and for fulfilling prudent international reserve requirements.

The heart of the IMF-led global monetary system was fixed exchange rates. That system died in the early 1970s with the de-linking of the US dollar from gold and with the introduction of floating exchange rates. All attempts since then to introduce a modicum of stability in the volatility of exchange rates have proved largely futile.

"the IMF in its present form is merely a pale shadow of Keynes' original vision"

The World Bank

Has the World Bank stuck closer to its original vision than the IMF? The World Bank was supposed to stand between the global capital markets and the developing countries and to recycle market funds to them by using its own creditworthiness, as well as by gradually building up the creditworthiness of these nations over time so they could have direct access to the private markets.

In some respects, the World Bank has done better than originally expected. It has helped raise market funds at lower cost, for longer maturity periods, and for some social sectors that private markets would not have touched, such as education, health, population and nutrition. It introduced the IDA in 1960 to subsidize its lending to poorer nations. Established as a bank, it has tended to become a development agency.

Where the World Bank is beginning to fail is in the transfer of any significant resources to developing nations. Recently its net resource transfers, including the funds of the IDA (the Bank's soft loan agency), have been negative, to the extent of one to two billion dollars a year. In fact, by now the Bank is recycling the repayment of its own debts rather than any new resources.

Private lending to developing countries has increased rapidly, and that is certainly a good development. But three-quarters of this private market lending is still to about 10 relatively well-off economies in Latin America and Southeast Asia. What about the other 117 developing countries? The Bank's role has been a modest one in these countries, and negative net resource transfers by the Bank to some poor nations have raised real questions about its development mandate.

The Bank was supposed to build up the creditworthiness of individual developing countries and enable them to walk with confidence into private capital markets. Except for South Korea, the Bank does not have many successes to boast of. Thanks to a severe global debt problem, most of its clients emerged in the 1980s with lower creditworthiness than they had enjoyed in the 1970s.

The resource profile of the Bank is inadequate in relation to the poverty profile of the developing world. According to the Bank's own estimates, the number of absolute poor in the developing world has been increasing. Yet in real terms IDA finance available per poor person has been shrinking. This is not a fault of the Bank management but of its donors who have refused to see the implications of such an imbalance.

The original Keynesian vision envisaged the World Bank as an institution for expansion of global growth and employment levels, rather than as an instrument for deflationary policies. One of the most scathing criticisms of the Bank in the developing countries these days is that it gets greatly browbeaten by the IMF in prescribing demand management and deflationary policies, particularly as a condition for its structural adjustment loans.

World Bank loans have encouraged the growth of industry in developing countries.
An aluminium smelter in Ghana.

© IBRD

The GATT

The third pillar of the Bretton Woods system, the GATT, has become even further removed from the original Keynesian vision than the IMF and the World Bank.

Keynes envisioned an ITO, which would not only maintain free trade but also help stabilize world commodity prices. That is why he linked the value of his world currency (the bancors) with the average price of 30 primary commodities, including gold and oil. In practice, the GATT excluded primary commodities altogether and only belatedly has an effort been made in the Uruguay Round of negotiations to include agriculture and tropical products in the global trade package.

The actual operations of the GATT system reflect the same disparity in global power structure as do the two other Bretton Woods institutions. The South and the former socialist bloc are opening up their markets; the North, according to a recent study by the Organization for Economic Cooperation and Development (OECD), has been restricting its markets during the 1980s and adopting greater trade protectionism.

The GATT has not been able to prevent beggar-my-neighbour policies or trade wars between powerful nations.

One distinguishing feature of the GATT is that overall it embraces at present only a small fraction of the total world production entering trade markets – excluding as it does primary commodities, gold, oil, textiles, services, capital flows, labour flows, intellectual property resources, etc. However, the new World Trade Organization (WTO) is likely to reverse this trend of the growing marginalization of the international trading regime.

"*severe global debt*"

Electricity of Portugal (EDP) is heir to the prestige, the vitality and the pioneering spirit that has long characterized the electricity sector in Portugal. Since its formation as an enterprise in 1976, EDP has played a major role in Portugal's development, bringing to all parts of the country the electrical infrastructure that has enabled vast improvements in the quality of life of the people of Portugal.

EDP, moreover, feels deeply involved with the people of Portugal and their economic endeavours. Not least, their deep and abiding urge to develop to the full, the potential of their country.

It is in this light that we see our own role as agents of development. We know that quality of life isn't built only by technological effort, but is also derived from many other social, cultural and human influences.

Nowadays, the economic and social value of electricity is widely recognized as an invaluable commodity for industrial and domestic purposes and as an important factor in the quality of life. Not only does it allow for the creation of wealth and growth of societies, electricity is also a vehicle of culture and wellbeing, spreading even further the powerful tools of progress and development. In Portugal the enterprises that over the years have made up the Portuguese electricity sector have always defended those values as part of the Portuguese quest for modernity.

Electricity of Portugal salutes the United Nations on the occasion of its 50th Anniversary. We are proud to associate ourselves with an organization whose principles contribute to a better understanding between people all over the world, in particular those values of solidarity, of justice and of equality for all humankind.

EDP - Electricidade de Portugal, S.A.

Apartado 4 205
1 506 LISBOA CODEX

Fatal flaws

There are two aspects of this 50-year evolution which should particularly concern us.

First, the IMF and the World Bank are no longer institutions of global governance; they are by now primarily institutions to police the developing world. In fact, no real institutions of global, economic, monetary and financial management exist today. The WTO may be an exception. But so far as the IMF is concerned, isn't it somewhat charitable to call a 10 per cent money manager – with influence only on the monetary policy of developing countries responsible for about 10 per cent of global liquidity – an International Monetary Fund? And isn't it somewhat optimistic to describe an institution recycling negative net financial transfers to the developing countries as the World Bank?

The plain truth is that, as global interdependence has increased, institutions of global governance have weakened. We are back to *ad hoc* improvisations by rich nations, either unilaterally or through a loose coordination by G-7, the grouping of the seven most powerful industrial nations.

A basic question today is whether we need Bretton Woods institutions only to influence the policies of the developing countries, which account for one-fifth of global output and one-tenth of global liquidity, or whether we need them as genuine institutions of global governance. Some of the criticism of these institutions in the enlightened lobbies of the Third World arises out of a perception that the industrial countries are largely independent of the discipline of the Bretton Woods institutions. Moreover, the industrial countries not only set their own rules, they also set the framework within which Bretton Woods institutions and developing countries can operate.

Second, the founders of the Bretton Woods institutions were searching for expansionary economic policies after a prolonged period of global deflation. Full employment was on top of the international agenda in the 1940s. In recent decades it seemed that world leaders, particularly in the industrial nations, became more preoccupied

with inflation than with jobs. The pendulum is now beginning to swing once again and jobs are moving to the top of the policy agenda.

The developing countries, unfortunately, have to live with the consequences of changing policy agendas in the industrial world. Most of them have been subjected by the Bretton Woods institutions to deflationary policy conditionality when their real need was for expansion of jobs and output. The demand management school often won over the

> ''*the seven most powerful industrial nations*''

supply expansion school. This was also because adjustment through supply expansion often takes a longer period and much larger resources than the Bretton Woods institutions could afford.

This is not to suggest that demand management is unnecessary. It may sometimes even be a pre-condition for sound supply expansion policies. After all, budgets must be balanced and borrowing must be curtailed. But the Bretton Woods institutions compounded their error of over-emphasizing demand management by accepting wrong policy choices for slashing budgetary expenditures. It does not take a genius to figure out how to balance budgets without unbalancing the lives of the people. There are many low-priority budget items. Military expenditures exceed expenditures on education and health in many developing countries. Budgetary subsidies to the rich often far exceed such subsidies to the poor. Yet education and health expenditures have been cut ahead of military expenditures during periods of adjustment, and food subsidies to the poor have been slashed in preference to cutting tax and interest rate subsidies to powerful landlords and industrialists. The social and human costs of the adjustment programmes have been unnecessarily high and the Bretton Woods institutions have been blamed for the consequences.

This image of political insensitivity has been rather unfair to both the IMF and the World Bank. It is not seriously credible that officials of the Bretton Woods institutions chuckle over the harsh human conditionality of their loans. One expert who has watched this game of mirrors from both sides – as a staff member of the World Bank for 12 years and as the Finance and Planning Minister of Pakistan for eight years – states that what really happens is that the governments of developing countries find it politically convenient to squeeze the poorer and weaker sections of their societies and to pretend that it is a part of external conditionality.

But the Bretton Woods institutions must accept their own part of the responsibility. They must pressure governments to cut their military spending rather than their social spending – something they have started doing only in the last few years. They must analyse subsidies to high and low income groups in a national budget and stand firm in slashing subsidies to the rich elitist groups in a society before subsidies to the poor are touched. They must at least encourage transparency of information and an open policy dialogue by giving various policy options for balancing budgets in their economic reports, with an analysis of their impact on various income groups in that society. They must spend as much time discussing politically sensitive issues of land reform and credit for all as they do now on distorted prices in an economic system.

These are not easy issues. They require skilful engineering and political alliances for change within the system. But unless the Bretton Woods institutions are willing to take some political heat on these issues, the cause of the poor – which is

© *Jeremy Hartley/Panos*

216

always poorly defended in their own systems – will go by default. In any case, if the Bretton Woods institutions are already taking so much abuse for human costs which they do not wish to cause, they may as well get more directly involved in the discussion of these politically sensitive areas.

There are many policies of the Bretton Woods institutions which require urgent re-examination and reform – from their conditions imposed for structural adjustment loans to their weighted voting structures. But whatever else is done, we must first rescue the Bretton Woods institutions from the swamp of global irrelevance into which they have been sinking fast in the last 50 years.

One of the central questions today is whether we should leave the fate of the global economic system to the *ad hoc* coordination of G-7 or to the free workings of the international markets, or whether we need a minimum of global economic management through professional analysis and consultative processes within international financial institutions.

It is rather alarming that such a question needs to be asked once again. Keynes and White thought they had settled this issue in 1944 by persuading the international community to reject unilateralism in favour of multilateralism. The experience of the 1920s and 1930s was never to be repeated.

As we celebrate the 50th anniversary of the Bretton Woods institutions, let us pause for a moment to review their original purpose. And let us think quite seriously what we need to do to shape these pale relics of a forgotten past into institutions of genuine global governance in the 21st century. In the next century, we need the IMF to evolve into an International Central Bank and the World Bank to become an International Investment Trust. And if these institutions are not up to this challenge, we may need to reinvent new institutions of global, financial and economic management.

It will be far better to build on the existing structures than to search for an entirely new edifice. We must recognize that an evolutionary change is our best hope. In this spirit, what reforms can we consider to reposition these institutions for the challenges of the 21st century?

Many developing countries are struggling to repay loans to the World Bank.
A woman weeding rice seedlings.

GRUPO FINANCIERO INTERACCIONES

Grupo Financiero Interacciones, one of Mexico's leading financial institutions, believes that the condition of a nation's infrastructure is a major factor in its economic wellbeing.

With divisions covering insurance, banking, brokerage, engineering, research, leasing and factoring, the **Group** is poised to play a key role in Mexico's infrastructural development.

INTERACCIONES
GRUPO FINANCIERO

The $1.7 billion international financing for Mexico's largest highway project— the 362 mile Mexico City-Guadalajara toll road—was undertaken by **Grupo Financiero Interacciones.** In addition, the company acted as financial consultants in the modernization of Mexico City's infrastructure development programme, positioning itself as a leader in the issue of medium- and long-term investment for infrastructure projects.

Having recently undergone a process of reorganization and consolidation, **Grupo Financiero Interacciones** continues its philosophy to create programmes to improve productivity, quality and profitability with a view to assisting Mexico's future development.

Let us take the IMF first. We do need a global institution that can ensure sound economic management and global monetary stability. Such an institution should be able to perform five functions:

■ help stabilize global economic activity

■ act as a lender of last resort to financial institutions

■ calm the financial markets when they become jittery or disorderly

■ regulate banks and financial institutions with an international scope

■ create and regulate new international liquidity.

These five functions are the proper role of a world central bank. Even if we de-emphasize the last function – of creating an international reserve currency – as it may be over-ambitious at this stage, the other four functions lie at the very heart of sound macro-economic management and must be carried out by the IMF if it is to reclaim its legitimate role in the global monetary system.

Whether or not we will eventually move towards a world central bank in the 21st century is an issue likely to excite a good deal of debate in the next decade. In a way, such a development is inevitable. But that is the ultimate goal. In the meantime, we should consider some cautious steps – and eminently logical ones – which can initiate a reform of the IMF in the right direction.

First, we must seriously consider a new issue of SDRs – in the range of 30 to 50 billion SDRs. This extra dose of global liquidity could help fuel world economic recovery at a time when global inflationary pressures are low, primary commodity prices have hit rock bottom and most industrial countries are reducing their budget deficits. There could also be innovations in the distribution of SDRs, with industrial countries passing on some of their allocations to developing countries through overdraft facilities.

Second, the Compensatory and Contingency Financial Facility (CCFF) of the IMF needs to be changed in several directions. There should be no quota restriction, so that a country could obtain full compensation for a shortfall in its exports. The loan period needs to be extended so that countries would not have to repay before the contingency is over. Even more important, it is somewhat illogical to attach policy conditionality to borrowing. If a country is reeling from external shocks outside its control, why add the shock of IMF conditionality as well?

Third, in collaboration with the Bank for International Settlements (BIS), the IMF should acquire some regulatory control over international banking activities. The IMF should also be applying the proposed 'Tobin Tax' of 0.5 per cent on international currency transactions to curb excessive speculation, if this eminently sensible proposal begins to catch the imagination of the international community. This would not only give the IMF some control over international flows of capital which are sweeping across global markets with hurricane force, it would also yield enormous revenue – about $1.5 trillion a year – which could help finance World Bank and UN development operations. Global prosperity would be taxed in an invisible and non-discriminatory manner to finance an attack on global poverty.

Fourth, the IMF needs to acquire a greater role in global macro-economic management – reviewing the policies of all countries, whether or not they are active borrowers, and particularly having some influence on the macro-economic policies of major industrial powers. One possible mechanism may be for the IMF to persuade the BIS to link the level of

"moving towards a world central bank – it must be the ultimate goal"

reserves that banks are required to hold against loans to these countries to the IMF's evaluation. This would affect the industrial countries' ability to raise funds from private banks and give the IMF substantial leverage over their policies.

These four steps would be only an initial move in the direction of IMF reform. They are not a blueprint for converting the IMF into a world central bank. These proposals are offered in the hope that it may be possible to move on some of them in the current environment.

Let us turn now to the World Bank. There are several areas of reform which are appropriate at this stage.

First, the Bank is by now certainly the finest institution in advising developing countries on economic growth policies. Where it needs to develop much greater sensitivity and expertise is in linking economic growth to human lives, in analysing the distribution and sustainability of growth, and in examining more participatory patterns of development. The issue is not growth *per se*. To address poverty, economic growth is an imperative. But what type of growth? To benefit the masses, growth opportunities must be more equitably distributed. And they must be sustainable from one generation to the next. The World Bank certainly talks about these issues. But its critics allege that its embrace of the issues of sustainable, people-centred development is less than enthusiastic. It regards such issues more as an irritation than as central themes. We could all gain a great deal if the Bank were to turn its professional rigour to the emerging concerns for sustainable human development.

Second, the Bank must find new ways of recycling much larger resources to the developing countries. We are reaching the end of an era where legislatures in the rich nations will keep voting larger IDA resources. In the 21st century we shall have to start looking for more innovative ways of raising global financing to address the issues of global poverty. Such proposals as the Tobin Tax, or an international tax on non-renewable energy or on the armament trade, or proceeds from environmental emission permits – which are still regarded with a good deal of healthy scepticism – are the kind of proposals which

Many African countries are rich in minerals and resources.
A mine in Zambia.

© Ron Giling/Panos

"*what type of growth?*"

EGYPTIAN ELECTRICITY AUTHORITY

 EEA, Egypt's public utility authority, is committed to promoting development through the generation and transmission of electrical energy.

Created more than 35 years ago, it aims to provide Egypt with a reliable electricity service.

Nowadays, EEA endeavours to enhance cross-boundary cooperation in electricity, providing environmentally-friendly solutions to dwindling conventional energy sources.

may move to the centre of the international debate when it is recognized that the new compulsions of global human security require some form of global financing. The Bank has been fairly conservative in its approach to new financing sources: in fact, after the launching of the IDA in 1960, it has considered no significant innovation in its approaches to funding. Many of its well-wishers would like to see the Bank as a leader in exploring new avenues for raising international finance.

Construction work in Chengdu, a city in western China.

© *Alain Le Garsmeur/Panos*

From agricultural peasant markets to metropolitan capitals of finance, commerce has been recognized as a major force in determining the future development of humanity.

© Martin Adler/Panos

Third, the Bank must start considering prudent ways to restructure its own debts. The Bank has advised all other creditors to restructure their debts to developing countries, but expressed an inability to reschedule its own debts because of its Charter limitations and its concerns about its triple-A credit rating in the capital markets. The result is obvious: the Bank will end up owning more and more debt of its member countries, its net transfers will decline significantly, and after some time it will be recycling its own debts rather than any new resources. It has already reached that position with several developing countries. The Bank must begin to convince its contributors and the capital markets that it has to act as a development agency, not a global moneylender, and that prudent rescheduling of debts must be a part of its operations.

Fourth, the Bank must take on the role of an international investment trust – selling bonds to nations with a surplus and lending the proceeds to developing countries. Developing countries could borrow from the trust on terms appropriate to their level of development. The newly industrializing countries could pay commercial rates, while low-income countries would pay less – a subsidy that richer members of the international community should be persuaded to cover. If some of the proposals regarding international fees or taxes prove to be acceptable to the

"it is time to begin designing the global institutions of the 21st century"

international community, a pool of resources would become available for such a subsidized recycling of market funds.

The founders of the Bretton Woods institutions and the UN were neither inhibited nor timid 50 years ago. When bombs were still raining on London, John Maynard Keynes was preparing the blueprint of the Bretton Woods institutions. When Europe was still at war, Jean Monnet was dreaming about a European Economic Community. When the dust of war had still not settled, the Marshall Plan for the reconstruction of Europe was taking shape. When the hostility of nations was still simmering, the hopeful design of a United Nations was being signed by the leaders of the world, led by President Truman.

We must admire the vision of those people today – and their courage to innovate. We see little of this intellectual ferment these days even though we have seen some unprecedented changes in the global environment – from the fall of the Berlin Wall to the end of apartheid in South Africa. The unthinkable is already becoming the commonplace. And yet our sources of creativity are curiously passive regarding the future shape of global economic governance. Maybe it is time to begin designing the global institutions of the 21st century.

The UN is unique in its capacity to mobilize an international response to crises.
UNHCR is overseeing the organization of scores of camps like this one in Tanzania for the millions of Rwandan refugees who fled the country in 1994.

businesslike ~ a management approach

- The need for change
- Innovative proposal
- A framework for action
- Coordination and control

© Howard Davies/Panos

The United Nations is, of course, not a business, in the sense that its purposes are commercial or profit-seeking. But in the broader sense the UN is the centrepiece of the most important business of all – that of ensuring that our global community provides hospitable, peaceful and equitable conditions of life for all of its people. It is surely therefore important, indeed imperative, that the UN draws upon the best of business practices and expertise in fulfilling its global mission. This is especially so at a time when that mission is becoming increasingly complex and the resources available to the UN to fulfil it ever more difficult to obtain.

Much has been said about the need to reform the UN and to effect changes in its Charter. Indeed, the 50th anniversary of the UN has given rise to a plethora of books, studies, seminars and learned papers focusing on the future of the UN and the reforms required to prepare it for that future. Particularly valuable and timely is the report of the Commission on Global Governance chaired by Prime Minister Ingvar Carlsson of Sweden and former Commonwealth Secretary-General Sir Shridath Ramphal.

This process has produced some thoughtful and innovative proposals which will give governments a rich body of analysis and a broad range of ideas from which to draw in taking the decisions concerning the future of the UN. It has concentrated largely on issues of structure, of process and of Charter change. There has been some, but too little, attention paid to the management dimension of these changes, even though the greatest and most immediate need in the UN is for improvements in its management. This is

"WE COMMIT OURSELVES
to serve our clients efficiently, explore new business opportunities, be a cornerstone of the community and an asset to South Africa."

Celebrating its fifth anniversary as a public company within the South African market, Transnet Limited has met the challenge to change from being a bureaucratic state-run organisation (South African Transport Services) into a dynamic group of businesses.

The Group consists of the holding company, Transnet, a public company of which the South African Government is the sole shareholder; six transport businesses - Spoornet (Rail Transport), Portnet (Harbours), Autonet (Road Transport), Petronet (Liquid Petroleum Transport), South African Airways (Air Transport) and PX (container shipments); and a number of related and support businesses.

A transport giant by any standards, Transnet handles 164 million tons of rail freight per year, 7 million tons by road, 3.8 million passengers by road, 120 million tons in the harbours, 14,000 million litres are pumped through its petrol pipelines and it flies 31,000 domestic and international flights per year. In total,Transnet is worth R40 billion in fixed assets and has a workforce of 115,000 employees.

Transnet is today recognised as the dominant player in the transport arena in Southern Africa. The role of a well-developed transport infrastructure, which provides a cost effective service in enhancing economic growth and improving the quality of life of all South Africans, cannot be over-emphasised.

Adding value to the lives of employees, their families and the community is part of the company's vision. The company goes beyond training and developing employees in the workplace, to developing the families of employees and the communities in which they live.

The company's social investment policy focuses on primary health care through operating a primary health care train in rural areas and skills development such as needlework, bricklaying, agriculture, welding and starting a business.

The company is also actively involved in developing sport, art and culture as a tool to uplift and involve communities.

Transnet strives in all its projects to empower communities to do more for themselves.

not in any way to detract from the importance of the structural and constitutional changes that must be made to enable the UN to function effectively in a world very different from that which gave rise to its creation half a century ago. In the meantime, improvements in management and the introduction of relevant practices and methods developed in the business world need not await structural and constitutional change.

Many, perhaps most, of the necessary management improvements can be carried out within the existing mandate and authority of the UN Secretary-General, although it would be important for him/her to have the broad support of member states if these

managed process of internal change would enhance the UN's effectiveness in the areas in which its services are most needed and most valued. The permanent staff of the UN is not excessive by the standards of government or other organizations, both private and public. The permanent staff of the UN is now at a level of some 10,609 permanent staff and a total of approximately 33,967 if the specialized agencies, excepting the World Bank and the International Monetary Fund (IMF), are included.[1] In the aggregate, the costs of the UN and its agencies amount to less than two dollars for each person in the world as compared with $150 per person for military expenditures. It represents 0.0005 per cent of the world's gross domestic product.[2]

"*a great deal can be done to make the UN more efficient*"

authorities are to be invoked fully and vigorously. At the same time, improvement in the management and cost-effectiveness of the UN would serve to strengthen political support for the kind of extended mandate and accompanying structural and constitutional changes that will be needed for the UN of the 21st century. The current financial crisis provides a strong impetus for greater cost-efficiency which can only be accomplished through major improvements in management. The need for such changes is likely to become more acute as budgetary constraints faced by virtually all member states point to even greater pressures on the UN's finances and much tougher requirements by governments for more efficient use of UN resources.

A great deal can be done to make the UN more efficient in its use of existing resources without impairing its overall effectiveness. Indeed, a well-

While it is useful to bear in mind that the cost of running the UN system represents only a very modest proportion of the total cost of global governance, this is really not the point in making the case for better management of the UN. The case rests on what governments actually get from their investment in the UN and what value they place on it in relation to alternative uses of their resources. Today all governments are facing severe budgetary pressures that are requiring them to re-examine their own priorities and provide much more rigorous and cost-effective management of their finances. It would be illusory to believe that the UN can be exempt from this process. It would be much more realistic to recognize the reality that in few, if any, nations does the UN have the kind of strong political constituency that can support its claim on the national budget against the competing claims of domestic constituencies.

Over the past 50 years the UN Secretariat has grown in response to the evolving priorities of the community of nations it serves, as reflected in the agendas and the resolutions of the General Assembly and other UN deliberative bodies. But priorities have changed and new issues have emerged. These have been reflected only to a very limited degree by corresponding changes in the deployment of secretariat resources. New secretariat units have been created while existing units have been retained to perform functions overlapping those of other units and often no longer accorded the level of priority that gave rise to their creation.

All organizations require periodic reform and in today's rapidly changing world the process must be a continuing one. But although the world has altered radically in the 50 years since the UN was established, changes within the UN have been minimal, certainly not radical. The time has clearly come for radical change. This change can and should begin at the management level. Many of the needs for change which drive the growing pressures for structural and constitutional reform can be met to a large extent through improvements in management. And while basic structural and constitutional change is indispensable, it will not come quickly or easily and would not in any event be effective without accompanying management changes. Such management changes can and should precede, and would help prepare the way for, basic structural and constitutional change.

A trimmed down UN

Secretary-General Boutros Boutros-Ghali is to be commended for initiating within the Secretariat a process of change more radical than that undertaken by any of his predecessors. In consolidating the departmental structure of the Secretariat, reducing the number of officials reporting directly to the Secretary-General and rationalizing the country-level representation of the UN, he has made a good start. But it is only a start.

The process of management change must be guided by an up-to-date evaluation of what each unit within the Secretariat actually does, what it produces, to what extent this overlaps with what others produce, how its products are actually used, how they are valued by those who use them and how this

relates to their cost. This is routine in most businesses and other organizations that are run in a businesslike manner.

Some will argue that it is not feasible or appropriate to quantify the output of the UN Secretariat, dealing as it does with major world issues which simply cannot be measured by the kind of quantitative standard which business applies. True, but only to a degree. It is entirely feasible to make a reasonably accurate assessment of the output of each unit in the Secretariat, to determine its cost and to ascertain from those who actually use its products how much they value them.

Such a process would undoubtedly reveal that much of the Secretariat's work involving perhaps half, or even more, of its staff members is devoted to areas and issues that are now accorded marginal priority by member states or can be done better by others either inside or outside the UN. It is likely that a very large proportion of the UN Secretariat, probably well over half, is now engaged in activities that would fall into these categories. And in most cases this would not be a reflection on the quality or performance of the people performing these tasks. In so many cases a very small, under-funded secretariat unit is expected to do meaningful work in areas in which other organizations with much larger budgets and capacities and stronger mandates are the prime actors.

The UN need not and cannot do everything. Its uniqueness and its comparative advantage lies in the fact that it is global in its mandate and is universal in its membership. Its resources should be concentrated in those areas in which these distinctive qualities enable it to perform for the international community, functions which other organizations are not geared to perform. But in doing so it should draw on and utilize, to a much greater extent than it now does, the capacities and contributions of other organizations, inter-governmental and non-governmental, which have the specialized knowledge, experience and constituencies which the UN does not have. Often the primary role of the UN will be to provide a global framework or context for actions that must be taken on other levels – regional, national or sectoral. It need not and cannot have in the Secretariat the capacities to deal with these issues in

International development cooperation, the environment, human rights and population are all areas that the UN has put firmly on the international agenda.
Unsafe barrels of waste, part of the trade in toxic waste that sends millions of contaminated barrels to the developing world.

their totality. Yet in all too many instances the UN purports to do so, maintaining secretariat units to deal with issues which it simply does not have the capacity to deal with effectively. The result is a dispersion of UN resources and a dilution of its effectiveness that has contributed significantly to the unsatisfactory performance of the UN in so many areas and the reduction of confidence in it.

The UN's track record

The experience of the UN's first 50 years surely points to the main areas in which the UN is at its best. There is no substitute for it as the global forum for leadership in identifying and legitimizing new issues for the international agenda – as it did in respect of international development cooperation, human rights, the environment, population and women's issues, to name but a few. It is also unique in its capacity to mobilize the international response to major peacekeeping, peacemaking and humanitarian needs and to provide the forum for the development of international law and the negotiation and administration of treaties and conventions. Virtually all of these areas have in common that the number of permanent secretariat members involved is relatively small and their principal task is to orchestrate and to service processes involving specialized representatives of member states and representatives and experts from other organizations, inter-governmental and non-governmental.

Three examples where the UN Secretariat has done this are the UN Conference on the Human Environment held in Stockholm in 1972, which placed the environment on the international agenda; the Office for Emergency Operations in Africa (OEOA), which led and coordinated the international response to the great African famine emergency of 1984-86 and the UN Conference on Environment and Development (UNCED) in Rio de Janeiro in 1992, which provided a broad global sanction for the concept of sustainable development and agreement on basic principles and actions to give effect to it. In each case, the central UN Secretariat unit was very small in relation to the magnitude of the task it was given – numbering from 20 to 30 people drawn from the permanent Secretariat. But in all cases, too, it engaged the active support and involvement of all parts of the UN system and a multiplicity of other actors and sources of expertise, national and

> ## *"no substitute for the UN as the global forum for leadership"*

international, governmental and non-governmental. What the UN provided was the leadership, the capacity for mobilization and orchestration of the contributions of other participants and the framework within which they could operate in a collaborative manner towards common goals and objectives.

An important feature of each of these examples is that the organizations responsible were *ad hoc* in nature and each was phased out after the task for which it was set up was completed.

All of the UN's peacekeeping operations are by their nature *ad hoc* responses to particular crisis situations. All are managed and orchestrated by a permanent UN headquarters staff that has never exceeded more than 314 professionals, even now that the UN is managing 16 peacekeeping and peacemaking operations involving a total of approximately 74,600 temporary personnel in the field.[3] The same has been true of virtually all humanitarian operations, global conferences and treaty negotiations. The point here is that many of the UN's most important and successful value-added activities have involved relatively small numbers of its permanent staff and correspondingly modest contributions from regular budgetary resources. At the same time, the successful launching and management of such

"the principal international forum – the place where voices can be most heard"

The UN Earth Summit in 1992 sketched out a global accord for dealing with environmental destruction.
A representative of the world's indigenous people at the Earth Summit's Global Forum.

© Dylan García/Panos

initiatives requires a permanent secretariat complement with special qualities of leadership and management, and the capacity to identify and command the respect and cooperation of the principal actors concerned both within and outside the UN system. Yet it is a quality that is not sufficiently valued, nurtured and supported by present UN personnel policies and practices.

The kind of management improvements the UN so clearly needs require significant changes in personnel policies, particularly through reduced politicization and improved professionalization of the staff appointments process. Recruitment, career development and training practices should be oriented towards producing within the Secretariat professionals with the integrative, mobilizing and orchestrating skills required to deal with issues that are increasingly complex and systemic in nature and involve a multiplicity of actors, disciplines and sectors. One way of improving the leadership capacities of the UN Secretariat would be to have an independent board review the professional qualifications of those being considered for senior appointments. The Secretary-General would, of course, retain final decision-making in respect of such appointments but his selections would be made from amongst those whose professional qualifications met certain objectively applied standards.

One of the principal challenges the UN faced in its early years was that of facilitating the transition of former colonies in the developing world to independence, supporting the establishment of their governments and launching them on the pathway to national development. The technical assistance offered by the UN and the development assistance it mobilized and helped to deploy made a critically important contribution to the emergence of these newly independent nations as full and influential participants in the community of nations. But the situation and the needs of developing countries have changed immensely during the past few decades. Developing countries, which comprise some three-quarters of the world's population, now represent a similar proportion of the membership of the UN. It has become their principal international forum, the place where their voices can be most heard and heeded and their influence most fully brought to bear.

The Yemen Bank for Reconstruction and Development (YBRD)
with its headquarters in Sana'a, is the largest bank in Yemen, offering banking facilities and investment, credits and securities. With five regional banks and 39 branch offices operating throughout the country, the YBRD has built a solid foundation for the country's new economy and become a starting point for the development of its multi-sector economy.

With its capital divided between the State, which has a 51% share, and the private sector with 49%, the YBRD has been a leader in building a national mixed economy.

The YBRD was set up after the September Revolution in 1962 as the sole moneylender to the Government of the young Yemen Republic. Since its creation, the YBRD has functioned as a catalyst in bringing together the economic, social, cultural and educational sectors. It has helped set up many key companies in Yemen which range from power generation to housing development. The Bank has also taken on the responsibility of helping the State to meet its foreign liabilities relating to the imports of a diversified range of products vital to the country's economic health.

Apart from its foreign investments, the YBRD has set up and been involved in the formation of 33 industrial, commercial and banking organizations. As far as the future activity of the Bank is concerned, it will continue to play an important role in the economic and social development process taking place in Yemen today.

Head Office: Sana'a
Republic of Yemen
Teleg. Add. Banyemen
P.O. Box 541
Tlx: 2202, 2291, 2533
Tel: 271662, 271601.

Yet the resources of the UN Secretariat have not been redeployed sufficiently to take account of the major changes in the needs and interests of developing countries, and the proportion of their external funding requirements provided by the UN has been reduced substantially. Economic and social development is and must be one of the highest priority tasks of the UN. Yet it is one in which the UN is a great deal less effective than it could be and should be, despite the large proportion of the Secretariat ostensibly devoted to it.

In a global economy in which knowledge is the principal source of added-value and competitiveness, developing countries, and particularly the least developed, are disadvantaged by a lack of the resources required to develop their scientific and technological capabilities, their institutional infrastructure and educational systems. Many of them lack the policy research capabilities required to assert and protect their own interests in a rapidly changing international policy and negotiating environment. Supporting developing countries in development and strengthening their capacities in these areas is, for most of them, their most critical need and highest priority. The UN Development Programme (UNDP), through its Capacity 21 and Sustainable Development Network initiatives, is giving special attention to mobilizing resources for these purposes. But so far the response has been disappointing.

The UN's funding challenge

Funding for the UN's development programmes is hard to get and is likely to be even harder to come by in future. At the same time, the proportion of funds made available for emergency assistance has been growing, much of it at the expense of development funding. The recent experience of the UN Children's Fund (UNICEF) is a case in point. The proportion of its budget devoted to emergency, as distinct from development, programmes has grown from just over five per cent to 28 per cent in the past 10 years. No one would argue with the need to meet humanitarian needs which are usually of a highly urgent and critical nature in terms of the immediate need to relieve human suffering and save lives. But when this is done at the expense of long-term development, which is the best means of ensuring against future humanitarian crises, it becomes a

vicious circle in which the lack of adequate funding for development sets the stage for even greater humanitarian needs in the future.

Against this background, it is imperative that the UN makes the best possible use of its financial and human resources in responding to both the humanitarian and development priorities of developing countries. There is a great potential for doing this through improved management practices and greater cost-efficiency. And, in doing this, the UN will also convince both donors and developing countries that it provides the most efficient and effective system for channelling resources to developing countries for both humanitarian and development purposes.

The UN must gear itself to become to a much greater extent a mobilizer and not just a dispenser of resources in the development field, as it has done so successfully in the humanitarian field. During the 1984-86 famine in Sub-Saharan Africa, the UN took the lead in mobilizing and deploying over four billion dollars of humanitarian assistance, only a modest portion of which was dispensed directly by the UN. Yet the UN was not nearly so effective in meeting the process of mobilizing the increased resources required for rehabilitation and long-term

"no one would argue with the need to meet humanitarian needs"

development in Africa following the famine. This is in part explained by the fact that during emergencies public and political pressures drive a coordination that has not been possible to achieve in development.

There is a promising step in the right direction in the Secretary-General's recent initiative creating a closer link between the policy and the funding functions of the UN and the broad responsibilities he has given to UN Administrator James Gustave Speth for development and coordination. It would be important to the effectiveness of, and confidence in, this new framework for coordination that policies and priorities set by member governments drive and guide funding, rather than the reverse. The time has come to bring all the UN funding functions within a common administrative framework, which would logically be provided by UNDP. This would produce significant savings in personnel and administrative costs. And, in consolidating the administration of funds in UNDP, the distinctiveness required to maintain the support of specialized constituencies can be preserved by maintaining separate 'windows'. Thus, for example, the fund of the UN Environment Programme (UNEP) would, for administrative purposes, become part of UNDP, while a separate window would be maintained at UNEP headquarters in Nairobi to respond to the specialized funding needs of UNEP's programmes. This would have the further benefit of ensuring the close coordination of UNEP's programmes with the growing amount of UNDP's development funding which has an environment dimension and can benefit from UNEP input.

There is a great potential for cost-effectiveness in rationalizing the UN's administrative and budgetary processes and developing a much more coherent system of programme-budgeting. Substantial savings and improved effectiveness could also be achieved through a greater degree of rationalization of secretariat and administrative resources as between the headquarters, the regional commissions and country-level missions. This three-tier administrative

The 16 current peacekeeping operations are orchestrated by a permanent staff of 314 people.
UN peacekeepers board a plane in Mozambique.

Sierra Leone's roads
have been in a state
of deterioration for
many years and have
been a severe obstacle
to the country's economic
progress. In 1992 all this
began to change when the
government put into effect
the recommendations of a
reorganisation study carried out by the

SIERRA LEONE ROADS AUTHORITY

United Nations Development Programme. The
Sierra Leone Roads Authority (SLRA) was set up to
develop, construct and maintain the country's roads.
The first phase of a seven-year road rehabilitation
and maintenance programme is now under way to
clear the backlog of road maintenance and return
Sierra Leone's roads to a satisfactory state. It will also
make sure they remain in good condition. To achieve
this goal, the bulk of road maintenance activity has been
switched from the public to the private sector and, with
gender participation in mind, a particular effort has been
made to hire women contractors. Already there is a visible
improvement in the quality of roads reflected in the rising living
standards of the rural population. A well maintained road network
is a catalyst for the increased movement of passengers, goods and
services that will all contribute to the development of Sierra Leone.
For this valuable work to continue, the SLRA continues to look to the
donor agencies to enhance its operational capacity and, in doing so, aid
the country's much needed economic recovery.

structure is one of the reasons for the high overhead costs of the UN in the economic and social development field in relation to the amount of funding it dispenses to developing countries.

Virtually all governments are at or near the limits of what they can do to meet the needs and expectations of their people and what their people are prepared to pay in taxes. Thus, the multiplicity of non-governmental actors that make up civil society are inevitably playing a much larger role, both in developing social policy directions and in mobilizing and deploying resources to meet particular societal needs and interests. In many areas their capacities today exceed those of governments. The same is true at the international level where today more humanitarian and development resources are channelled to developing countries through non-governmental organizations (NGOs) than through the UN. Thus the UN has a primary role in providing credible, objective and well-informed leadership and a coherent framework for mobilization and deployment of international resources from a variety of sources around particular objectives. It must learn to play this role much more effectively.

The UN needs to adapt to the sea-change that has taken place in the flow of resources to developing countries. Private investment has become by far the principal source of external financing for the rapidly growing economies of Asia and Latin America, which are also generating substantially growing earnings from their export trade. While these rapidly developing countries continue to require external support in meeting their social needs, their capacity to do this from their own

resources is improving. Meanwhile the least developed countries, particularly those of Sub-Saharan Africa, remain heavily dependent on Official Development Assistance (ODA). And the countries in transition in Eastern Europe and the former Soviet Union require specialized technical policy support as well as infusions of private and public capital to help them rebuild and restructure their economies. The UN must therefore be in a position to provide a more diverse range of support targeted to the particular needs and interests of each of these categories of countries.

> "*the UN must provide a more diverse range of support*"

The UN itself is not likely to become a channel for substantially increased flows of funds to developing countries. But it has the unique capacity, which needs to be vastly strengthened, to provide a forum in which the interests of developing countries can be defended and championed, to mobilize support for developing those countries' own institutional capabilities, and to supplement their individual capacities for protecting and asserting their interests in the multiplicity of international negotiations in areas where their lack of adequate institutional and policy expertise puts them at a disadvantage. It is also in the best position to create the leadership and cooperative framework for mobilizing and deploying the resources of the entire international community, including non-governmental actors, around particular needs and objectives. This would mean building the new UN around the best experiences of its past while shedding much of the costly and bureaucratic baggage that has developed over the years and which is now more an impediment than a contributor to the UN's effectiveness.

Coordination and a common focus

An indispensable key to the UN's success in undertaking this role in leading and catalyzing action by the entire world community is for it to become the primary source of objective, credible information on major global trends and issues. The basis and tools for such leadership would be the advances made in recent years in information sciences and telecommunications, combined with the confidence and respect earned over the years by the Statistical Division of the UN Department of Economic and Social Information and Policy Analysis as one of the UN's quietest but most consistently valuable performers. But it will require strong leadership, mandated directly by the Secretary-General, to rationalize the current conglomeration of information services within the UN which, despite the high quality of some of them, has so far defied any attempt at coordination, consistency and common focus. Here, too, the potential for improved cost-effectiveness is so great that it is likely that the kind of leadership and strategic purposes foreseen for the UN in this field could be achieved within existing budgets.

As the experience of OEOA demonstrated, information is the key to coordination. Nothing is more characteristic of calls for UN reform than exhortations for more 'coordination'. Yet, with some notable exceptions, mostly of an *ad hoc* nature, the UN has a dismal record in effecting coordination. Nevertheless, when the UN can dispense timely and reliable information which other actors find useful in their own decision-making, it thereby exercises a *de facto* coordinating role that most other actors would not accord to it in any formal sense. The OEOA had no formal mandate for coordination. Yet virtually all the major organizations – bilateral, intergovernmental and non-governmental – providing humanitarian and relief assistance to Africa during the 1984-86 famine looked to OEOA for information about needs, and actions to meet those needs which were planned or already under way, as the basis for decisions on deployment of their own assistance. This in turn enabled that assistance to be targeted to the people most in need. It was the key to the central role played by the UN in helping some 30 million people whose lives were at risk to survive the famine.

The UN could achieve even greater efficiency in the use and the effectiveness of secretariat resources if governments were to agree on consolidating and

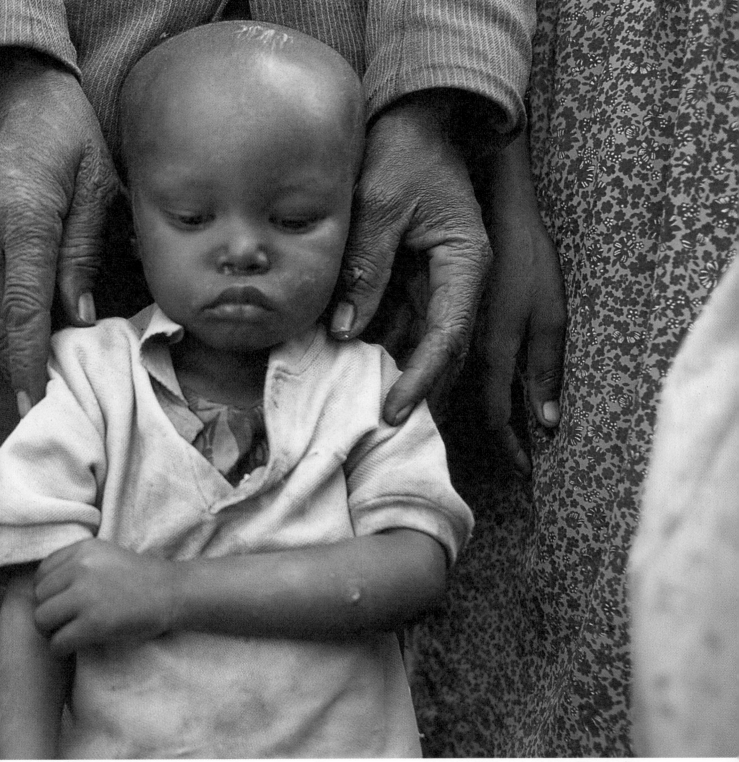

© Betty Press/Panos

Funds are increasingly being channelled into emergency relief at the expense of development programmes.
In the past 10 years, UNICEF's emergency relief programme has grown from five per cent to 28 per cent of its total expenditure.

When human crises erupt, the world needs a UN that can provide increasingly fast, efficient and well coordinated intervention

© *Philip Wolmuth/Panos*

rationalizing the work and meetings of the various committees, commissions, conferences and governing bodies which have proliferated over the years and

contribute significantly to the dispersion of the efforts of the Secretariat, as well as of governments themselves. A good deal of such rationalization could be accomplished by the decision of member states in the General Assembly and other UN bodies without Charter change.

Introducing business-like management principles and practices into the UN may seem somewhat mundane in light of the broad global purposes the UN was established to serve and the ideals enshrined in its Charter. But as the UN has reached the important milestone of its 50th anniversary, it must prepare itself to make radical changes in the manner in which it manages its awesome responsibilities if it is to meet the challenges of the much more demanding, complex and interdependent world of the 21st century. Indeed, it is precisely because its task as the centrepiece of an effective global system of governance is so vitally important to the human future that it requires the very best of management and should settle for nothing less. After all, no business is more important than the business with which the UN is entrusted.

© Betty Press/Panos

During the 1984-86 famine in Sub-Saharan Africa, the drought combined with conflict was a deadly combination for millions in Ethiopia.

ETHIOPIA'S

MODERN

TELECOMMUNICATIONS

FOR FULL

ACCESSIBILITY

▼

ACCESS ANY PLACE

IN THE

WORLD

FROM ETHIOPIA

OR

ACCESS ANY TOWN

IN ETHIOPIA

FROM ANY

PART OF

THE WORLD

▲

100 Years of Telecommunications Service in Ethiopia

1994 marked the 100th Anniversary of the introduction of the telephone to Ethiopia. An extensive open-wire line system was laid, linking the capital with all the important administrative towns of the country. However most of the system was wrecked during the patriotic war of resistance against Fascist aggression. As a result, Ethiopia had to rebuild its telecommunications network and in 1952 the Ethiopian Telecommunications Authority (ETA) was established by government decree.

Even though ETA has undertaken six five-year development programs over the past 40 years, the rural telecommunications system is still largely served by open-wire transmission systems and manual switchboards. In the urban centres there is a digital transmission and switching system, linking the capital Addis Ababa to all the administrative centres of the country. For its international traffic, ETA uses two Standard A Earth Stations accessing INTELSAT satellites, while submarine cable and terrestrial microwave systems are also used for links to neighbouring countries.

ETA's current five-year 7th Development Program, 1993-97, aims at modernizing the network with further expansion of the international, domestic and, more significantly, the rural transmission and switching facilities to help keep pace with the development requirements of the country. The funds required for this program are expected to come mainly from international financing and donor organizations with which ETA traditionally has enjoyed a reputation for prompt loan repayment. However, because of the magnitude of the programs, ETA invites all new international financing and donor organizations to support its development efforts, aimed at promoting the country's untapped potential for growth.

ETHIOPIAN TELECOMMUNICATIONS AUTHORITY
Telephone: 51 05 00   Fax: 515777   Telex: 21000
P.O. Box 1047   ADDIS ABABA — ETHIOPIA

Endnotes

1 UN Document A/49/527 *Human Resources Management: Composition of the Secretariat.*

2 Erskine Childers and Brian Urquhart, *Renewing the United Nations System, Development Dialogue 1994:1* (Uppsala, Sweden: Dag Hammarskjold Foundation, 1994) p.143.

3 UN Department of Peacekeeping Operations, *Summary of Contributions to Peacekeeping Operations by Countries* (as of 30 November 1994).

Food distribution at Nyacyonga Camp in Rwanda.

© *David Orr/Panos*

Employment is moving in the direction of household enterprises and small private firms and cooperatives.
A Bolivian weaver at work.

responsibilities of the corporate sector

© Sean Sprague/Panos

- Corporate citizenship
- Sustainable development
- New partnerships
- Responsible investment

D "Downsizing and lay-offs continue even as corporate performance improves...stock prices gyrate wildly irrespective of supply and demand of goods and services...global currency markets are in upheaval... population growth and civil unrest are creating a litany of social problems...cities around the world are in trouble...the burden of national debt rises around the world."

At a time of unprecedented change and upheaval in the world, business managers are frequently uncertain as to where their responsibilities lie. On the one hand, business leaders are encouraged to become 'good corporate citizens' and direct their companies' significant resources towards addressing and solving social problems. On the other hand, the financial and competitive pressures on them are stronger than ever before. In what London Business School's Charles Handy calls 'the age of paradox' what, if anything, are a business's social obligations? And how have these obligations evolved over time?

To these queries, there exist two opposed viewpoints that have been argued back and forth for years. The traditional response has been that business's sole responsibility is to make a profit – and thus business has no social obligations. To justify and prove this view, economists and business leaders refer to the works of Adam Smith, Milton Friedman and others. At the other end of the spectrum is the view that business has purposely exploited and destroyed the system in a selfish attempt to maximize profits at the expense of society.

BRIDGING THE CONTINENTS.

In all parts of the world, tyres and cables are essential in the areas of transportation of people and goods, and transmission of energy and information. Pirelli's business is centred on these key markets in which we are among the world leaders and innovators. Our mission is therefore to manufacture and market good value, high quality products which can link people and countries drawing them closer together and bringing down barriers. Pirelli is therefore proud to take part in the celebrations of the 50th Anniversary of the United Nations fostering a vision of hope.

A more accurate interpretation of the social obligation of business is a path between these two extremes. What results is neither a condemnation of business nor an attack on profit-making. Rather, what emerges is a fresh and enlightened understanding of both economics and the purpose of business in our globalized society. The shift in thinking which will occur is that one cannot separate the social obligations of business from the financial, ethical or management obligations – it is all part of the whole package. As such it is not a question as to whether or not business has social obligations because, quite clearly, all institutions in society have social obligations. The choice for business becomes whether to address their social obligations proactively through such innovations as public-private partnerships, privatization efforts and the creation of pollution rights markets, or passively and reactively, via taxes, fines and other regulatory requirements.

Business functions by public consent and its basic purpose is to serve, constructively, the needs of society – to the satisfaction of society not merely to maximize profits. This fundamental shift in the view and understanding of the purpose of business has profound implications on how business is managed and perceived. Additionally, this definition presents a very different set of expectations for shareholders and stakeholders of corporations. Keeping this definition in mind, most would agree that the social order is imbalanced. A greater affluence for a small group of individuals amid a deteriorating environment and decaying community life just does not make sense. Indeed, the sluggishness of social progress is producing rising criticism from all major institutions in society: government, schools, churches, as well as business. In this context, companies are undergoing the most searching public scrutiny. Certainly, statistics show that the majority of the public think that corporations have not been sufficiently concerned about the problems society faces. Two-thirds believe business now has a moral obligation to help achieve progress in society even at the expense of profitability.

So business is being asked to contribute more to the quality of life than just supplying quantities of goods and services and, insomuch as it exists to serve society, the future of business will depend on its sensitivity to the changing demands of the consumer. It is, after all, in the interests of business to enlarge its markets and improve its workforce by helping disadvantaged people to develop into customers and workers and to fulfil their economic potential. Likewise, it is in the direct self-interest of companies to help reduce the mounting costs of welfare, crime, disease and homelessness, for much of the cost of these maladies is placed on business through higher taxation rates and increasing expenditures on security. It is therefore not unreasonable to suggest that if business does not accept a fair measure of responsibility for social improvement, then the interests of the corporation may actually be jeopardized.

Public-private partnership

One of the significant outcomes of the 1992 UN Conference on Environment and Development (UNCED) in Rio de Janeiro was the agreement that business was given a role in shaping the new agenda and a responsibility for making it happen – both in its own everyday operations, by moving towards eco-efficient processes and products, as well as in consort with the public sector in addressing specific problems on the ground. A stable policy regime enables and encourages business and industry to operate responsibly and efficiently and implement long-term policies.

There has also been a fundamental shift in the way governments perceive the role of private capital in economic development, especially foreign investment. More and more state economies are abandoning central planning as a way of bringing prosperity to the economy at large. Foreign investment is now looked upon as the engine of growth and the agent of advancement.

Transnational corporations are playing a central role in this change. Since the 1970s, economic growth has been increasingly associated with new technologies rather than with the use of such natural resources as energy and minerals. Production has become less materials-intensive and more skill- and technology-intensive. New communication technologies are inducing a far greater degree of economic internationalization than was previously possible. Transnational corporations and their global strategies are a major vehicle for transfer and diffusion of technology in developing countries.

The widespread liberalization and the internationalization of production has accorded greater freedom to business. More freedom also means more responsibility, including social responsibility. The term 'good corporate citizen' suggests that the transnational corporations have an obligation to act as responsible members of societies that grant them legal standing. True, business cannot redress every social ill and thus substitute for the government's role, but businesses are increasingly adopting their own codes of conduct. Among them, those relating to employment and human resources development are particularly pronounced. Basic terms of employment are governed by local laws. But corporate standards can impart norms that are considered to be desirable from an international perspective. Elimination of child labour and forced labour by prisoners is an example of where the global production system has positively imposed values on national standards. Both in hiring practices and in treatment of workers, social responsibility standards could be expected to prohibit discrimination on the basis of such factors as race, sex, religion or ethnicity. The challenge is in instituting this where discrimination is legally sanctioned or socially entrenched, setting in motion a ripple reaction that goes far beyond the immediate domain of the factories.

It is generally agreed that the workforce directly employed by transnational corporations enjoys superior wages and benefits relative to the conditions prevailing in local firms. Business has accepted the tenet that a well-trained and well-motivated workforce is an invaluable asset. Therefore going beyond the minimal compliance with the local labour laws to provide better working conditions, imparting better training and better health care facilities is in its own self-interest. This, in turn, facilitates improvement of the infrastructure and transfer of technology to developing countries. In a similar vein, corporations are increasingly taking steps to reduce their adverse effects on the environment and to put in place effective environmental management. This is a positive sign that business has come to recognize the fragility of the environment and the eco-systems. Forestry companies are instituting policies to regenerate tree species if only out of self-interest. Mining and chemical companies are taking steps to clean up the environment. The cost of achieving higher-than-necessary compliance with environmental guidelines is viewed as a form of insurance, a reserve against changing public opinion and social values.

Agribusiness can often be a significant creator of seasonal jobs and improve self-employment opportunities among the rural poor. Plantation-based, vertically-integrated marketing systems dominated by transnational corporations can increase rural employment opportunities for many of the landless poor in a number of developing countries. Contract farming arrangements in the cultivation of labour-intensive crops can increase the returns of smallholders in certain developing countries.

Human resource development is also central to economic growth and development. Human capital created through investment in education and the development of skills emerges as one of the most significant factors not only of economic development but also of international competitiveness. But building up a stock of human capital requires more than just public investment in education. Specialized training is fundamental to the creation of sustainable competitiveness advantage. The business community is in an excellent position to judge priorities in skill formation and therefore has an important complementary role to play in the provision of education and training.

To understand why big businesses, and transnational corporations in particular, wield such an influence, one need only look at the reach of transnational corporations across national boundaries.

The universe of transnational corporations is now estimated to comprise about 37,000 parent firms which control over 200,000 foreign affiliates worldwide. The top hundred transnational corporations now hold about $3.4 trillion in global assets, about $1.3 trillion of which is held outside of their respective home countries. Foreign affiliates generated sales of more than $4.8 trillion in 1991, slightly more than world exports of goods and non-factor services. Transnational corporations are estimated to employ around 73 million people directly and control some one-third of world output. The number of jobs created by them indirectly is much greater – estimated to be around 150 million.

In 1995, 37,000 transnational firms controlled over 200,000 foreign affiliates worldwide.
A transnational car plant in Trinidad.

© *Philip Wolmuth/Panos*

STATNETT

P.O.Box 5192 Majorstua
N-0302 Oslo
Norway

Tel: +47 22 52 70 00
Fax: +47 22 52 70 01

CONSULTING & ENGI-
NEERING SERVICES;
INSTITUTIONAL DEVEL-
OPMENT; TRANSMISSION
& DISTRIBUTION; OPERA-
TION & MAINTENANCE

Statnett (the Norwegian Power Grid Company) is internationally recognized for its expertise in electro-technical construction technology. The company offers: planning and assessment of major electro-technical construction projects, as well as construction of power lines, sea cables, transformer stations, substations and switching stations. Statnett's assets exceed USD 1.47 billion and the company has an annual turnover of 400 million.

Taste for Competition

The company has extensive experience in planning, building and managing electricity networks, both in Norway and

abroad. Through field experience as well as development and research in the areas of transmission, distribution, planning and construction, Statnett is continuously sharpening its competitive edge in these areas.

Conduit of Heavy Power Equipment

A significant amount of the road and sea transport of heavy electrical equipment within, to and from Norway is carried out by Statnett. The company

owns and operates the specially designed freight ships *M/S Elektron* and *C/S Skagerrak*. While the Ro-Ro ship *M/S Elektron* (449 BRT) was designed to carry trucks with a total capacity up to 500 tons, the *C/S Skagerrak* was built for laying and repairing subsea cable connections. The company also operates advanced equipment for stretching power lines across fjords. This equipment, among the largest of its kind in the world, has a winch capacity of 50 tons.

Corridors of Power

Statnett is responsible for coordinating the operation of the entire Norwegian power system, which comprises more than 600 power plants with a collective generator effect of 27 million kW. The company also manages the main electricity networks that transmit power around the country. In 1993, the total production in this system was 120 TWh. Statnett owns and operates 8 500 km of power lines and sea cables as well as 80 distribution sub-stations. Conversion systems for domestic and international power sources are also among the company's specialities.

Laying subsea cable off the coast of Denmark.

The role of the United Nations

As the UN agency charged with accelerating and coordinating industrialization, the UN Industrial Development Organization (UNIDO) has played a part in encouraging multinationals and foreign investors to invest their capital in the South.

The agency overrode doubts about the benefits of multinational investment in the South, and, in 1978, created a worldwide network of investment offices – in close cooperation with the World Bank – to help open the doors to foreign investors. In 1986, when UNIDO was transformed into a specialized agency of the UN, its mandate was broadened to include working with the private – as well as with the public and cooperative – sectors of industry.

The guiding principle behind UNIDO's approach to investment is to develop the most effective channel for transferring know-how, managerial expertise, market access and manufacturing capacities to developing nations, while providing local sponsors with reliable overseas partners. Through its World Investment Network Service (WINS), UNIDO links businesses around the world and swaps country data, industrial technology and financing opportunities. It encourages governments and business to adopt policies for environmental management with emphasis on pollution prevention, assisting and supporting business associations to put cleaner production programmes into practice. According to UNIDO, the agency generated nearly $5,500 million worth of investments for more than 1,600 projects between 1986 and 1993.

With the majority of UNIDO's clients being small- and medium-scale enterprises (SMEs), investment goes straight to the heart of development needs. SMEs often out-perform larger enterprises because of their potential to respond more quickly to market changes and opportunities to develop specialized products, and to absorb technological innovations. This adaptability also means more jobs as smaller businesses expand. For example, a UNIDO training programme for Kenyan entrepreneurs in the small-scale textile sector has given some 400 businesswomen the chance to acquire a comprehensive set of skills ranging from product design and development, through management and financing to marketing and presentation. They in turn are passing these newly acquired skills on to other women opening up opportunities for greater female participation in the country's development.

The UN Development Programme (UNDP) works closely with Sustainable Project Management (SPM), an initiative created by the Business Council for Sustainable Development (BCSD) to aid greater private sector involvement in support of sustainable development. The focus is to identify and prepare bankable projects which result in the establishment of new profitable companies, owned partly by municipal authorities and partly by private interests, that help provide urban and industrial infrastructure services in three key areas: water treatment/recycling, waste management/minimization and energy efficiency/demand management.

In Wuhan and Shanghai, China, a new public-private service company will manage eco-efficiency improvements to thermal power plants in the city, including improving generation capacity, energy efficiency, flue gas and dust control, and waste water treatment. The project also includes the installation of a co-generation unit for district heating in Wuhan and the nearby industrial estate. Similar projects are planned for four more cities in China.

"to help open the doors to foreign investors"

In Madras, India, SPM expects to establish a new public-private company to recycle waste water and sewage water from the city for reuse by industry. This project enjoys strong support from the municipal authorities, local industry and government at central and state levels. It is expected that the project will be duplicated in other cities in India through similar companies working with the Confederation of Indian Industry (CII) and the private sector.

In Colombia, a public-private company is being set up to introduce new eco-efficient technologies to decontaminate waste water from the coffee industry and provide clean supplies for the local people. This project will shortly be replicated in three other states of Colombia as well as in other coffee-producing countries.

Reviewing these programmes, Gus Speth, the UNDP Administrator, has stated: 'These initiatives are the result of our assessment of the needs and opportunities for greater private sector involvement in support of sustainable development.... The innovative perspective of this programme is that it allows for a direct communication channel between local authorities and the private sector at various levels – creating opportunities for technology dissemination and a positive impact on the most pressing urban environmental problems.'

Further examples include introducing energy management programmes and new technologies for suburban electrification in the Andean countries, recycling sewage water using zoo plankton technology in Costa Rica, establishing an urban capacity building centre for eco-efficiency in Gaza and Jericho, introducing new technologies for peri-urban electrification in South Africa and dealing with solid waste problems in the Czech Republic.

This type of public-private sector cooperation turns problems in the developing world and emerging economies into viable business opportunities. In the process, it makes a real difference to many of our most vulnerable fellow citizens. It is indeed a fresh approach to tackle some of the most pressing social ills because the old approach has failed: purely public sector projects are subject to budgetary constraints, while totally private sector projects emphasize short-term profitability.

Human resourcefulness and initiative are the motor that drives successful business
An old woman recycling metal from used drink cans in Phnom Penh, Cambodia.

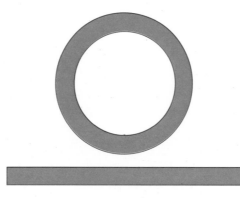

THE BENJELLOUN GROUP

The Benjelloun Group, with its headquarters in Morocco, has interests in banking, insurance, manufacturing, international trade, agriculture, construction, real estate, leisure and telecommunications. Associated with European, Japanese and US corporations including AT&T, Citibank, General Motors, Goodyear, Mercedes Benz, Volvo, Isuzu, Itochu & Westinghouse, the Group has recently privatized the leading commercial bank in Morocco.

Mr Othman Benjelloun, Chairman and CEO of the Benjelloun Group, created the Moroccan-American Foundation and was its first Co-Chairman with Henry Kissinger. Currently Chairman of the US-Morocco Council for Trade and Investment, Mr Benjelloun is also Councillor at the Center for Strategic and International Studies, Washington, DC.

The Benjelloun Group believes that the UN is vital to the advancement of international humanitarian standards and moral and social values, with particular emphasis on education, environment, health care and food supply. The Group also considers that the UN has an important role to play in the sectors of telecommunications, scientific research and technology.

As Othman Benjelloun has stated: 'It is only with the ongoing contribution of the UN that the world can look forward to a future that is ecologically, economically and socially viable for all.'

THE BENJELLOUN GROUP

RMA - 69 Avenue des F.A.R., Casablanca, Morocco
Tel. (212-2) 75 35 84   Fax. (212-2) 75 35 74

New business agenda in Asia

Today, most of the nations which make up East Asia are considered the world's fastest growing economies. Eight Asian countries have achieved annual average growth rates of over five per cent from 1965 onwards to 1989, with some of the tiger economies in southeast Asia growing at significantly higher rates of six per cent to eight per cent a year.

But progress has also had some negative impact and raises new challenges on the economic, political and social front. Poverty, particularly rural poverty, remains the region's largest problem. The effects of rapid growth in the region have largely been felt in urban areas, while rural areas continue to wallow in relative or absolute poverty. Because growth is directed towards urban areas, internal migration flows into cities will result in even more rapid

of society – concerns that often escape the attention of the corporate manager. These are the issues of relevance to billions of poor, issues such as endemic poverty, population growth and basic human rights.

Business has often distanced itself from the bigger moral obligation to help the government solve such an overwhelming challenge. However, government cannot do it alone. Unless the business world is willing to do more to alleviate the burden of poverty, many of the societies in which they operate will not move beyond current hand-to-mouth existence. Business that exists in such a precarious environment will eventually be forced to bow out.

Hence, poverty, population and environment are all intertwined. One is affected by the progress or

"a new trend emerging in business"

urbanization of the region. By the turn of the century, all the countries of southeast Asia will be at least 50 per cent urbanized. While that creates larger consumer markets which are good for business, it also creates strains on the system as transport, water, power, education, housing and health care resources are stretched to their limits. Rapid economic development is also placing more strain on environmental resources.

The Earth Summit inspired the Association of Southern Asian Nations (ASEAN) Chamber of Commerce and Industry to adopt Business Principles on Sustainable Development. As a result, individual ASEAN countries have each set up sustainable development councils to ensure corporations keep an eye on their environmental and social responsibilities.

While it may be significant to see this new trend emerging in business, there is still considerable neglect for areas that are deemed priority concerns

degeneration of the other. UN initiatives have shown that only through the improved standards of living in developing countries can population growth be slowed down and the environmental consequences of poverty be avoided.

One of the best examples of a business-led partnership in Asia that has focused on helping alleviate the plight of the poor is the Philippine Business for Social Progress (PBSP). It has mobilized the financial, technical and managerial resources of companies for over 20 years in partnership programmes to promote sustainable development at the grassroots level in urban and rural communities. Today it has some 120 member companies, each pledging one per cent of its net profit to social development, of which 20 per cent goes to PBSP and hundreds of non-governmental organization (NGO) partnerships which have worked together to implement approximately 3,000 rural and urban development projects benefiting 1.5 million people.

Because business and economic growth thrive in an environment of peace and stability, the business community will also need to speak up and be heard on issues it does not normally address. In the Philippines, the business community has been involved in exercises such as the peace process and elections because of the community's underlying belief that there can be no prosperity without political stability.

In the early 1980s, business groups, civic associations, NGOs, educational and religious institutions, and professional and trade associations banded together to form a movement which became known as the National Citizens Movement for Free Elections (NAMFREL).

Since 1984, NAMFREL has been active in voter education, legislative reforms and poll-watching, and holds an independent parallel count of election returns. The business community has supported NAMFREL in these projects, not only through financial assistance but, more importantly, by seconding managers to help run its operations and lending equipment and facilities for the critical task of protecting the integrity of the ballots and the electoral count. At every election in the Philippines, poll-watching groups, such as NAMFREL, the Parish Pastoral Council for Responsible Voting and all their affiliates and partner organizations, have mobilized up to half a million volunteers to safeguard the polls.

But the business community also realized that stability had to go beyond safeguarding the ballot. A multisectoral effort was put together under the government's auspices. This became known as the National Unification Commission (NUC). As part of its mission to oversee the entire peace process, NUC drew on the support and feedback of many sectors – including the business community – to search for ways to attain a sustainable peace.

This new advocacy role will bring new demands on the business community as well as non-traditional constituencies to deal with. If, in the past, individual businesses lobbied governments for vested interests, today businesses will need more and more to deal with governments and consider the national interest. Moreover, NGOs and community-based peoples' organizations are becoming increasingly a

Business is gradually becoming aware of its social obligations.
A steel recycling plant in Tanzania creates jobs and prevents waste.

fact of life in many countries and therefore business will have to work with them as partners in nation building.

Within the region, a strong tradition has already been established where businesses support many community projects. For instance, foundations established by corporations in the Philippines and Thailand encourage them to set aside a fixed percentage of their profits annually, which are then devoted to community projects. If the top 1,000 companies in ASEAN set aside one per cent of their profits a year, business corporations could inject over $80 million into community projects.

There is another task which the business community may have to face. As standards of living rise, so will expectations of political and individual freedoms. Is it possible to liberalize continually the economy and still maintain a closed society? Obviously each country will have to make its own choice. The relevant question for the business sector, however, is what role, if any, it should play in this regard. Political instability automatically translates to economic uncertainty. Should business stand aside and simply allow events to transpire and do its best to pick up the pieces after a political upheaval? The Philippine and Eastern European experience would seem to indicate the opposite course of action. Similarly, after Korea attained a high degree of economic development and liberalization, democratization of the political process quickly followed. In the long run, empirical evidence shows that free markets and political freedom can co-exist and reinforce each other.

In India, the CII invited the resident representative of UNDP in India to be a member of various committees overseeing the formulation and implementation of a number of corporate citizenship programmes. In 1991, the CII mounted a study to examine the benefits that business derives by adopting a socially responsible attitude. The study revealed that every dollar invested by companies in these 'Community Through Employee' activities brings a benefit of five dollars directly or indirectly. The survey convinced a number of businesses that these activities were as important as manufacturing and marketing and that such investments were akin to 'an insurance premium'.

© Ron Giling/Panos

*Administración Nacional
de Usinas y Trasmisiones Eléctricas
Gerencia General*

Our support for the United Nations on its 50th Anniversary represents a display of our dedication to the United Nations' fundamental principles and objectives to promote international cooperation towards a better world.

UTE has played a fundamental role in the economic and social development of Uruguay over the last 80 years. We have the largest electrical grid in Latin America and one of the largest in the world. In particular, the electrification of rural areas has taken on a special significance. We provide a strategic input to the areas where the basic instruments of economic development depend on our facilities. And we ensure that people in rural areas have the same rights to comfort, information, communication and cultural development as our major urban areas.

UTE has developed a multi-disciplinary team which ensures that environmental concerns are integrated into our management structure. This guarantees that the environment forms a key part of the planning and development of new projects as well as making sure environmental costs are incorporated into the selection process during the quest for alternatives. At the same time, the team has forged a partnership with the University of the Republic in order to establish renewable energy research programmes and to evaluate solar and wind power as potential sources of energy.

Furthermore, with our continuing endeavour to ensure quality of service and respect for the environment, we are promoting and encouraging a better future for the national and regional community of which we form a part.

Eng. Ruperto Long
President of UTE

For example, in the city of Pune in western India, business is spearheading an effort called Total Quality Community Project, aimed at poverty alleviation, education and environmental improvement. Similarly in Bombay, business has committed itself to converting Bombay, the big eyesore, to Bombay, the big apple. In rural areas business has been proactive in introducing programmes ranging from the adoption of villages for comprehensive development, to initiatives such as the provision of safe drinking water, afforestation and maternal and child health care programmes, including family planning, adult education and literacy campaigns for women. This renewed vigour on the part of Indian industry has sprung not merely out of a sense of moral responsibility but from a realization that such long-term investments result in a more conducive industrial climate, lower absenteeism, good industrial relations and a sustained rise in productivity.

The Latin American story

Latin America is the most urbanized region of the developing world. More than 73 per cent of the population of Brazil and Mexico and 86 per cent in Chile and Argentina live in cities. São Paulo, Mexico City and Buenos Aires are among the 10 largest cities in the world. Together with Uruguay and Venezuela, these four countries have the most developed economies in Latin America with very similar per capita incomes.

The World Business Council for Sustainable Development (WBCSD) of Latin America argues that, in order to promote efficient trading and environmental policies, it is important to minimize subsidies, to improve regulations and to abolish the vested interests that result from them. Their damaging effects are most keenly felt in agriculture, energy and in public sector purchases. Indeed, business leaders believe that government interference prevents private companies and most citizens from participating in open markets, and that the restrictive regulations impair not only economic growth but also social improvement.

The definition of property rights is also a controversial issue that has to be tackled. The opening up of markets without a clear or equitable definition of property rights – especially those relating to land – often fails to result in sustainable growth in important sectors. Lack of an ownership stake in resources has also been shown to contribute to marginalization of the poor and to exert pressure on natural resources. For example, in many rural areas of Latin America, farmers have no recognized title to land. In view of the uncertainty of the prevailing conditions, countless smallholders are prepared to invest only small amounts of money short-term, to the serious detriment of the economy, the environment and society as a whole.

Clearer ground rules would also stimulate cooperation among companies in the Americas. A good example is the 'CO$_2$ trading schemes' which have drawn on the findings of recent research to facilitate more efficient use of environmentally-sound investment. Instead of investing additional capital in end-of-the-pipe measures and factories in the North, money could be invested more profitably, and with greater marginal utility, in forestry and timber projects in the South. This would not only improve the CO$_2$ balance in the atmosphere but also make a great contribution towards development. But projects like this cannot be implemented until clearly defined legal title is extended to more types of property.

Funding for the environment has been one of the issues covered by the North American Free Trade Agreement (NAFTA) and special attention has been paid to the US-Mexico border, an area with significant local and cross-border environmental problems. A number of promising initiatives – some based on regional cooperation, others from the private sector and the use of market incentives – have already been proposed. One of these would address the critical air pollution problems in the El Paso/Juarez, US-Mexico border.

The WBCSD has taken a leadership role in devising innovative ways to encourage partnership projects with the private sector, especially in developing countries. Since its inception, it has seen the need to establish a strong relationship with such organizations as UNDP and the World Bank, to encourage and facilitate technology cooperation and to continue a high level policy dialogue.

The South African model

In 1995, with the dramatic political changes in the country, freer dialogue between South Africa and the UN and its agencies is now possible. This has been met with scepticism in some South African quarters where the UN has not historically been seen as an ally. Nonetheless there is also evident enthusiasm in other quarters to contribute to international initiatives.

Traditionally, the UN and its agencies have worked with governments, not the private sector. However there is a need for the UN and business to review their links and develop active, practical, goal-oriented approaches. Governments' responsibilities essentially rest within national boundaries – they may influence broader fields but legitimately they are nationally focused. The activities of the multinational, private sector, on the other hand, regularly transcend such political boundaries, as do many environmental concerns.

Officially absent from the Earth Summit in Rio de Janeiro in 1992, the majority of South Africans remain unaware of their responsibilities in terms of the resultant conventions and Agenda 21. However, a South African business delegation was at Rio, clearly conscious that the principal responsibility for converting Rio's outputs into meaningful outcomes would rest with the business community, not government.

It is clear, therefore, that nowhere will there be a sustained political settlement without sustained economic growth driven by the private sector. In turn, sustained economic growth cannot be achieved without wise environmental management. Poverty forces people to disregard the sustainability of the resources around them in their quest to survive from day to day.

In addition, there is a need to build strong partnerships between the NGO community and the private sector. Yet the history of adversity between the two and the ostensible monopoly on the moral high ground claimed by the NGOs complicates this process. It is essential that the NGO community better understands the needs and constraints of business, while the business community develops a more sympathetic approach to popular concerns. As

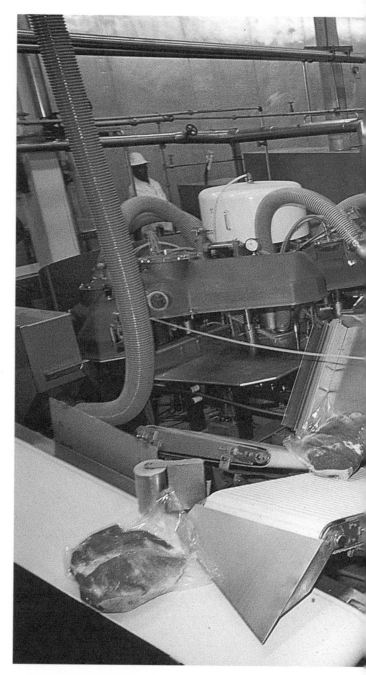

all South Africans now have a say in their future, fairer access to gainful employment and the ability to acquire property give them a vested interest in the quality of their environment.

According to some estimates, up to 50 per cent of South Africa's population do not have formal employment. Apartheid had largely denied black entrepreneurs business opportunity. The lack of business outlets within townships resulted in not only transport problems, but also a lack of a viable tax base with which to support local government

High business standards enable countries to succeed in a competitive world market.
A meat factory in Botswana.   © David Reed/Panos

services. The financial sector has been reluctant to offer high risk loans to black entrepreneurs who could not provide collateral – a situation now being addressed by the development of the 'community' and 'micro' banks to encourage small business development and a move away from perpetually sponsoring unemployment.

It is in the area of creating small-scale, income-generating enterprises where attention is most needed. These new enterprises could involve converting one company's waste into another's input (making compost from abattoir wastes is one recent example in Johannesburg) or developing sanitation, water purification and recycling schemes. The major electrification programme under way in South Africa increases access to affordable electricity for numerous potential enterprises, while some paper and pulp companies are encouraging the development of small-scale nurseries of indigenous, medicinal plants on the periphery of their forest operations to protect indigenous species (which provide seed banks) in enclaves within their commercial forests.

COMMUNICATION

BELGACOM knows it

In the early days of the United Nations, development meant physical mobility and communications meant motorways. Fifty years later, it is communication, and in particular telecommunications, that is the key to development.

Today's telecommunications users define their own need and demand additional services. Consequently, many of Europe's telecommunications companies are embracing privatization and competition as the best means of ensuring their customers are provided with a cost-effective and efficient service.

In line with this, BELGACOM, until recently a public telephone company protected by various monopolies, is now a new public limited company with three priorities – high technology, competitive tariffs and, above all, a commitment to customer service. With modern management, a new personnel charter and a vastly improved service, our subscribers are now looked upon as our clients.

But there remains much to be done and BELGACOM is on line to achieve its two objectives – to continue as the No. 1 national and international telecommunications company in Belgium, and to acquire a significant and profitable share in the competitive markets.

John J. Goossens, President & C.E.O.

BELGACOM

A final word

As a result of the dramatic, political, military and economic shifts of the past decade, an opportunity presents itself for a new breed of global leaders to emerge. The skills necessary to lead in this new era – diplomacy, negotiation, financial leverage, management, persuasiveness, relationship building, communicating and a respect for individuals – are not limited to the world's politicians or government bureaucracies. These skills are shared by people throughout the world regardless of profession, nationality, gender or race.

Indeed, as borders between nations lose their significance in terms of economic importance, businessmen and women are being thrust into a position of stewardship for the citizens of the world. As US Secretary of Labour Robert Reich notes in his book *The Wealth of Nations*, business leaders are becoming transnational statesmen of this and future generations.

Farsighted corporate leaders are not blind to the systemic, societal disorders of this generation, fully realizing that business cannot flourish in a climate of turmoil and poverty where resources are being channelled destructively. Regardless of implicit or explicit acknowledgement, all businesses in all countries operate and exist in a public policy environment. Thus, becoming actively involved in the successful resolution of geo-political issues to further global stability is in the direct self-interest of international business.

Because business and the UN both seek world peace and prosperity, it is natural that they support each others' activities. Already the UN is assisting the business community in many ways through the World Bank, the International Finance Corporation (IFC), the International Monetary Fund (IMF) and UNIDO. Similarly, the diverse activities of UN agencies dealing with labour, human rights, food and agriculture, health, civil aviation, telecommunications, intellectual property and industrial development have advanced international trade and commerce.

The UN Secretary-General recently stated that 'Never before in its history has the United Nations been so action-oriented, so actively engaged, and so widely expected to respond to needs both immediate and persuasive. Clearly, it is in our power to bring about a renaissance – to create a new United Nations for a new international era.'

If business is to respond positively to this challenge, it will require greater efforts, a closer cooperation and the development of new and innovative approaches in its relationship with the UN and its agencies.

An African NGO works in partnership with business to help people in marginalized communities in Zimbabwe develop income opportunities.
A team working on a low-cost solar energy system for recharging batteries.

Children in many developing countries are forced to work to meet family bills.
A child labourer in a brick-kiln.

World Economy ~ a global compact

- Economics and society
- The pace of change
- Integrating policies
- The unemployment crisis

Economic policy exists to deliver social progress. Social progress is denied where there is high persistent unemployment. In the mid-1990s, high unemployment characterizes the economies of the world's richest and poorest countries alike. Something is badly wrong. The UN-sponsored World Summit for Social Development held in Copenhagen in March 1995 firmly placed this subject centre stage. It made it clear that unemployment is the number one social problem of our age.

Unemployment has risen, and stubbornly persisted, as the world's economies grow increasingly interdependent. National economies are being ever more closely tied to each other by global pacts – such as that which concluded the Uruguay Round of the General Agreement on Tariffs and Trade (GATT) – and by regional arrangements – such as the European Union (EU) and the North American Free Trade Agreement (NAFTA).

Even without such arrangements, new technologies by their own momentum promote economic integration. The revolution in communications moves goods, services and capital around the world at a rate never seen in history. New manufacturing techniques make possible unprecedented increases in productivity. Humankind can at last hope for a future in which poverty will be abolished.

But the immediate problem is of too little production and too few jobs. Economic integration makes it impossible for any one country on its own to make a dash for growth and jobs. The problem is global. The solution must be global too.

© Trygve Bolstad/Panos

The United Nations continues to awaken our dreams. Ontario Hydro shares your vision of hope, and of a sustainable future. We are proud to help celebrate your 50th anniversary

Of course, things look different in different places. In East and Southeast Asia (including China) output and employment have been growing dramatically, but parts of that successful region lag sadly behind. In South Asia, absolute poverty is being reduced, but the growth of employment is precarious and much valuable work is paid at levels barely sufficient to keep families alive. The relative success of those regions, containing almost half of the world's people, proves that there is no reason to despair. But the achievement is fragile. Even there, far more remains to be done before the unemployment crisis can be considered solved.

In the rest of the world, entire generations of people are growing up believing that it is unrealistic to hope for productive, remunerative and reasonably secure jobs. Societies that fail to offer that prospect are bound to be socially unstable and economically insecure. The pace of change is overwhelming whole sectors of economic activity. Those displaced from their jobs are often not equipped to work in the new activities that emerge. When new jobs are created they are often less well paid, less secure and of lower quality than those that disappear.

Without concerted international action, across national frontiers and occupational differences, unemployment and its attendant miseries seem bound to persist, even to get worse. The prospect is intolerable. The techniques exist for improving it.

World problems, world solutions

The trend towards world economic integration gathered pace in the early 1990s, promoted by international agreements and circumstances. The following are some examples:

- The completion in early 1994 of the Uruguay Round of negotiations in the GATT has set the scene for a worldwide opening of trade.

- Regional blocs (in North America, for example) have been set up to foster free trade.

- Trade in services, although not adequately measured, seems to have grown much faster than trade in goods.

- The formerly centrally-planned economies are being integrated, although at a low level of activity, with the rest of the world economy.

- Barriers to the international movement of capital have been much reduced.

- The international migration of labour has grown fast, although subjected to new restrictions.

These developments impose new constraints upon purely national economic policies. They limit taxation, interest rates, exchange rates and public-sector deficits. They make protected industries unviable and unable to sustain their labour forces, however lavishly governments may support them. In particular, they make it almost impossible to increase the relative price of labour in one country. Solutions must be sought across national frontiers, by concerted action.

Recent history shows what happens when countries try, and fail, to escape on their own from the unemployment trap. The economic woes of the 1980s followed the economic shocks of the 1970s. The sudden rise and subsequent fall of energy prices after 1973 encouraged massive and unsustainable international lending. Soaring interest rates and huge government deficits in countries at all stages of development were followed by a worldwide epidemic of inflation.

In reaction, many governments suddenly retrenched, often under pressure from international lenders. Stability, not dynamism, became the watchword. World trade slowed down. The annual average rate of growth in world merchandise exports was 6.6 per cent in the 1965-80 period and 4.1 per cent between 1980 and 1991. As industrial activity declined in the industrialized nations, the prices of primary commodities fell, impoverishing the producing countries.

Seeking to redress the harm done by inflation, the industrialized countries tolerated what they hoped would be temporarily high levels of unemployment. Many of them raised new protective barriers against imports: the World Bank in 1991 estimated that in the previous decade 20 of the 24 member countries of the Organization for Economic Cooperation and Development (OECD) became more protectionist, especially against competing products from developing countries.

None of these restrictive policies worked as it was meant to. True, as inflation was curbed almost everywhere, governments prophesied that monetary stability would, of its own accord, stimulate growth. But unemployment went on rising, and where, as in the United States, it eventually started to roll back, rates of pay for the new unskilled jobs were far lower than those prevailing before the recession. Inequality increased and so did the sense of deprivation. Meanwhile, in the poorest countries things got worse in absolute terms. The picture is gloomy.

© Trygve Bolstad/Panos

'Jobless growth' or benign transition?

The contrast in performance between the world's most and least successful regions is sharp and bitter. East and Southeast Asia are enjoying unprecedented growth in both real incomes and employment. **Africa and the Middle East confront a potential catastrophe of demographic growth and economic failure. Meanwhile, the industrial countries of OECD are baffled by the persistence of unemployment amid prosperity.**

The facts, however, do not support the view that the world is inexorably set on a path of 'jobless growth', by which technological progress will benefit a few and disadvantage many. New technologies have created, and made possible, many millions of jobs in most regions. Employment has grown in the economies that have grown fastest.

Where the unemployment crisis exists, it has been created not by chance but by error; by incentives that distort and institutions that are inadequate. For example, national policies have often been mistakenly devised to promote capital investment, when labour-intensive production was what the country needed. Before the debt shock of the late 1970s, the economies of Latin America were growing fast but they created far fewer jobs than have recently been created in Asia's economic boom.

National governments borrowed imprudently, for unproductive purposes, and thus made necessary the structural adjustment programmes of which their successor governments now understandably complain. Excessive borrowing fostered domestic inflation. The attempt to curb that inflation brought about recession. And the fight against inflation continues, even now that the battle is largely won, and the job crisis is more menacing than the monetary one.

External influences imposed the debt crisis. External considerations have helped to impose its successor, the employment crisis. Monetary restraint in the industrial countries brought growth there to a halt. They therefore reduced their imports from primary-producing developing countries. Those developing countries – especially the weakest of them, heavily dependent on commodity exports – in turn suffered recession.

Bonded labour still exists as a modern form of slavery.
This man has worked for 30 years as a bonded labourer.

On behalf of the Hellenic Bottling Company, I would like to congratulate the United Nations on the occasion of its 50th Anniversary. May it long prosper in the cause of unifying the nations and people of the world.

I would also like to take this opportunity to describe our commitment to the UN's ideals. As an organization, Hellenic Bottling Company is fully committed to the concept of 'good corporate citizenship', playing an active role in the Greek community and taking our environmental responsibilities seriously.

It is a measure of our community spirit that social responsibility is one of the six key corporate values of our company. We have firmly instilled this value in our employees, a fact that has been clearly recognized by our many clients.

By way of illustration, we give full support to humanitarian causes within the Greek community. As the company grows, so does our need to contribute to the social, cultural and educational advancement of our country.

We are proud of our achievements, believing that our actions and values reflect the spirit of A Vision of Hope.

Christos A. Komninos

Managing Director

HELLENIC BOTTLING COMPANY S.A.

In particular, OECD countries limited domestic borrowing by increasing their interest rates. Consequently, interest rates rose everywhere, above all in the developing countries that had borrowed heavily, especially those in Latin America. Capital stopped flowing from OECD countries to the developing world, limiting the developing countries' ability to buy goods and services from OECD countries and making their recovery harder. It became – and remains – a vicious circle. Future policy must break out of it.

Domestic policies

The importance of domestic policies is self-evident. The East Asian economies that in the 1980s avoided stagnation and unemployment did so because they got their domestic policies right. Prudent borrowing, creative use of exchange rates, promotion of exports, protection of food producers, restraint of nominal wages – all these factors combined to keep the growth of employment in step with overall economic growth. Other nations and regions should look carefully at the implications.

Without sound domestic policies, no country will progress towards the goal of prosperity and full employment. A stable and non-inflationary currency, a high rate of savings and investment, as well as prudent management of exchange rates, are necessary preconditions for sustained growth. All that goes without saying.

Yet many countries still lack civil peace, the rule of law and the efficient delivery of public administration. In so far as the international community can help to install good governance, it should endeavour to do so.

The most important contribution that national government can make to economic growth and the efficiency of the labour market is through education and training. There is overwhelming evidence that the best investment countries can make is in basic education, especially of women. Women's education reduces birth rates and improves children's health. The *World Development Report* issued by the World Bank in 1992 noted that improving girls' education contributed to environmental conservation and sustainable development.

Governments can ease the transfer of employment from declining to growing sectors by new forms of social security and temporary income supplements, and by ensuring the transferability of pensions and benefits such as health insurance.

As some economic sectors decline and others rise, the opportunities to increase employment in declining sectors should not be forgotten. For example, investment in irrigation may create new jobs in labour-intensive agriculture, while the general farm labour force continues to decline. Equally, service industries can often develop new and profitable markets, with a high potential for employment, by adapting to match new forms of demand.

"women's education reduces birth rates and improves children's health"

International policies

Interdependence between nations has increased and will continue to increase. No solution can work unless it takes that into consideration. In the 1980s, the growth of world trade slowed markedly for most groups of countries (see table below) and where trade faltered unemployment rose.

Between 1980 and 1991:

- OECD's share of world exports increased sharply, from 63 per cent to 72 per cent. Meanwhile OECD's trade with the developing countries fell sharply, from 30 per cent to 24 per cent as a share of OECD's imports. Falling oil prices speeded this decline. Asia's share of world exports rose, while that of the other developing countries declined. In particular, OECD imports of Asian manufactured goods rose sharply.

- As the developing countries' trade with OECD countries declined, trade amongst themselves increased significantly from a low base. This increase was wholly accounted for by Asian countries.

- The largest proportional increase in international trade took place between China and the rest of East and Southeast Asia. But the figures may be deceptive: much trade with China was not recorded, for political reasons.

- OECD's terms of trade improved, while the terms of trade of Africa and the Middle East grew dramatically worse.

- OECD countries reduced their imports because they were in recession, then reduced them still further by protectionist import restrictions. Non-Asian developing countries failed to increase their exports.

- Capital flowed from the developing to the developed nations. In 1985, largely because of heavy debt repayments, the reverse flows of capital towards the rich nations was as high as $30.2 billion.

Exports of country groups as a percentage of world exports

	1980	1991
OECD countries	62.9	71.5
Former Soviet Union and Eastern Europe	7.8	5.0
Developing countries	29.3	23.5
Latin America and the Caribbean	5.4	3.9
Asia	8.7	14.9
Africa	4.7	1.9
West Asia	10.5	2.8

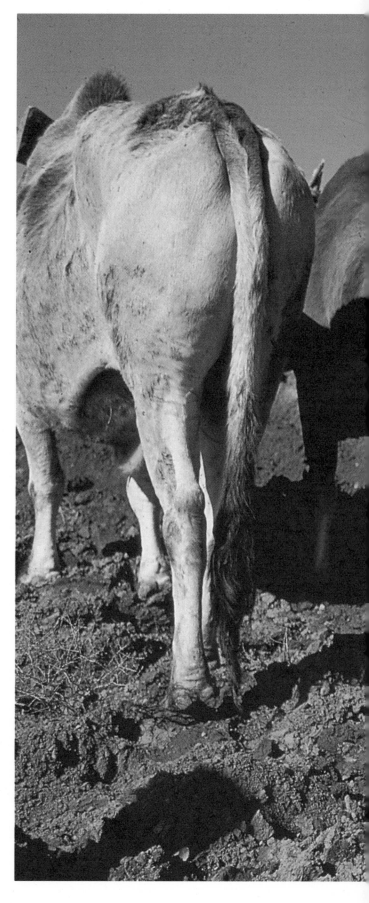

Most wealth is concentrated in urban areas worldwide, while millions of rural workers eke out a meagre existence.

© Kay Muldoon/IBRD

Power of hope

ENEL is the world's second largest electric power company

28 million residential and industrial customers
34,000 billion lira (US$ 21 billion) revenue
198 billion kWh of electric power sold
52,000 MW of net capacity **106**,000 employees

For 32 years, ENEL's advanced technology, innovation, organization and professional skills have been at the service of the "Italian System", responding to its needs, contributing to its growth. ENEL is now ready to offer its services to help the sustainable growth of the world.

Italian Electric Power Company

Yet the worst may be over. Recently there has been a general, if fragile, recovery in most commodity prices but not in oil. Real interest rates fell dramatically in the early 1990s but may be heading up again. Capital is flowing again towards the developing countries, by $26.8 billion in 1992, but much of that was short-term lending and the poorest countries of Africa felt little benefit. Several heavily indebted countries have escaped from the trap; strengthened by capital inflows, they are borrowing again on international markets.

A few developing countries achieved high growth of employment and their economies generally while OECD's recession was at its height. Now OECD's recession is over, the World Bank has recently projected an overall annual growth rate of 2.6 per cent for OECD economies in the 1994-2003 period. Yet if growth is to gather pace throughout the developing world, faster OECD growth is essential.

"the worst may be over"

In particular, economic expansion in OECD countries would revive Africa's export performance and improve Africa's terms of trade. Among the main beneficiaries would be OECD countries themselves, whose African markets would expand quickly.

The governments of the industrial world have got ready to fight the last battle: the battle against inflation. But the real enemy in the mid-1990s is not inflation but unemployment.

Careful monetary expansion by OECD countries would entail risk of renewing inflation. But high unemployment throughout OECD should help to ensure that wage increases do not contribute to inflation. And the risk of inflation would be much reduced if the expanding countries kept pace with each other and did not seek to gain a competitive advantage in the process. At the same time, by increasing domestic demand, they would put to work large numbers of their own unemployed. Soon that increased demand would translate itself into higher commodity prices, enabling the poorest developing countries to increase their imports. This, in turn, would promote the non-inflationary growth of exports from OECD countries. Everybody would gain – especially the unemployed in rich and poor countries alike.

Free trade, better aid

With the conclusion of the Uruguay Round of bargaining in the GATT, conditions have been established for worldwide free trade in goods and services. That was a necessary precondition for speeding the growth of economic activity. International cooperation is more necessary than ever if full advantage is to be taken of this opportunity to put more people to work.

We have seen that, in the bad years of the 1980s, many industrialized countries sought to mitigate the effects of recession by restricting imports and thus made recovery harder for themselves.

Opening borders to the flow of trade would reverse that damage. In 1993, the World Bank made the following estimate: 'Total exports from China, Jamaica, Pakistan, Thailand and the Philippines would increase by at least 40 per cent if OECD tariff barriers were removed. Other countries would gain even more...'. In particular, several countries specializing in exports of textiles and clothing would benefit dramatically, with corresponding gains in their ability to import from OECD itself.

Poor countries, where real wages are low, have a competitive advantage in labour-intensive manufacturing. If rich countries import more low-price manufactured goods, they will obviously employ fewer of their own people in low-wage jobs. If economic growth is fast enough, the lost jobs will be replaced by new jobs demanding high skills and paying higher wages. But this process cannot be left to chance. Governments and social partners must work together to ease the transition, especially in retraining displaced workers and ensuring that labour markets operate humanely and efficiently.

In the industrialized countries, ill-considered protectionist measures are often called for as a response to cheap imports, or against the failure of exporting countries to safeguard workers' rights. But trade restrictions defeat their own objective. They reduce the rate of economic growth and thus in turn increase unemployment. When unemployment is high, workers' conditions rarely improve and their rights are rarely acknowledged. In this respect, too, progress can best be made by cooperation, not confrontation. Exporting and importing countries must work together to raise standards without resorting to protectionism. Only exceptional circumstances can justify restraints on the growth of trade.

With the conclusion of the Uruguay Round of the GATT and the strengthening of regional free trade pacts, trade should grow rapidly in the coming decade. According to the GATT Secretariat, the agreement should, by the year 2000, boost world merchandise trade by an extra 12 per cent. The benefits could be larger still.

The GATT agreement permits some discriminatory trade barriers against developing country exports of textiles, garments and footwear – labour-intensive products, in which low pay gives the poorest countries a competitive advantage. Even where, as is certainly the case, workers are at present exploited in such countries, the fastest way to end the exploitation is to increase the demand for labour and thus raise its price. Those trade barriers should be lowered.

Special attention must furthermore be paid to the effect of the Uruguay Round on the food-importing countries of Sub-Saharan Africa. By raising world food prices, the agreement may, in the short term, harm the trade balances of these countries, for which compensatory arrangements should be made.

"progress can best be made by cooperation"

Women are increasingly joining the paid workforce but often lack the legal protection given to men.
A woman feeds silkworms.

© Neil Cooper/Panos

Aid and its conditions

Official Development Assistance (ODA) is defined as net disbursement of grants and loans made on concessional financial terms. In 1991, the world total of ODA was US$58.2 billion, the vast majority of it from member countries of OECD. Overall, this was equal to 0.33 per cent of those countries' total Gross National Product (GNP).

Private flows of capital to the developing world were much larger, at $113 billion in 1992-93. After the low period of the 1980s, this was a return to the level seen before the debt crisis. The flow may once more prove unsustainable. In any case, most of it

went to a few countries whose national incomes are already classed in the middle income category and above. Private capital hardly benefitted the poor.

A high proportion of ODA, too, flows towards relatively prosperous countries. During the days of the Cold War, aid was sent mainly to boost political allies or with the aim of maintaining regional stability. With that confrontation over, it is a good time to focus aid deliberately upon those who most need help – in particular, the 48 countries (containing 72 per cent of the people in the developing world) that in 1991 had a per capita income below $1,000.

The relatively successful developing countries would, in this case, rely mainly on flows of private capital, which we have seen to be larger in total than ODA. If ODA were clearly seen as an instrument of economic development, rather than of military or political manipulation, its allocation would be much simpler. Aid would go to the countries that most need it and use it best.

One of the main tests of performance could be the expansion of productive employment. Other relevant social achievements are those analysed in the annual *Human Development Report* issued by the UN Development Programme (UNDP). Put simply, ODA to countries that create jobs and improve the lot of the poor among their people should be conceded entirely as grants, rather than as loans that have often served mainly to plunge indebted countries even deeper into debt.

Most of the world's most severely indebted countries are in Sub-Saharan Africa. The Uruguay Round will not greatly benefit them and may, by raising world food prices, make their lives yet harder. Few of them were ever able to borrow much from private creditors. Their debts to individual donor countries have mostly been forgiven or deferred. Their main outstanding debts are, therefore, owed largely to the multilateral aid agencies, which at present are not allowed formally to write off debt. It would be reasonable and prudent, and a great saving of administrative time and ingenuity, if a way could be found of eliminating those debts altogether.

Get in touch with your family.

With your friends.

With your loved ones.

This way,

we can share

a real vision of hope.

Peace.

With communication, Telecom makes it possible.

TELECOM
MAKES
THE
WORLD
SMALLER

TELECOM

Colombia, South America.

A Vision of Hope: The Fiftieth Anniversary of the United Nations.

IT IS THE PEOPLE'S TIME

Fitting jobs to people

People come first. Governments must create the conditions in which all their citizens have the opportunity to find reasonably secure, remunerative and productive employment. Yet it is not states but families that decide how many citizens there shall be.

Several countries in different parts of the world have dramatically reduced the rate of growth of their population. Success is most likely in economies that are growing and where educational opportunities are improving. Yet even where birth rates have fallen, the number of children born each year will go on rising, as the many women born in past years reach the age of parenthood.

And for many nations – especially in Africa – the demographic time-bomb has already exploded. There are too few jobs for too many young people who see almost no chance of finding secure employment. Many governments have made things worse by attempting to become the employers of last resort. For those who could find productive work, they have created jobs with no identifiable purpose, producing no goods that people want and no useful services.

A swollen and under-employed public service imposes an inflationary burden on national exchequers and rates of pay are therefore kept very low, adding to the frustration of those intended to be the beneficiaries. The social consequences are worst when, as is often the case, government jobs are offered automatically to all those completing a specified level of education. Past policies of this kind are regarded as significant contributors to social unrest.

Without underlying economic growth, the attempt to increase state employment is unsustainable and self-defeating. The way forward must be by increasing productive activity and offering an appropriate education to those who will work in it. The best way to strengthen labour markets – and to satisfy individuals – is by providing basic education for all.

Women and other disadvantaged groups

It is of course a human and moral imperative to encourage full participation of women in all aspects of society. Improving women's participation on equal terms in the labour force is the key both to limiting the growth of population and to improving the welfare of coming generations. Female advancement has a quick and lasting effect on birth rates and well-educated mothers improve the educational chances of the children they bear. It is the most significant single way to bring about general social advancement.

Yet in most regions women suffer disadvantages. In the Middle East and in most of Africa they are in practice largely excluded from paid employment. Almost everywhere, and notably in East Asia, women's wages are discriminatorily low. Even in many otherwise enlightened societies, their educational opportunities are limited. Very rarely are they offered the child-care facilities they need if they are to compete on equal terms with men.

Many societies treat members of certain ethnic and religious groups with equal unfairness: examples are indigenous people in Latin American countries and gypsies in Eastern Europe. Members of traditionally disadvantaged groups tend to suffer long-term unemployment, giving rise to further social disadvantage.

Legislation against discrimination is only the start of a comprehensive policy for the protection of disadvantaged groups, including women. They need better access to education and to productive resources if they are to make their full contribution to society.

"*women's wages are discriminatorily low*"

Labour markets

Like all markets, the market for jobs works best when demand roughly matches supply. At times of high unemployment that is not the case and the fault lies with governments. It means that their macro-economic policies are failing to ensure the efficient use of resources, especially of labour.

Inappropriate government policies may also distort labour markets so badly as to contribute to mass unemployment. Especially in Western Europe, labour-market policies have often been enactments of agreements between organizations of workers and of employers. Laws and regulations formalize massive social gains made over many years.

It is often argued that, as technology and the economic environment change, such policies need changing. But it is extremely difficult to tell whether labour-market distortions are caused by inappropriate regulation or by general market failures. It must be frankly recognized that labour-market flexibility means different things to different people. The creation of new job opportunities is essential, but so is the protection of existing workers' rights. It is important to recognize, and reject, the version of flexibility that implies only reductions in pay and in workers' rights. It is not progress to replace secure employment by other jobs of lower quality at lower pay.

East Asia has shown in recent years that labour mobility can be compatible with increased employment and rising pay – but only in the context of rapid economic expansion. In most other developing countries, where growth is sluggish, labour mobility is also slow. Most new jobs are generated through self-employment and the informal sector. Sometimes, but too rarely, the informal sector achieves high productivity and dynamic growth. But, mostly, informal-sector work is relatively unproductive and low paid.

Appropriate responses should be devised in the light of several considerations:

- The method by which wages and conditions of work are set in any country should respect local traditions. Growth in developing countries might be hampered by rules copied from those prevailing in economies with more highly developed labour markets.

- Restricting labour mobility by employment quotas, or by guaranteeing employment in unviable enterprises, may reduce overall economic activity and deny job opportunities to new entrants in the labour market.

- If public-sector pay is disproportionately high, it can distort labour markets and contribute to unproductive public expenditure, and if public-sector employment is too high a proportion of total employment, it may lead to inefficiency in public services and further labour-market distortions.

- The most effective government action to improve the working of the labour market is by promoting basic education and encouraging the retraining of workers bypassed by technical or economic change.

- Legislation, and persuasion, can help to ensure that members of disadvantaged groups have a fair chance to find work.

- Exceptional problems may call for special labour-market policies. Examples include natural disasters, where well-established public works programmes can be efficiently expanded to both relieve distress and build capital assets such as roads or dams, and economic disaster such as that affecting much of Eastern Europe. Jobs have been eliminated in the region by harsh but necessary reforms and savings by hyper-inflation. There, as the World Bank has argued, it may be impossible to find even short-term work for those affected and cash income supplements may be the only way to avoid distress. The overriding rule is that emergency relief be finite, offering the beneficiaries a strong incentive to return actively to the labour market as soon as possible.

Many workers in the developing world are poorly paid and lack labour laws.

The dignity of human labour lies at the heart of the UN's efforts to provide international standards for protection of workers

© Chris Stowers/Panos

An outline for global action

Nations that act together can greatly increase their chances of providing remunerative and sustainable work for all their citizens. Full employment is possible only if economic growth is rapid. The world has become a global market in which trade transfers the benefits of growth – and its risks – from one economy to another.

Certainly individual countries can exclude themselves from the growth process by, for example, bad macro-economic management, bureaucratic rigidity or institutional corruption. Good governance and the rule of law are the domestic basis for growth. But no one country can keep growing for long on its own. The approach to full employment in an interdependent world must start with an international compact.

The 1995 World Summit for Social Development in Copenhagen has provided the opportunity for agreement on an agenda for worldwide growth. The industrial countries of OECD must coordinate their policies for faster growth. The momentum towards freer trade must be sustained, with reductions in tariffs and other barriers by countries at all levels of development. The system of ODA should be reformed to concentrate the resources available on the countries and people most in need. The outstanding debts of the poorest developing countries should be reduced or, better, eliminated. Basic education for all, especially for women, and retraining for adults, are essential preconditions for increasing and upgrading employment everywhere. They should be supported by more and better technical assistance, including the transfer of educational technology.

An integrated world demands concerted action. All nations, enterprises, national and multinational, and workers' organizations have a common interest in the growth of trade and of economic activity. Faster growth will put the jobless to work.

To promote global growth, a global compact is needed. No country, or sector, can on its own fulfil its potential and provide the jobs that people need. All can succeed if they pull together. Now is the time to start. The aims of a global compact would be to speed the growth of employment, reduce poverty and improve the quality of the jobs provided. The subjects it would need to consider are wide-ranging but closely interwoven. They include trade, aid, the operation of labour markets, migration, the movement of capital and the safeguarding of the environment.

In all these areas there are shared risks to be avoided and mutual advantages to be obtained. Global action must be defined by a global forum. The Copenhagen Summit has drawn up an agenda and started a process. We now have to give it the impetus it needs to succeed.

© *Peter Barker/Panos*

Employment remains precarious in areas of Asia, despite high growth rates.
River stone collection for the construction industry.

Abdullah Said Bugshan & Bros.

A chapter of Saudi Arabia's
Economic Development

In the forefront of applied telecommunications

In the days before oil dominated the economy of Saudi Arabia, Makkah, situated on one of the oldest trade routes between Asia and Europe and an annual meeting place of many thousands of pilgrims to the Holy Mosques in Makkah and Medina, was an important commercial centre of the Arab peninsula. One of the ancient Makkah trading families to make the transition from a family firm to a modern, prestigious, highly diversified group of companies is Abdullah Said Bugshan & Bros. founded over six decades ago.

Today Saudi Arabia, under the wise leadership of the Custodian of the Two Holy Mosques, King Fahd Ibn Abdulaziz, experiences great progress and development. In a country that is now at the forefront of applied telecommunications technology, Abdullah Said Bugshan & Bros. has emerged as a leader in telecommunications, civil and electro-mechanical design, construction, operation and maintenance.

Cooperating with such pioneers of telecommunications technology as AT&T International of the United States, Consultel (Telecom Italia) and others, the BUGSHAN Telecommunications Division is in a position to execute the most demanding large-scale telecommunications projects on a turnkey basis. Its scope of work comprises the installation of integrated communications systems followed up by comprehensive maintenance and support services.

This Division has engineered, furnished and installed the King Fahd Satellite Telecommunications City, comprising two Intelsat stations, one Arabsat station, central equipment, buildings and a digital microwave link together with the communication systems for the King Khalid International Airport (KKIA) in Riyadh. These achievements add to an already impressive list of projects including meteorological satellite systems, rural radio telephone service systems, and the operation and maintenance of the telex and Al-Waseet network throughout the Kingdom.

As the major subcontractor in the scheme and AT&T's local agent, BUGSHAN is proud of the confidence placed in the company by the Custodian of the Two Holy Mosques, King Fahd Ibn Abdulaziz and his Government, having been awarded the $4 billion telephone expansion project contract under the Economic Offset Program, the largest of its kind in the Kingdom's history.

Jeddah: P.O Box 378, Jeddah 21411   Riyadh: P.O Box 80, Riyadh 11411   Dammam: P.O Box 103, Dammam 31411
           Telephone: 6473840, Fax: 6479379   Telephone: 4787711, Fax: 4774225   Telephone: 8576180, Fax: 8575475
           Telex: 602677 ASBROS SJ,   Telex: 401144 BGSHAN SJ,   Telex: 801065 BGSHAN SJ,
           Cable: BUGSHAN   Cable: BUGSHAN   Cable: BUGSHAN

Reference

In the words of the Charter, the UN is to be "a centre for harmonizing the actions of nations in the attainment of these common ends." That role is reflected first and foremost in the international agreements which resulted from the painstaking deliberations of its founders.

This final section reproduces the two key agreements on which the central work of the UN is based: the Charter of the UN and the Statute of the International Court of Justice. These spell out the structures and governing principles by which the UN takes decisions, divides powers between its main organs, and provides an international judicial body to adjudicate on disputes between sovereign nations.

In addition to these fundamental documents, the section includes the ground-breaking statement entitled **An Agenda for Peace** made by the UN Secretary-General, Boutros Boutros-Ghali, in 1992. The report was submitted to the Security Council as it faced the challenges of peacemaking, peacekeeping and preventive diplomacy in the post-Cold War era.

The section concludes with an up-to-date listing of the names of officers and member associations of the World Federation of United Nations Associations (WFUNA). It is from this listing that readers can find the appropriate UNA from which to obtain further information on the work of the UN and activities to mark the 50th Anniversary.

Chapters

The Charter of the UN

PREAMBLE TO THE CHARTER OF THE UNITED NATIONS

WE THE PEOPLES OF THE UNITED NATIONS DETERMINED

to save succeeding generations from the scourge of war, which twice in our lifetime has brought untold sorrow to mankind, and
to reaffirm faith in fundamental human rights, in the dignity and worth of the human person, in the equal rights of men and women and of nations large and small, and
to establish conditions under which justice and respect for the obligations arising from treaties and other sources of international law can be maintained, and
to promote social progress and better standards of life in larger freedom,

AND FOR THESE ENDS

to practice tolerance and live together in peace with one another as good neighbours, and
to unite our strength to maintain international peace and security, and
to ensure, by the acceptance of principles and the institution of methods, that armed force shall not be used, save in the common interest, and
to employ international machinery for the promotion of the economic and social advancement of all peoples,

HAVE RESOLVED TO COMBINE OUR EFFORTS TO ACCOMPLISH THESE AIMS

Accordingly, our respective Governments, through representatives assembled in the city of San Francisco, who have exhibited their full powers found to be in good and due form, have agreed to the present Charter of the United Nations and do hereby establish an international organization to be known as the United Nations.

CHAPTER I
PURPOSES AND PRINCIPLES

Article I

The Purposes of the United Nations are:

1. To maintain international peace and security, and to that end: to take effective collective measures for the prevention and removal of threats to the peace, and for the suppression of acts of aggression or other breaches of the peace, and to bring about by peaceful means, and in conformity with the principles of justice and international law, adjustment or settlement of international disputes or situations which might lead to a breach of the peace;

2. To develop friendly relations among nations based on respect for the principle of equal rights and self-determination of peoples, and to take other appropriate measures to strengthen universal peace;

3. To achieve international co-operation in solving international problems of an economic, social, cultural, or humanitarian character, and in promoting and encouraging respect for human rights and for fundamental freedoms for all without distinction as to race, sex, language, or religion; and

4. To be a centre for harmonizing the actions of nations in the attainment of these common ends.

Article 2

The Organization and its Members, in pursuit of the Purposes stated in Article 1, shall act in accordance with the following Principles.

1. The Organization is based on the principle of the sovereign equality of all its Members.

2. All Members, in order to ensure to all of them the rights and benefits resulting from membership, shall fulfill in good faith the obligations assumed by them in accordance with the present Charter.

3. All Members shall settle their international disputes by peaceful means in such a manner that international peace and security, and justice, are not endangered.

4. All Members shall refrain in their international relations from the threat or use of force against the territorial integrity or political independence of any state, or in any other manner inconsistent with the Purposes of the United Nations.

5. All Members shall give the United Nations every assistance in any action it takes in accordance with the present Charter, and shall refrain from giving assistance to any state against which the United Nations is taking preventive or enforcement action.

6. The Organization shall ensure that states which are not Members of the United Nations act in accordance with these Principles so far as may be necessary for the maintenance of international peace and security.

7. Nothing contained in the present Charter shall authorize the United Nations to intervene in matters which are essentially within the domestic jurisdiction of any state or shall require the Members to submit such matters to settlement under the present Charter; but this principle shall not prejudice the application of enforcement measures under Chapter Vll.

CHAPTER II
MEMBERSHIP

Article 3

The original Members of the United Nations shall be the states which, having participated in the United Nations Conference on International Organization at San Francisco, or having previously signed the Declaration by United Nations of 1 January 1942, sign the present Charter and ratify it in accordance with Article 110.

Article 4

1. Membership in the United Nations is open to all other peace-loving states which accept the obligations contained in the present Charter and, in the judgment of the Organization, are able and willing to carry out these obligations.

2. The admission of any such state to membership in the United Nations will be effected by a decision of the General Assembly upon the recommendation of the Security Council.

Article 5

A Member of the United Nations against which preventive or enforcement action has been taken by the Security Council may be suspended from the exercise of the rights and privileges of membership by the General Assembly upon the recommendation of the Security Council. The exercise of these rights and privileges may be restored by the Security Council.

Article 6

A Member of the United Nations which has persistently violated the Principles contained in the present Charter may be expelled from the Organization by the General Assembly upon the recommendation of the Security Council.

CHAPTER III
ORGANS

Article 7

1. There are established as the principal organs of the United Nations: a General Assembly, a Security Council, an Economic and Social Council, a Trusteeship Council, an International Court of Justice, and a Secretariat.

2. Such subsidiary organs as may be found necessary may be established in accordance with the present Charter.

Article 8

The United Nations shall place no restrictions on the eligibility of men and women to participate in any capacity and under conditions of equality in its principal and subsidiary organs.

CHAPTER IV
THE GENERAL ASSEMBLY

Composition

Article 9

1. The General Assembly shall consist of all the Members of the United Nations.

2. Each Member shall have not more than five representatives in the General Assembly.

Functions and Powers

Article 10

The General Assembly may discuss any questions or any matters within the scope of the present Charter or relating to the powers

we the peoples

and functions of any organs provided for in the present Charter, and, except as provided in Article 12, may make recommendations to the Members of the United Nations or to the Security Council or to both on any such questions or matters.

Article 11

1. The General Assembly may consider the general principles of co-operation in the maintenance of international peace and security, including the principles governing disarmament and the regulation of armaments, and may make recommendations with regard to such principles to the Members or to the Security Council or to both.
2. The General Assembly may discuss any questions relating to the maintenance of international peace and security brought before it by any Member of the United Nations, or by the Security Council, or by a state which is not a Member of the United Nations in accordance with Article 35, paragraph 2, and, except as provided in Article 12, may make recommendations with regard to any such questions to the state or states concerned or to the Security Council or to both. Any such question on which action is necessary shall be referred to the Security Council by the General Assembly either before or after discussion.
3. The General Assembly may call the attention of the Security Council to situations which are likely to endanger international peace and security.
4. The powers of the General Assembly set forth in this Article shall not limit the general scope of Article 10.

Article 12

1. While the Security Council is exercising in respect of any dispute or situation the functions assigned to it in the present Charter, the General Assembly shall not make any recommendation with regard to that dispute or situation unless the Security Council so requests.
2. The Secretary-General, with the consent of the Security Council, shall notify the General Assembly at each session of any matters relative to the maintenance of international peace and security which are being dealt with by the Security Council and shall similarly notify the General Assembly, or the Members of the United Nations if the General Assembly is not in session, immediately the Security Council ceases to deal with such matters.

Article 13

1. The General Assembly shall initiate studies and make recommendations for the purpose of:
a. promoting international co-operation in the political field and encouraging the progressive development of international law and its codification;
b. promoting international co-operation in the economic, social, cultural, educational, and health fields, and assisting in the realization of human rights and fundamental freedoms for all without distinction as to race, sex, language, or religion.
2. The further responsibilities, functions and powers of the General Assembly with respect to matters mentioned in paragraph I (b) above are set forth in Chapters IX and X.

Article 14

Subject to the provisions of Article 12, the General Assembly may recommend measures for the peaceful adjustment of any situation, regardless of origin, which it deems likely to impair the general welfare or friendly relations among nations, including situations resulting from a violation of the provisions of the present Charter setting forth the Purposes and Principles of the United Nations.

Article 15

1. The General Assembly shall receive and consider annual and special reports from the Security Council; these reports shall include an account of the measures that the Security Council has decided upon or taken to maintain international peace and security.
2. The General Assembly shall receive and consider reports from the other organs of the United Nations.

Article 16

The General Assembly shall perform such functions with respect to the international trusteeship system as are assigned to it under Chapters XII and XIII, including the approval of the trusteeship agreements for areas not designated as strategic.

Article 17

1. The General Assembly shall consider and approve the budget of the Organization.

2. The expenses of the Organization shall be borne by the Members as apportioned by the General Assembly.
3. The General Assembly shall consider and approve any financial and budgetary arrangements with specialized agencies referred to in Article 57 and shall examine the administrative budgets of such specialized agencies with a view to making recommendations to the agencies concerned.

Voting

Article 18

1. Each member of the General Assembly shall have one vote.
2. Decisions of the General Assembly on important questions shall be made by a two-thirds majority of the members present and voting. These questions shall include: recommendations with respect to the maintenance of international peace and security, the election of the non-permanent members of the Security Council, the election of the members of the Economic and Social Council, the election of members of the Trusteeship Council in accordance with paragraph I (c) of Article 86, the admission of new Members to the United Nations, the suspension of the rights and privileges of membership, the expulsion of Members, questions relating to the operation of the trusteeship system, and budgetary questions.
3. Decisions on other questions, including the determination of additional categories of questions to be decided by a two-thirds majority, shall be made by a majority of the members present and voting.

Article 19

A Member of the United Nations which is in arrears in the payment of its financial contributions to the Organization shall have no vote in the General Assembly if the amount of its arrears equals or exceeds the amount of the contributions due from it for the preceding two full years. The General Assembly may, nevertheless, permit such a Member to vote if it is satisfied that the failure to pay is due to conditions beyond the control of the Member.

Procedure

Article 20

The General Assembly shall meet in regular annual sessions and in such special sessions as occasion may require. Special sessions shall be convoked by the Secretary-General at the request of the Security Council or of a majority of the Members of the United Nations.

Article 21

The General Assembly shall adopt its own rules of procedure. It shall elect its President for each session.

Article 22

The General Assembly may establish such subsidiary organs as it deems necessary for the performance of its functions.

CHAPTER V

THE SECURITY COUNCIL

Composition

Article 23

1. The Security Council shall consist of fifteen Members of the United Nations. The Republic of China, France, the Union of Soviet Socialist Republics, the United Kingdom of Great Britain and Northern Ireland, and the United States of America shall be permanent members of the Security Council. The General Assembly shall elect ten other Members of the United Nations to be non-permanent members of the Security Council, due regard being specially paid, in the first instance, to the contribution of Members of the United Nations to the maintenance of international peace and security and to the other purposes of the Organization, and also to equitable geographical distribution.
2. The non-permanent members of the Security Council shall be elected for a term of two years. In the first election of the non-permanent members after the increase of the membership of the Security Council from eleven to fifteen, two of the four additional members shall be chosen for a term of one year. A retiring member shall not be eligible for immediate re-election.
3. Each member of the Security Council shall have one representative.

WE ARE PROUD TO BE A PROJECT SPONSOR OF U.N. 50 AND *A VISION OF HOPE.*

Berlitz has been helping people with their language, cultural and business needs for over 115 years. As the world's premier language services company, we have:

- Over 320 Centers in 32 countries
- Instruction in English and 50 other languages
- Cross-Cultural training
- Translation/interpretation services
- Product localization capabilities
- Travel and language products and self-study courses

Berlitz International, Inc.

293 Wall Street

Princeton, New Jersey 08540 USA

Phone 609-497-9941 Fax 609-683-0983

Berlitz®

Helping the World Communicate

Instruction
Translation
Publishing

Functions and Powers
Article 24
1. In order to ensure prompt and effective action by the United Nations, its Members confer on the Security Council primary responsibility for the maintenance of international peace and security, and agree that in carrying out its duties under this responsibility the Security Council acts on their behalf.
2. In discharging these duties the Security Council shall act in accordance with the Purposes and Principles of the United Nations. The specific powers granted to the Security Council for the discharge of these duties are laid down in Chapters VI, VII, VIII, and XII.
3. The Security Council shall submit annual and, when necessary, special reports to the General Assembly for its consideration.

Article 25
The Members of the United Nations agree to accept and carry out the decisions of the Security Council in accordance with the present Charter.

Article 26
In order to promote the establishment and maintenance of international peace and security with the least diversion for armaments of the world's human and economic resources, the Security Council shall be responsible for formulating, with the assistance of the Military Staff Committee referred to in Article 47, plans to be submitted to the Members of the United Nations for the establishment of a system for the regulation of armaments.

Voting
Article 27
1. Each member of the Security Council shall have one vote.
2. Decisions of the Security Council on procedural matters shall be made by an affirmative vote of nine members.
3. Decisions of the Security Council on all other matters shall be made by an affirmative vote of nine members including the concurring votes of the permanent members; provided that, in decisions under Chapter VI, and under paragraph 3 of Article 52, a party to a dispute shall abstain from voting.

Procedure
Article 28
1. The Security Council shall be so organized as to be able to function continuously. Each member of the Security Council shall for this purpose be represented at all times at the seat of the Organization.
2. The Security Council shall hold periodic meetings at which each of its members may, if it so desires, be represented by a member of the government or by some other specially designated representative.
3. The Security Council may hold meetings at such places other than the seat of the Organization as in its judgment will best facilitate its work.

Article 29
The Security Council may establish such subsidiary organs as it deems necessary for the performance of its functions.

Article 30
The Security Council shall adopt its own rules of procedure, including the method of selecting its President.

Article 31
Any Member of the United Nations which is not a member of the Security Council may participate, without vote, in the discussion of any question brought before the Security Council whenever the latter considers that the interests of that Member are specially affected.

Article 32
Any Member of the United Nations which is not a member of the Security Council or any state which is not a Member of the United Nations, if it is a party to a dispute under consideration by the Security Council, shall be invited to participate, without vote, in the discussion relating to the dispute. The Security Council shall lay down such conditions as it deems just for the participation of a state which is not a Member of the United Nations.

CHAPTER VI
PACIFIC SETTLEMENT OF DISPUTES
Article 33
1. The parties to any dispute, the continuance of which is likely to endanger the maintenance of international peace and security, shall, first of all, seek a solution by negotiation, enquiry, media-tion, conciliation, arbitration, judicial settlement, resort to regional agencies or arrangements, or other peaceful means of their own choice.
2. The Security Council shall, when it deems necessary, call upon the parties to settle their dispute by such means.

Article 34
The Security Council may investigate any dispute, or any situation which might lead to international friction or give rise to a dispute, in order to determine whether the continuance of the dispute or situation is likely to endanger the maintenance of international peace and security.

Article 35
1. Any Member of the United Nations may bring any dispute, or any situation of the nature referred to in Article 34, to the attention of the Security Council or of the General Assembly.
2. A state which is not a Member of the United Nations may bring to the attention of the Security Council or of the General Assembly any dispute to which it is a party if it accepts in advance, for the purposes of the dispute, the obligations of pacific settlement provided in the present Charter.
3. The proceedings of the General Assembly in respect of matters brought to its attention under this Article will be subject to the provisions of Articles 11 and 12.

Article 36
1. The Security Council may, at any stage of a dispute of the nature referred to in Article 33 or of a situation of like nature, recommend appropriate procedures or methods of adjustment.
2. The Security Council should take into consideration any procedures for the settlement of the dispute which have already been adopted by the parties.
3. In making recommendations under this Article the Security Council should also take into consideration that legal disputes should as a general rule be referred by the parties to the International Court of Justice in accordance with the provisions of the Statute of the Court.

Article 37
1. Should the parties to a dispute of the nature referred to in Article 33 fail to settle it by the means indicated in that Article, they shall refer it to the Security Council.
2. If the Security Council deems that the continuance of the dispute is in fact likely to endanger the maintenance of international peace and security, it shall decide whether to take action under Article 36 or to recommend such terms of settlement as it may consider appropriate.

Article 38
Without prejudice to the provisions of Articles 33 to 37, the Security Council may, if all the parties to any dispute so request, make recommendations to the parties with a view to a pacific settlement of the dispute.

CHAPTER VII
ACTION WITH RESPECT TO THREATS TO THE PEACE, BREACHES OF THE PEACE, AND ACTS OF AGGRESSION
Article 39
The Security Council shall determine the existence of any threat to the peace, breach of the peace, or act of aggression and shall make recommendations, or decide what measures shall be taken in accordance with Articles 41 and 42, to maintain or restore international peace and security.

Article 40
In order to prevent an aggravation of the situation, the Security Council may, before making the recommendations or deciding upon the measures provided for in Article 39, call upon the parties concerned to comply with such provisional measures as it deems necessary or desirable. Such provisional measures shall be without prejudice to the rights, claims, or position of the parties concerned. The Security Council shall duly take account of failure to comply with such provisional measures.

Article 41
The Security Council may decide what measures not involving the use of armed force are to be employed to give effect to its decisions, and it may call upon the Members of the United Nations to apply such measures. These may include complete or partial interruption of economic relations and of rail, sea, air, postal, telegraphic, radio, and other means of communication, and the severance of diplomatic relations.

Article 42
Should the Security Council consider that measures provided for in Article 41 would be inadequate or have proved to be inadequate, it may take such action by air, sea, or land forces as may

be necessary to maintain or restore international peace and security. Such action may include demonstrations, blockade, and other operations by air, sea, or land forces of Members of the United Nations.

Article 43

1. All Members of the United Nations, in order to contribute to the maintenance of international peace and security, undertake to make available to the Security Council, on its call and in accordance with a special agreement or agreements, armed forces, assistance, and facilities, including rights of passage, necessary for the purpose of maintaining international peace and security.
2. Such agreement or agreements shall govern the numbers and types of forces, their degree of readiness and general location, and the nature of the facilities and assistance to be provided.
3. The agreement or agreements shall be negotiated as soon as possible on the initiative of the Security Council. They shall be concluded between the Security Council and Members or between the Security Council and groups of Members and shall be subject to ratification by the signatory states in accordance with their respective constitutional processes.

Article 44

When the Security Council has decided to use force it shall, before calling upon a Member not represented on it to provide armed forces in fulfilment of the obligations assumed under Article 43, invite that Member, if the Member so desires, to participate in the decisions of the Security Council concerning the employment of contingents of that Member's armed forces.

Article 45

In order to enable the United Nations to take urgent military measures, Members shall hold immediately available national air-force contingents for combined international enforcement action. The strength and degree of readiness of these contingents and plans for their combined action shall be determined, within the limits laid down in the special agreement or agreements referred to in Article 43, by the Security Council with the assistance of the Military Staff Committee.

Article 46

Plans for the application of armed force shall be made by the Security Council with the assistance of the Military Staff Committee.

Article 47

1. There shall be established a Military Staff Committee to advise and assist the Security Council on all questions relating to the Security Council's military requirements for the maintenance of international peace and security, the employment and command of forces placed at its disposal, the regulation of armaments, and possible disarmament.
2. The Military Staff Committee shall consist of the Chiefs of Staff of the permanent members of the Security Council or their representatives. Any Member of the United Nations not permanently represented on the Committee shall be invited by the Committee to be associated with it when the efficient discharge of the Committee's responsibilities requires the participation of that Member in its work.
3. The Military Staff Committee shall be responsible under the Security Council for the strategic direction of any armed forces placed at the disposal of the Security Council. Questions relating to the command of such forces shall be worked out subsequently.
4. The Military Staff Committee, with the authorization of the Security Council and after consultation with appropriate regional agencies, may establish regional sub-committees.

Article 48

1. The action required to carry out the decisions of the Security Council for the maintenance of international peace and security shall be taken by all the Members of the United Nations or by some of them, as the Security Council may determine.
2. Such decisions shall be carried out by the Members of the United Nations directly and through their action in the appropriate international agencies of which they are members.

Article 49

The Members of the United Nations shall join in affording mutual assistance in carrying out the measures decided upon by the Security Council.

Article 50

If preventive or enforcement measures against any state are taken by the Security Council, any other state, whether a Member of the United Nations or not, which finds itself confronted with special economic problems arising from the carrying out of those measures shall have the right to consult the Security Council with regard to a solution of those problems.

Article 51

Nothing in the present Charter shall impair the inherent right of individual or collective self-defence if an armed attack occurs against a Member of the United Nations, until the Security Council has taken measures necessary to maintain international peace and security. Measures taken by Members in the exercise of this right of self-defence shall be immediately reported to the Security Council and shall not in any way affect the authority and responsibility of the Security Council under the present Charter to take at any time such action as it deems necessary in order to maintain or restore international peace and security.

CHAPTER VIII
REGIONAL ARRANGEMENTS

Article 52

1. Nothing in the present Charter precludes the existence of regional arrangements or agencies for dealing with such matters relating to the maintenance of international peace and security as are appropriate for regional action, provided that such arrangements or agencies and their activities are consistent with the Purposes and Principles of the United Nations.
2. The Members of the United Nations entering into such arrangements or constituting such agencies shall make every effort to achieve pacific settlement of local disputes through such regional arrangements or by such regional agencies before referring them to the Security Council.
3. The Security Council shall encourage the development of pacific settlement of local disputes through such regional arrangements or by such regional agencies either on the initiative of the states concerned or by reference from the Security Council.
4. This Article in no way impairs the application of Articles 34 and 35.

Article 53

1. The Security Council shall, where appropriate, utilize such regional arrangements or agencies for enforcement action under its authority. But no enforcement action shall be taken under regional arrangements or by regional agencies without the authorization of the Security Council, with the exception of measures against any enemy state, as defined in paragraph 2 of this Article, provided for pursuant to Article 107 or in regional arrangements directed against renewal of aggressive policy on the part of any such state, until such time as the Organization may, on request of the Governments concerned, be charged with the responsibility for preventing further aggression by such a state.
2. The term enemy state as used in paragraph 1 of this Article applies to any state which during the Second World War has been an enemy of any signatory of the present Charter.

Article 54

The Security Council shall at all times be kept fully informed of activities undertaken or in contemplation under regional arrangements or by regional agencies for the maintenance of international peace and security.

CHAPTER IX
INTERNATIONAL ECONOMIC AND SOCIAL CO-OPERATION

Article 55

With a view to the creation of conditions of stability and well-being which are necessary for peaceful and friendly relations among nations based on respect for the principle of equal rights and self-determination of peoples, the United Nations shall promote:

a. higher standards of living, full employment, and conditions of economic and social progress and development;
b. solutions of international economic, social, health, and related problems; and international cultural and educational cooperation; and
c. universal respect for, and observance of, human rights and fundamental freedoms for all without distinction as to race, sex, language, or religion.

Article 56

All Members pledge themselves to take joint and separate action in co-operation with the Organization for the achievement of the purposes set forth in Article 55.

Article 57

1. The various specialized agencies, established by intergovernmental agreement and having wide international responsibilities, as defined in their basic instruments, in economic, social, cultural, educational, health, and related fields, shall be brought into relationship with the United Nations in accordance with the provisions of Article 63.
2. Such agencies thus brought into relationship with the United Nations are hereinafter referred to as specialized agencies.

Article 58

The Organization shall make recommendations for the co-ordination of the policies and activities of the specialized agencies.

Article 59

The Organization shall, where appropriate, initiate negotiations among the states concerned for the creation of any new specialized agencies required for the accomplishment of the purposes set forth in Article 55.

Article 60

Responsibility for the discharge of the functions of the Organization set forth in this Chapter shall be vested in the General Assembly and, under the authority of the General Assembly, in the Economic and Social Council, which shall have for this purpose the powers set forth in Chapter X.

CHAPTER X

THE ECONOMIC AND SOCIAL COUNCIL

Composition

Article 61

1. The Economic and Social Council shall consist of fifty-four Members of the United Nations elected by the General Assembly.
2. Subject to the provisions of paragraph 3, eighteen members of the Economic and Social Council shall be elected each year for a term of three years. A retiring member shall be eligible for immediate re-election.
3. At the first election after the increase in the membership of the Economic and Social Council from twenty-seven to fifty-four members, in addition to the members elected in place of the nine members whose term of office expires at the end of that year, twenty-seven additional members shall be elected. Of these twenty-seven additional members, the term of office of nine members so elected shall expire at the end of one year, and of nine other members at the end of two years, in accordance with arrangements made by the General Assembly.
4. Each member of the Economic and Social Council shall have one representative.

Functions and Powers

Article 62

1. The Economic and Social Council may make or initiate studies and reports with respect to international economic, social, cultural, educational, health, and related matters and may make recommendations with respect to any such matters to the General Assembly, to the Members of the United Nations, and to the specialized agencies concerned.
2. It may make recommendations for the purpose of promoting respect for, and observance of, human rights and fundamental freedoms for all.
3. It may prepare draft conventions for submission to the General Assembly, with respect to matters falling within its competence.
4. It may call, in accordance with the rules prescribed by the United Nations, international conferences on matters falling within its competence.

Article 63

1. The Economic and Social Council may enter into agreements with any of the agencies referred to in Article 57, defining the terms on which the agency concerned shall be brought into relationship with the United Nations. Such agreements shall be subject to approval by the General Assembly.
2. It may co-ordinate the activities of the specialized agencies through consultation with and recommendations to such agencies and through recommendations to the General Assembly and to the Members of the United Nations.

Article 64

1. The Economic and Social Council may take appropriate steps to obtain regular reports from the specialized agencies. It may make arrangements with the Members of the United Nations and with the specialized agencies to obtain reports on the steps taken to give effect to its own recommendations and to recommendations on matters falling within its competence made by the General Assembly.
2. It may communicate its observations on these reports to the General Assembly.

Article 65

The Economic and Social Council may furnish information to the Security Council and shall assist the Security Council upon its request.

Article 66

1. The Economic and Social Council shall perform such functions as fall within its competence in connexion with the carrying out of the recommendations of the General Assembly.
2. It may, with the approval of the General Assembly, perform services at the request of Members of the United Nations and at the request of specialized agencies.
3. It shall perform such other functions as are specified elsewhere in the present Charter or as may be assigned to it by the General Assembly.

Voting

Article 67

1. Each member of the Economic and Social Council shall have one vote.
2. Decisions of the Economic and Social Council shall be made by a majority of the members present and voting.

Procedure

Article 68

The Economic and Social Council shall set up commissions in economic and social fields and for the promotion of human rights, and such other commissions as may be required for the performance of its functions.

Article 69

The Economic and Social Council shall invite any Member of the United Nations to participate, without vote, in its deliberations on any matter of particular concern to that Member.

Article 70

The Economic and Social Council may make arrangements for representatives of the specialized agencies to participate, without vote, in its deliberations and in those of the commissions established by it, and for its representatives to participate in the deliberations of the specialized agencies.

Article 71

The Economic and Social Council may make suitable arrangements for consultation with non-governmental organizations which are concerned with matters within its competence. Such arrangements may be made with international organizations and, where appropriate, with national organizations after consultation with the Member of the United Nations concerned.

Article 72

1. The Economic and Social Council shall adopt its own rules of procedure, including the method of selecting its President.
2. The Economic and Social Council shall meet as required in accordance with its rules, which shall include provision for the convening of meetings on the request of a majority of its members.

CHAPTER XI

DECLARATION REGARDING NON-SELF-GOVERNING TERRITORIES

Article 73

Members of the United Nations which have or assume responsibilities for the administration of territories whose peoples have not yet attained a full measure of self-government recognize the principle that the interests of the inhabitants of these territories are paramount, and accept as a sacred trust the obligation to promote to the utmost, within the system of international peace and security established by the present Charter, the well-being of the inhabitants of these territories, and, to this end:

a. to ensure, with due respect for the culture of the peoples concerned, their political, economic, social, and educational advancement, their just treatment, and their protection against abuses;
b. to develop self-government, to take due account of the political aspirations of the peoples, and to assist them in the progressive development of their free political institutions, according to the particular circumstances of each territory and its peoples and their varying stages of advancement;
c. to further international peace and security;
d. to promote constructive measures of development, to encourage research, and to co-operate with one another and, when and where appropriate, with specialized international bodies with a view to the practical achievement of the social, economic, and scientific purposes set forth in this Article; and
e. to transmit regularly to the Secretary-General for information purposes, subject to such limitation as security and constitutional considerations may require, statistical and other information of a technical nature relating to economic, social, and educational conditions in the territories for which they are respectively responsible other than those territories to which Chapters XII and XIII apply.

Article 74

Members of the United Nations also agree that their policy in re-

BANCO ECONOMICO S.A.

At a time when the United Nations celebrates its 50th Anniversary, it is universally recognized that the major problems facing humanity today are related mainly to environmental conservation and social and economic development. In many of the emerging nations, including Brazil, it is necessary for governments •to involve the business sector in order to bring about improvements, especially in the areas of education and health.

Business also needs to be more responsible in matters of environmental conservation, acknowledging that most environmental damage has been caused by a lack of concern by corporations.

However it is in relation to social issues, particularly with underprivileged communities, that the Brazilian Development Bank, together with the support of the business community, has been able to assist. This principle is very much in line with that of The Prince of Wales Business Leaders Forum, an organization formed by HRH Prince Charles of the United Kingdom and operating in countries worldwide.

Angelo Calmon de Sá
Chairman & C.E.O.

In the same way that the United Nations seeks to involve the business community, we wish to bring together corporations from all over the world to begin this task. Each one of us, by supporting social projects within underprivileged communities, particularly in the developing countries, can make a contribution, whether it be in the form of leadership or by way of financial assistance. In our experience there is no other kind of social intervention that can produce such dividends at so little cost.

By way of example, some fifteen years ago in the town of Feira de Santana, a nun started a project involving the care of the elderly and a small number of children. It now provides a formal education, both vocational and religious, for five hundred children at a cost of only US$10 per child, including food and job training. It is only through the involvement of all those taking part, giving their time voluntarily, that such a miracle has been made possible.

We believe that no government department or private company alone can carry out projects like this at such a low cost. It is only by business and government working together that real progress can be made.

Rua Miguel Calmon, 285 - 11º andar- Tel 55 (71) 242 1834 - Telex (71) 1741
Fax 55 (71) 243 3788 - 40004-900 - Salvador - Bahia - Brazil

spect of the territories to which this Chapter applies, no less than in respect of their metropolitan areas, must be based on the general principle of good-neighbourliness, due account being taken of the interests and well-being of the rest of the world, in social, economic, and commercial matters.

CHAPTER XII
INTERNATIONAL TRUSTEESHIP SYSTEM

Article 75
The United Nations shall establish under its authority an international trusteeship system for the administration and supervision of such territories as may be placed thereunder by subsequent individual agreements. These territories are hereinafter referred to as trust territories.

Article 76
The basic objectives of the trusteeship system, in accordance with the Purposes of the United Nations laid down in Article I of the present Charter, shall be:
a. to further international peace and security;
b. to promote the political, economic, social, and educational advancement of the inhabitants of the trust territories, and their progressive development towards self-government or independence as may be appropriate to the particular circumstances of each territory and its peoples and the freely expressed wishes of the peoples concerned, and as may be provided by the terms of each trusteeship agreement;
c. to encourage respect for human rights and for fundamental freedoms for all without distinction as to race, sex, language, or religion, and to encourage recognition of the interdependence of the peoples of the world; and
d. to ensure equal treatment in social, economic, and commercial matters for all Members of the United Nations and their nationals, and also equal treatment for the latter in the administration of justice, without prejudice to the attainment of the foregoing objectives and subject to the provisions of Article 80.

Article 77
1. The trusteeship system shall apply to such territories in the following categories as may be placed thereunder by means of trusteeship agreements:
a. territories now held under mandate;
b. territories which may be detached from enemy states as a result of the Second World War; and
c. territories voluntarily placed under the system by states responsible for their administration.
2. It will be a matter for subsequent agreement as to which territories in the foregoing categories will be brought under the trusteeship system and upon what terms.

Article 78
The trusteeship system shall not apply to territories which have become Members of the United Nations, relationship among which shall be based on respect for the principle of sovereign equality.

Article 79
The terms of trusteeship for each territory to be placed under the trusteeship system, including any alteration or amendment, shall be agreed upon by the states directly concerned, including the mandatory power in the case of territories held under mandate by a Member of the United Nations, and shall be approved as provided for in Articles 83 and 85.

Article 80
1. Except as may be agreed upon in individual trusteeship agreements, made under Articles 77, 79, and 81, placing each territory under the trusteeship system, and until such agreements have been concluded, nothing in this Chapter shall be construed in or of itself to alter in any manner the rights whatsoever of any states or any peoples or the terms of existing international instruments to which Members of the United Nations may respectively be parties.
2. Paragraph 1 of this Article shall not be interpreted as giving grounds for delay or postponement of the negotiation and conclusion of agreements for placing mandated and other territories under the trusteeship system as provided for in Article 77.

Article 81
The trusteeship agreement shall in each case include the terms under which the trust territory will be administered and designate the authority which will exercise the administration of the trust territory. Such authority, hereinafter called the administering authority, may be one or more states or the Organization itself.

Article 82
There may be designated, in any trusteeship agreement, a strategic area or areas which may include part or all of the trust territory to which the agreement applies, without prejudice to any special agreement or agreements made under Article 43.

Article 83
1. All functions of the United Nations relating to strategic areas, including the approval of the terms of the trusteeship agreements and of their alteration or amendment, shall be exercised by the Security Council.
2. The basic objectives set forth in Article 76 shall be applicable to the people of each strategic area.
3. The Security Council shall, subject to the provisions of the trusteeship agreements and without prejudice to security considerations, avail itself of the assistance of the Trusteeship Council to perform those functions of the United Nations under the trusteeship system relating to political, economic, social, and educational matters in the strategic areas.

Article 84
It shall be the duty of the administering authority to ensure that the trust territory shall play its part in the maintenance of international peace and security. To this end the administering authority may make use of volunteer forces, facilities, and assistance from the trust territory in carrying out the obligations towards the Security Council undertaken in this regard by the administering authority, as well as for local defence and the maintenance of law and order within the trust territory.

Article 85
1. The functions of the United Nations with regard to trusteeship agreements for all areas not designated as strategic, including the approval of the terms of the trusteeship agreements and of their alteration or amendment, shall be exercised by the General Assembly.
2. The Trusteeship Council, operating under the authority of the General Assembly, shall assist the General Assembly in carrying out these functions.

CHAPTER XIII
THE TRUSTEESHIP COUNCIL

Composition

Article 86
1. The Trusteeship Council shall consist of the following Members of the United Nations:
a. those Members administering trust territories;
b. such of those Members mentioned by name in Article 23 as are not administering trust territories; and
c. as many other Members elected for three-year terms by the General Assembly as may be necessary to ensure that the total number of members of the Trusteeship Council is equally divided between those Members of the United Nations which administer trust territories and those which do not.
2. Each member of the Trusteeship Council shall designate one specially qualified person to represent it therein.

Functions and Powers

Article 87
The General Assembly and, under its authority, the Trusteeship Council, in carrying out their functions, may:
a. consider reports submitted by the administering authority;
b. accept petitions and examine them in consultation with the administering authority;
c. provide for periodic visits to the respective trust territories at times agreed upon with the administering authority; and
d. take these and other actions in conformity with the terms of the trusteeship agreements.

Article 88
The Trusteeship Council shall formulate a questionnaire on the political, economic, social, and educational advancement of the inhabitants of each trust territory, and the administering authority for each trust territory within the competence of the General Assembly shall make an annual report to the General Assembly upon the basis of such questionnaire.

Voting

Article 89
1. Each member of the Trusteeship Council shall have one vote.
2. Decisions of the Trusteeship Council shall be made by a majority of the members present and voting.

Procedure

Article 90
1. The Trusteeship Council shall adopt its own rules of procedure, including the method of selecting its President.
2. The Trusteeship Council shall meet as required in accordance

with its rules, which shall include provision for the convening of meetings on the request of a majority of its members.

Article 91

The Trusteeship Council shall, when appropriate, avail itself of the assistance of the Economic and Social Council and of the specialized agencies in regard to matters with which they are respectively concerned.

CHAPTER XIV
THE INTERNATIONAL COURT OF JUSTICE

Article 92

The International Court of Justice shall be the principal judicial organ of the United Nations. It shall function in accordance with the annexed Statute, which is based upon the Statute of the Permanent Court of International Justice and forms an integral part of the present Charter.

Article 93

1. All Members of the United Nations are *ipso facto* parties to the Statute of the International Court of Justice.
2. A state which is not a Member of the United Nations may become a party to the Statute of the International Court of Justice on conditions to be determined in each case by the General Assembly upon the recommendation of the Security Council.

Article 94

1. Each Member of the United Nations undertakes to comply with the decision of the International Court of Justice in any case to which it is a party.
2. If any party to a case fails to perform the obligations incumbent upon it under a judgment rendered by the Court, the other party may have recourse to the Security Council, which may, if it deems necessary, make recommendations or decide upon measures to be taken to give effect to the judgment.

Article 95

Nothing in the present Charter shall prevent Members of the United Nations from entrusting the solution of their differences to other tribunals by virtue of agreements already in existence or which may be concluded in the future.

Article 96

1. The General Assembly or the Security Council may request the International Court of Justice to give an advisory opinion on any legal question.
2. Other organs of the United Nations and specialized agencies, which may at any time be so authorized by the General Assembly, may also request advisory opinions of the Court on legal questions arising within the scope of their activities.

CHAPTER XV
THE SECRETARIAT

Article 97

The Secretariat shall comprise a Secretary-General and such staff as the Organization may require. The Secretary-General shall be appointed by the General Assembly upon the recommendation of the Security Council. He shall be the chief administrative officer of the Organization.

Article 98

The Secretary-General shall act in that capacity in all meetings of the General Assembly, of the Security Council, of the Economic and Social Council, and of the Trusteeship Council, and shall perform such other functions as are entrusted to him by these organs. The Secretary-General shall make an annual report to the General Assembly on the work of the Organization.

Article 99

The Secretary-General may bring to the attention of the Security Council any matter which in his opinion may threaten the maintenance of international peace and security.

Article 100

1. In the performance of their duties the Secretary-General and the staff shall not seek or receive instructions from any government or from any other authority external to the Organization. They shall refrain from any action which might reflect on their position as international officials responsible only to the Organization.
2. Each Member of the United Nations undertakes to respect the exclusively international character of the responsibilities of the Secretary-General and the staff and not to seek to influence them in the discharge of their responsibilities.

Article 101

1. The staff shall be appointed by the Secretary-General under regulations established by the General Assembly.

2. Appropriate staffs shall be permanently assigned to the Economic and Social Council, the Trusteeship Council, and, as required, to other organs of the United Nations. These staffs shall form a part of the Secretariat.
3. The paramount consideration in the employment of the staff and in the determination of the conditions of service shall be the necessity of securing the highest standards of efficiency, competence, and integrity. Due regard shall be paid to the importance of recruiting the staff on as wide a geographical basis as possible.

CHAPTER XVI
MISCELLANEOUS PROVISIONS

Article 102

1. Every treaty and every international agreement entered into by any Member of the United Nations after the present Charter comes into force shall as soon as possible be registered with the Secretariat and published by it.
2. No party to any such treaty or international agreement which has not been registered in accordance with the provisions of paragraph 1 of this Article may invoke that treaty or agreement before any organ of the United Nations.

Article 103

In the event of a conflict between the obligations of the Members of the United Nations under the present Charter and their obligations under any other international agreement, their obligations under the present Charter shall prevail.

Article 104

The Organization shall enjoy in the territory of each of its Members such legal capacity as may be necessary for the exercise of its functions and the fulfilment of its purposes.

Article 105

1. The Organization shall enjoy in the territory of each of its Members such privileges and immunities as are necessary for the fulfilment of its purposes.
2. Representatives of the Members of the United Nations and officials of the Organization shall similarly enjoy such privileges and immunities as are necessary for the independent exercise of their functions in connexion with the Organization.
3. The General Assembly may make recommendations with a view to determining the details of the application of paragraphs 1 and 2 of this Article or may propose conventions to the Members of the United Nations for this purpose.

CHAPTER XVII
TRANSITIONAL SECURITY ARRANGEMENTS

Article 106

Pending the coming into force of such special agreements referred to in Article 43 as in the opinion of the Security Council enable it to begin the exercise of its responsibilities under Article 42, the parties to the Four-Nation Declaration, signed at Moscow, 30 October 1943, and France, shall, in accordance with the provisions of paragraph 5 of that Declaration, consult with one another and as occasion requires with other Members of the United Nations with a view to such joint action on behalf of the Organization as may be necessary for the purpose of maintaining international peace and security.

Article 107

Nothing in the present Charter shall invalidate or preclude action, in relation to any state which during the Second World War has been an enemy of any signatory to the present Charter, taken or authorized as a result of that war by the Governments having responsibility for such action.

CHAPTER XVIII
AMENDMENTS

Article 108

Amendments to the present Charter shall come into force for all Members of the United Nations when they have been adopted by a vote of two thirds of the members of the General Assembly and ratified in accordance with their respective constitutional processes by two thirds of the Members of the United Nations, including all the permanent members of the Security Council.

Article 109

1. A General Conference of the Members of the United Nations for the purpose of reviewing the present Charter may be held at a date and place to be fixed by a two-thirds vote of the members of the General Assembly and by a vote of any nine members of the Security Council. Each Member of the United Nations shall have one vote in the conference.

2. Any alteration of the present Charter recommended by a two-thirds vote of the conference shall take effect when ratified in accordance with their respective constitutional processes by two thirds of the Members of the United Nations including all the permanent members of the Security Council.

3. If such a conference has not been held before the tenth annual session of the General Assembly following the coming into force of the present Charter, the proposal to call such a conference shall be placed on the agenda of that session of the General Assembly, and the conference shall be held if so decided by a majority vote of the members of the General Assembly and by a vote of any seven members of the Security Council.

CHAPTER XIX
RATIFICATION AND SIGNATURE
Article 110

1. The present Charter shall be ratified by the signatory states in accordance with their respective constitutional processes.

2. The ratifications shall be deposited with the Government of the United States of America, which shall notify all the signatory states of each deposit as well as the Secretary-General of the Organization when he has been appointed.

3. The present Charter shall come into force upon the deposit of ratifications by the Republic of China, France, the Union of Soviet Socialist Republics, the United Kingdom of Great Britain and Northern Ireland, and the United States of America, and by a majority of the other signatory states. A protocol of the ratifications deposited shall thereupon be drawn up by the Government of the United States of America which shall communicate copies thereof to all the signatory states.

4. The states signatory to the present Charter which ratify it after it has come into force will become original Members of the United Nations on the date of the deposit of their respective ratifications.

Article 111

The present Charter, of which the Chinese, French, Russian, English, and Spanish texts are equally authentic, shall remain deposited in the archives of the Government of the United States of America. Duly certified copies thereof shall be transmitted by that Government to the Governments of the other signatory states.

IN FAITH WHEREOF the representatives of the Governments of the United Nations have signed the present Charter.

DONE at the city of San Francisco the twenty-sixth day of June, one thousand nine hundred and forty-five.

STATUTE OF THE INTERNATIONAL COURT OF JUSTICE

Article I

The International Court of Justice established by the Charter of the United Nations as the principal judicial organ of the United Nations shall be constituted and shall function in accordance with the provisions of the present Statute.

CHAPTER I
ORGANIZATION OF THE COURT
Article 2

The Court shall be composed of a body of independent judges, elected regardless of their nationality from among persons of high moral character, who possess the qualifications required in their respective countries for appointment to the highest judicial offices, or are jurisconsults of recognized competence in international law.

Article 3

1. The Court shall consist of fifteen members, no two of whom may be nationals of the same state.

2. A person who for the purposes of membership in the Court could be regarded as a national of more than one state shall be deemed to be a national of the one in which he ordinarily exercises civil and political rights.

Article 4

1. The members of the Court shall be elected by the General Assembly and by the Security Council from a list of persons nominated by the national groups in the Permanent Court of Arbitration, in accordance with the following provisions.

2. In the case of Members of the United Nations not represented in the Permanent Court of Arbitration, candidates shall be nominated by national groups appointed for this purpose by their governments under the same conditions as those prescribed for members of the Permanent Court of Arbitration by Article 44 of the Convention of The Hague of 1907 for the pacific settlement of international disputes.

3. The conditions under which a state which is a party to the present Statute but is not a Member of the United Nations may participate in electing the members of the Court shall, in the absence of a special agreement, be laid down by the General Assembly upon recommendation of the Security Council.

Article 5

1. At least three months before the date of the election, the Secretary-General of the United Nations shall address a written request to the members of the Permanent Court of Arbitration belonging to the states which are parties to the present Statute, and to the members of the national groups appointed under Article 4, paragraph 2, inviting them to undertake, within a given time, by national groups, the nomination of persons in a position to accept the duties of a member of the Court.

2. No group may nominate more than four persons, not more than two of whom shall be of their own nationality. In no case may the number of candidates nominated by a group be more than double the number of seats to be filled.

Article 6

Before making these nominations, each national group is recommended to consult its highest court of justice, its legal faculties and schools of law, and its national academies and national sections of international academies devoted to the study of law.

Article 7

1. The Secretary-General shall prepare a list in alphabetical order of all the persons thus nominated. Save as provided in Article 12, paragraph 2, these shall be the only persons eligible.

2. The Secretary-General shall submit this list to the General Assembly and to the Security Council.

Article 8

The General Assembly and the Security Council shall proceed independently of one another to elect the members of the Court.

Article 9

At every election, the electors shall bear in mind not only that the persons to be elected should individually possess the qualifications required, but also that in the body as a whole the representation of the main forms of civilization and of the principal legal systems of the world should be assured.

Article 10

1. Those candidates who obtain an absolute majority of votes in the General Assembly and in the Security Council shall be considered as elected.

2. Any vote of the Security Council, whether for the election of judges or for the appointment of members of the conference envisaged in Article 12, shall be taken without any distinction between permanent and non-permanent members of the Security Council.

3. In the event of more than one national of the same state obtaining an absolute majority of the votes both of the General Assembly and of the Security Council, the eldest of these only shall be considered as elected.

Article 11

If, after the first meeting held for the purpose of the election, one or more seats remain to be filled, a second and, if necessary, a third meeting shall take place.

Article 12

1. If, after the third meeting, one or more seats still remain unfilled, a joint conference consisting of six members, three appointed by the General Assembly and three by the Security Council, may be formed at any time at the request of either the General Assembly or the Security Council, for the purpose of choosing by the vote of an absolute majority one name for each seat still vacant, to submit to the General Assembly and the Security Council for their respective acceptance.

2. If the joint conference is unanimously agreed upon any person who fulfils the required conditions, he may be included in its list, even though he was not included in the list of nominations referred to in Article 7.

3. If the joint conference is satisfied that it will not be successful in procuring an election, those members of the Court who have already been elected shall, within a period to be fixed by the Security Council, proceed to fill the vacant seats by selection from among those candidates who have obtained votes either in the General Assembly or in the Security Council.

4. In the event of an equality of votes among the judges, the eldest judge shall have a casting vote.

Article 13

1. The members of the Court shall be elected for nine years and may be re-elected; provided, however, that of the judges elected at the first election, the terms of five judges shall expire at the end of three years and the terms of five more judges shall expire at the end of six years.

Consolidated Contractors Group

A Proud Past   An Active Present   A Promising Future

Forty years' experience in the construction of civil engineering, mechanical, offshore and industrial projects throughout the world.

Throughout its history, the Consolidated Contractors Group has been committed to improving the quality of life within developing countries through the construction of major infrastructure such as hospitals, universities, water treatment plants and distribution networks, petrochemical plants and refineries, power plants, marine docks, harbours and airports. Its vision for the future includes the welfare of 25,000 employees of 30 nationalities located on projects worldwide and at its headquarters in Athens, Greece.

On behalf of all its operating group members and associates, the Consolidated Contractors Group salutes the United Nations on its 50th Anniversary and is proud to be a part of its commemoration.

2. The judges whose terms are to expire at the end of the above-mentioned initial periods of three and six years shall be chosen by lot to be drawn by the Secretary-General immediately after the first election has been completed.
3. The members of the Court shall continue to discharge their duties until their places have been filled. Though replaced, they shall finish any cases which they may have begun.
4. In the case of the resignation of a member of the Court, the resignation shall be addressed to the President of the Court for transmission to the Secretary-General. This last notification makes the place vacant.

Article 14
Vacancies shall be filled by the same method as that laid down for the first election, subject to the following provision: the Secretary-General shall, within one month of the occurrence of the vacancy, proceed to issue the invitations provided for in Article 5, and the date of the election shall be fixed by the Security Council.

Article 15
A member of the Court elected to replace a member whose term of office has not expired shall hold office for the remainder of his predecessor's term.

Article 16
1. No member of the Court may exercise any political or administrative function, or engage in any other occupation of a professional nature.
2. Any doubt on this point shall be settled by the decision of the Court.

Article 17
1. No member of the Court may act as agent, counsel, or advocate in any case.
2. No member may participate in the decision of any case in which he has previously taken part as agent, counsel, or advocate for one of the parties, or as a member of a national or international court, or of a commission of enquiry, or in any other capacity.
3. Any doubt on this point shall be settled by the decision of the Court.

Article 18
1. No member of the Court can be dismissed unless, in the unanimous opinion of the other members, he has ceased to fulfil the required conditions.
2. Formal notification thereof shall be made to the Secretary-General by the Registrar.
3. This notification makes the place vacant.

Article 19
The members of the Court, when engaged on the business of the Court, shall enjoy diplomatic privileges and immunities.

Article 20
Every member of the Court shall, before taking up his duties, make a solemn declaration in open court that he will exercise his powers impartially and conscientiously.

Article 21
1. The Court shall elect its President and Vice-President for three years; they may be re-elected.
2. The Court shall appoint its Registrar and may provide for the appointment of such other officers as may be necessary.

Article 22
1. The seat of the Court shall be established at The Hague. This, however, shall not prevent the Court from sitting and exercising its functions elsewhere whenever the Court considers it desirable.
2. The President and the Registrar shall reside at the seat of the Court.

Article 23
1. The Court shall remain permanently in session, except during the judicial vacations, the dates and duration of which shall be fixed by the Court.
2. Members of the Court are entitled to periodic leave, the dates and duration of which shall be fixed by the Court, having in mind the distance between The Hague and the home of each judge.
3. Members of the Court shall be bound, unless they are on leave or prevented from attending by illness or other serious reasons duly explained to the President, to hold themselves permanently at the disposal of the Court.

Article 24
1. If, for some special reason, a member of the Court considers that he should not take part in the decision of a particular case, he shall so inform the President.
2. If the President considers that for some special reason one of the members of the Court should not sit in a particular case, he shall give him notice accordingly.
3. If in any such case the member of the Court and the President disagree, the matter shall be settled by the decision of the Court.

Article 25
1. The full Court shall sit except when it is expressly provided otherwise in the present Statute.
2. Subject to the condition that the number of judges available to constitute the Court is not thereby reduced below eleven, the Rules of the Court may provide for allowing one or more judges, according to circumstances and in rotation, to be dispensed from sitting.
3. A quorum of nine judges shall suffice to constitute the Court.

Article 26
1. The Court may from time to time form one or more chambers, composed of three or more judges as the Court may determine, for dealing with particular categories of cases; for example, labour cases and cases relating to transit and communications.
2. The Court may at any time form a chamber for dealing with a particular case. The number of judges to constitute such a chamber shall be determined by the Court with the approval of the parties.
3. Cases shall be heard and determined by the chambers provided for in this article if the parties so request.

Article 27
A judgment given by any of the chambers provided for in Articles 26 and 29 shall be considered as rendered by the Court.

Article 28
The chambers provided for in Articles 26 and 29 may, with the consent of the parties, sit and exercise their functions elsewhere than at The Hague.

Article 29
With a view to the speedy dispatch of business, the Court shall form annually a chamber composed of five judges which, at the request of the parties, may hear and determine cases by summary procedure. In addition, two judges shall be selected for the purpose of replacing judges who find it impossible to sit.

Article 30
1. The Court shall frame rules for carrying out its functions. In particular, it shall lay down rules of procedure.
2. The Rules of the Court may provide for assessors to sit with the Court or with any of its chambers, without the right to vote.

Article 31
1. Judges of the nationality of each of the parties shall retain their right to sit in the case before the Court.
2. If the Court includes upon the Bench a judge of the nationality of one of the parties, any other party may choose a person to sit as judge. Such person shall be chosen preferably from among those persons who have been nominated as candidates as provided in Articles 4 and 5.
3. If the Court includes upon the Bench no judge of the nationality of the parties, each of these parties may proceed to choose a judge as provided in paragraph 2 of this Article.
4. The provisions of this Article shall apply to the case of Articles 26 and 29. In such cases, the President shall request one or, if necessary, two of the members of the Court forming the chamber to give place to the members of the Court of the nationality of the parties concerned, and, failing such, or if they are unable to be present, to the judges specially chosen by the parties.
5. Should there be several parties in the same interest, they shall, for the purpose of the preceding provisions, be reckoned as one party only. Any doubt upon this point shall be settled by the decision of the Court.
6. Judges chosen as laid down in paragraphs 2, 3, and 4 of this Article shall fulfil the conditions required by Articles 2, 17 (paragraph 2), 20, and 24 of the present Statute. They shall take part in the decision on terms of complete equality with their colleagues.

Article 32
1. Each member of the Court shall receive an annual salary.
2. The President shall receive a special annual allowance.
3. The Vice-President shall receive a special allowance for every day on which he acts as President.
4. The judges chosen under Article 31, other than members of the Court, shall receive compensation for each day on which they exercise their functions.
5. These salaries, allowances, and compensation shall be fixed by the General Assembly. They may not be decreased during the term of office.
6. The salary of the Registrar shall be fixed by the General Assembly on the proposal of the Court.
7. Regulations made by the General Assembly shall fix the conditions under which retirement pensions may be given to members of the Court and to the Registrar, and the conditions under which

GDP ✒ GÁS DE PORTUGAL, SA

A PROJECT FOR THE FUTURE

GÁS DE PORTUGAL, a company with a long tradition as producer and distributor of city gas in Lisbon, is a pioneer in the field of studies for the introduction of natural gas in Portugal.

As the main shareholder and with its concession for the import and transportation of natural gas to the north, south and central Lisbon, the objectives of GÁS DE PORTUGAL are as follows:-

- to ensure that as from 1997, natural gas becomes a reality in Portugal.

- to provide a high quality, piped gas industry in Portugal.

Within the European Union, natural gas already represents twenty per cent of primary energy, being a clean, combustible fuel of high efficiency. Its use in the production of electricity for industry and the domestic market is an important factor in both economic and social progress whilst at the same time helping to alleviate environmental degradation.

With its key role in the Portuguese energy sector, together with its entrepreneurial vision, GÁS DE PORTUGAL supports the efforts of the UN in its promotion of social progress and sustainable development.

We believe that together we can contribute to a better future for humankind.

Valdemar Neves, President

GDP ✒ GÁS DE PORTUGAL, SA

Av. Marechal Gomes da Costa, Cabo Ruivo, 1800 Lisbon, Portugal
Tel. 351 (1) 858 4321, Fax. 351 (1) 858 6743, Telex. 12864 PETRO P

members of the Court and the Registrar shall have their travelling expenses refunded.

8. The above salaries, allowances, and compensation shall be free of all taxation.

Article 33
The expenses of the Court shall be borne by the United Nations in such a manner as shall be decided by the General Assembly.

CHAPTER II
COMPETENCE OF THE COURT

Article 34
1. Only states may be parties in cases before the Court.
2. The Court, subject to and in conformity with its Rules, may request of public international organizations information relevant to cases before it, and shall receive such information presented by such organizations on their own initiative.
3. Whenever the construction of the constituent instrument of a public international organization or of an international convention adopted thereunder is in question in a case before the Court, the Registrar shall so notify the public international organization concerned and shall communicate to it copies of all the written proceedings.

Article 35
1. The Court shall be open to the states parties to the present Statute.
2. The conditions under which the Court shall be open to other states shall, subject to the special provisions contained in treaties in force, be laid down by the Security Council, but in no case shall such conditions place the parties in a position of inequality before the Court.
3. When a state which is not a Member of the United Nations is a party to a case, the Court shall fix the amount which that party is to contribute towards the expenses of the Court. This provision shall not apply if such state is bearing a share of the expenses of the Court.

Article 36
1. The jurisdiction of the Court comprises all cases which the parties refer to it and all matters specially provided for in the Charter of the United Nations or in treaties and conventions in force.
2. The states parties to the present Statute may at any time declare that they recognize as compulsory *ipso facto* and without special agreement, in relation to any other state accepting the same obligation, the jurisdiction of the Court in all legal disputes concerning:
a. the interpretation of a treaty;
b. any question of international law;
c. the existence of any fact which, if established, would constitute a breach of an international obligation;
d. the nature or extent of the reparation to be made for the breach of an international obligation.
3. The declarations referred to above may be made unconditionally or on condition of reciprocity on the part of several or certain states, or for a certain time.
4. Such declarations shall be deposited with the Secretary-General of the United Nations, who shall transmit copies thereof to the parties to the Statute and to the Registrar of the Court.
5. Declarations made under Article 36 of the Statute of the Permanent Court of International Justice and which are still in force shall be deemed, as between the parties to the present Statute, to be acceptances of the compulsory jurisdiction of the International Court of Justice for the period which they still have to run and in accordance with their terms.
6. In the event of a dispute as to whether the Court has jurisdiction, the matter shall be settled by the decision of the Court.

Article 37
Whenever a treaty or convention in force provides for reference of a matter to a tribunal to have been instituted by the League of Nations, or to the Permanent Court of International Justice, the matter shall, as between the parties to the present Statute, be referred to the International Court of Justice.

Article 38
1. The Court, whose function is to decide in accordance with international law such disputes as are submitted to it, shall apply:
a. international conventions, whether general or particular, establishing rules expressly recognized by the contesting states;
b. international custom, as evidence of a general practice accepted as law;
c. the general principles of law recognized by civilized nations;
d. subject to the provisions of Article 59, judicial decisions and the teachings of the most highly qualified publicists of the various nations, as subsidiary means for the determination of rules of law.
2. This provision shall not prejudice the power of the Court to decide a case *ex aequo et bono*, if the parties agree thereto.

CHAPTER III
PROCEDURE

Article 39
1. The official languages of the Court shall be French and English. If the parties agree that the case shall be conducted in French, the judgment shall be delivered in French. If the parties agree that the case shall be conducted in English, the judgment shall be delivered in English.
2. In the absence of an agreement as to which language shall be employed, each party may, in the pleadings, use the language which it prefers; the decision of the Court shall be given in French and English. In this case the Court shall at the same time determine which of the two texts shall be considered as authoritative.
3. The Court shall, at the request of any party, authorize a language other than French or English to be used by that party.

Article 40
1. Cases are brought before the Court, as the case may be, either by the notification of the special agreement or by a written application addressed to the Registrar. In either case the subject of the dispute and the parties shall be indicated.
2. The Registrar shall forthwith communicate the application to all concerned.
3. He shall also notify the Members of the United Nations through the Secretary-General, and also any other states entitled to appear before the Court.

Article 41
1. The Court shall have the power to indicate, if it considers that circumstances so require, any provisional measures which ought to be taken to preserve the respective rights of either party.
2. Pending the final decision, notice of the measures suggested shall forthwith be given to the parties and to the Security Council.

Article 42
1. The parties shall be represented by agents.
2. They may have the assistance of counsel or advocates before the Court.
3. The agents, counsel, and advocates of parties before the Court shall enjoy the privileges and immunities necessary to the independent exercise of their duties.

Article 43
1. The procedure shall consist of two parts: written and oral.
2. The written proceedings shall consist of the communication to the Court and to the parties of memorials, counter-memorials and, if necessary, replies; also all papers and documents in support.
3. These communications shall be made through the Registrar, in the order and within the time fixed by the Court.
4. A certified copy of every document produced by one party shall be communicated to the other party.
5. The oral proceedings shall consist of the hearing by the Court of witnesses, experts, agents, counsel, and advocates.

Article 44
1. For the service of all notices upon persons other than the agents, counsel, and advocates, the Court shall apply direct to the government of the state upon whose territory the notice has to be served.
2. The same provision shall apply whenever steps are to be taken to procure evidence on the spot.

Article 45
The hearing shall be under the control of the President or, if he is unable to preside, of the Vice-President; if neither is able to preside, the senior judge present shall preside.

Article 46
The hearing in Court shall be public, unless the Court shall decide otherwise, or unless the parties demand that the public be not admitted .

Article 47
1. Minutes shall be made at each hearing and signed by the Registrar and the President.
2. These minutes alone shall be authentic.

Article 48
The Court shall make orders for the conduct of the case, shall decide the form and time in which each party must conclude its arguments, and make all arrangements connected with the taking of evidence.

Article 49
The Court may, even before the hearing begins, call upon the agents to produce any document or to supply any explanations. Formal note shall be taken of any refusal.

Article 50
The Court may, at any time, entrust any individual, body, bureau,

commission, or other organization that it may select, with the task of carrying out an enquiry or giving an expert opinion.

Article 51

During the hearing any relevant questions are to be put to the witnesses and experts under the conditions laid down by the Court in the rules of procedure referred to in Article 30.

Article 52

After the Court has received the proofs and evidence within the time specified for the purpose, it may refuse to accept any further oral or written evidence that one party may desire to present unless the other side consents.

Article 53

1. Whenever one of the parties does not appear before the Court, or fails to defend its case, the other party may call upon the Court to decide in favour of its claim.
2. The Court must, before doing so, satisfy itself, not only that it has jurisdiction in accordance with Articles 36 and 37, but also that the claim is well founded in fact and law.

Article 54

1. When, subject to the control of the Court, the agents, counsel, and advocates have completed their presentation of the case, the President shall declare the hearing closed.
2. The Court shall withdraw to consider the judgment.
3. The deliberations of the Court shall take place in private and remain secret.

Article 55

1. All questions shall be decided by a majority of the judges present.
2. In the event of an equality of votes, the President or the judge who acts in his place shall have a casting vote.

Article 56

1. The judgment shall state the reasons on which it is based.
.2. It shall contain the names of the judges who have taken part in the decision.

Article 57

If the judgment does not represent in whole or in part the unanimous opinion of the judges, any judge shall be entitled to deliver a separate opinion.

Article 58

The judgment shall be signed by the President and by the Registrar. It shall be read in open court, due notice having been given to the agents.

Article 59

The decision of the Court has no binding force except between the parties and in respect of that particular case.

Article 60

The judgment is final and without appeal. In the event of dispute as to the meaning or scope of the judgment, the Court shall construe it upon the request of any party.

Article 61

1. An application for revision of a judgment may be made only when it is based upon the discovery of some fact of such a nature as to be a decisive factor, which fact was, when the judgment was given, unknown to the Court and also to the party claiming revision, always provided that such ignorance was not due to negligence.
2. The proceedings for revision shall be opened by a judgment of the Court expressly recording the existence of the new fact, recognizing that it has such a character as to lay the case open to revision, and declaring the application admissible on this ground.
3. The Court may require previous compliance with the terms of the judgment before it admits proceedings in revision.
4. The application for revision must be made at latest within six months of the discovery of the new fact.
5. No application for revision may be made after the lapse of ten years from the date of the judgment.

Article 62

1. Should a state consider that it has an interest of a legal nature which may be affected by the decision in the case, it may submit a request to the Court to be permitted to intervene.
2. It shall be for the Court to decide upon this request.

Article 63

1. Whenever the construction of a convention to which states other than those concerned in the case are parties is in question, the Registrar shall notify all such states forthwith.
2. Every state so notified has the right to intervene in the proceedings; but if it uses this right, the construction given by the judgment will be equally binding upon it

Article 64

Unless otherwise decided by the Court, each party shall bear its own costs.

CHAPTER IV
ADVISORY OPINIONS

Article 65

1. The Court may give an advisory opinion on any legal question at the request of whatever body may be authorized by or in accordance with the Charter of the United Nations to make such a request.
2. Questions upon which the advisory opinion of the Court is asked shall be laid before the Court by means of a written request containing an exact statement of the question upon which an opinion is required, and accompanied by all documents likely to throw light upon the question.

Article 66

1. The Registrar shall forthwith give notice of the request for an advisory opinion to all states entitled to appear before the Court.
2. The Registrar shall also, by means of a special and direct communication, notify any state entitled to appear before the Court or international organization considered by the Court, or, should it not be sitting, by the President, as likely to be able to furnish information on the question, that the Court will be prepared to receive, within a time limit to be fixed by the President, written statements, or to hear, at a public sitting to be held for the purpose, oral statements relating to the question.
3. Should any such state entitled to appear before the Court have failed to receive the special communication referred to in paragraph 2 of this Article, such state may express a desire to submit a written statement or to be heard; and the Court will decide.
4. States and organizations having presented written or oral statements or both shall be permitted to comment on the statements made by other states or organizations in the form, to the extent, and within the time limits which the Court, or, should it not be sitting, the President, shall decide in each particular case. Accordingly, the Registrar shall in due time communicate any such written statements to states and organizations having submitted similar statements.

Article 67

The Court shall deliver its advisory opinions in open court, notice having been given to the Secretary-General and to the representatives of Members of the United Nations, of other states and of international organizations immediately concerned.

Article 68

In the exercise of its advisory functions the Court shall further be guided by the provisions of the present Statute which apply in contentious cases to the extent to which it recognizes them to be applicable.

CHAPTER V
AMENDMENT

Article 69

Amendments to the present statute shall be effected by the same procedure as is provided by the Charter of the United Nations for amendments to that Charter, subject however to any provisions which the General Assembly upon recommendation of the Security Council may adopt concerning the participation of states which are parties to the present Statute but are not Members of the United Nations.

Article 70

The Court shall have power to propose such amendments to the present Statute as it may deem necessary, through written communications to the Secretary-General, for consideration in conformity with the provisions of Article 69.

An Agenda for Peace ~ *the tasks ahead*

Boutros Boutros-Ghali

Preventive Diplomacy, Peacemaking and Peace-keeping

Report of the Secretary-General pursuant to the statement adopted by the Summit Meeting of the Security Council on 31 January 1992

Introduction

1. IN ITS STATEMENT of 31 January 1992, adopted at the conclusion of the first meeting held by the Security Council at the level of Heads of State and Government, I was invited to prepare, for circulation to the Members of the United Nations by 1 July 1992, an "analysis and recommendations on ways of strengthening and making more efficient within the framework and provisions of the Charter the capacity of the United Nations for preventive diplomacy, for peacemaking and for peace-keeping."

2. The United Nations is a gathering of sovereign States and what it can do depends on the common ground that they create between them. The adversarial decades of the cold war made the original promise of the Organization impossible to fulfil. The January 1992 Summit therefore represented an unprecedented recommitment, at the highest political level, to the Purposes and Principles of the Charter.

3. In these past months a conviction has grown, among nations large and small, that an opportunity has been regained to achieve the great objectives of the Charter - a United Nations capable of maintaining international peace and security, of securing justice and human rights and of promoting, in the words of the Charter, "social progress and better standards of life in larger freedom". This opportunity must not be squandered. The Organization must never again be crippled as it was in the era that has now passed.

4. I welcome the invitation of the Security Council, early in my tenure as Secretary-General, to prepare this report. It draws upon ideas and proposals transmitted to me by Governments, regional agencies, non-governmental organizations, and institutions and individuals from many countries. I am grateful for these, even as I emphasize that the responsibility for this report is my own.

5. The sources of conflict and war are pervasive and deep. To reach them will require our utmost effort to enhance respect for human rights and fundamental freedoms, to promote sustainable economic and social development for wider prosperity, to alleviate distress and to curtail the existence and use of massively destructive weapons. The United Nations Conference on Environment and Development, the largest summit ever held, has just met at Rio de Janeiro. Next year will see the second World Conference on Human Rights. In 1994 Population and Development will be addressed. In 1995 the World Conference on Women will take place, and a World Summit for Social Development has been proposed. Throughout my term as Secretary-General I shall be addressing all these great issues. I bear them all in mind as, in the present report, I turn to the problems that the Council has specifically requested I consider: preventive diplomacy, peacemaking and peace-keeping – to which I have added a closely related concept, post-conflict peace-building.

6. The manifest desire of the membership to work together is a new source of strength in our common endeavour. Success is far from certain, however. While my report deals with ways to improve the Organization's capacity to pursue and preserve peace, it is crucial for all Member States to bear in mind that the search for improved mechanisms and techniques will be of little significance unless this new spirit of commonality is propelled by the will to take the hard decisions demanded by this time of opportunity.

7. It is therefore with a sense of moment, and with gratitude, that I present this report to the Members of the United Nations.

I. The changing context

8. IN THE COURSE of the past few years the immense ideological barrier that for decades gave rise to distrust and hostility-and the terrible tools of destruction that were their inseparable companions-has collapsed. Even as the issues between States north and south grow more acute, and call for attention at the highest levels of government, the improvement in relations between States east and west affords new possibilities, some already realized, to meet successfully threats to common security.

9. Authoritarian regimes have given way to more democratic forces and responsive Governments. The form, scope and intensity of these processes differ from Latin America to Africa to Europe to Asia, but they are sufficiently similar to indicate a global phenomenon. Parallel to these political changes, many States are seeking more open forms of economic policy, creating a worldwide sense of dynamism and movement.

10. To the hundreds of millions, who gained their independence in the surge of decolonization following the creation of the United Nations, have been added millions more who have recently gained freedom. Once again new States are taking their seats in the General Assembly. Their arrival reconfirms the importance and indispensability of the sovereign State as the fundamental entity of the international community.

11. We have entered a time of global transition marked by uniquely contradictory trends. Regional and continental associations of States are evolving ways to deepen cooperation and ease some of the contentious characteristics of sovereign and nationalistic rivalries. National boundaries are blurred by advanced communications and global commerce, and by the decisions of States to yield some sovereign prerogatives to larger, common political associations. At the same time, however, fierce new assertions of nationalism and sovereignty spring up, and the cohesion of States is threatened by brutal ethnic, religious, social, cultural or linguistic strife. Social peace is challenged on the one hand by new assertions of discriminating and exclusion and, on the other, by acts of terrorism seeking to undermine evolution and change through democratic means.

12. The concept of peace is easy to grasp; that of international security is more complex, for a pattern of contradictions has arisen here as well. As major nuclear powers have begun to negotiate arms reduction agreements, the proliferation of weapons of mass destruction threatens to increase and conventional arms continue to be amassed in many parts of the world. As racism becomes recognized for the destructive force it is and as apartheid is being dismantled, new racial tensions are rising and finding expression in violence. Technological advances are altering the nature and expectation of life all over the globe. The revolution in communications has united the world in awareness, in aspiration and in greater solidarity against injustice. But progress also brings new risks for stability: ecological damage, disruption of family and community life, greater intrusion into the lives and rights of individuals.

13. This new dimension of insecurity must not be allowed to obscure the continuing and devastating problems of unchecked population growth, crushing debt burdens, barriers to trade, drugs and the growing disparity between rich and poor. Poverty, disease, famine, oppression and despair abound, joining to produce 17 million refugees, 20 million displaced persons and massive migrations of peoples within and beyond national borders. These are both sources and consequences of conflict that require the ceaseless attention and the highest priority in the efforts of the United Nations. A porous ozone shield could pose a greater threat to an exposed population than a hostile army. Drought and disease can decimate no less mercilessly than the weapons of war. So at this moment of renewed opportunity, the efforts of the Organization to build peace, stability and security must encompass matters beyond military threats in order to break the fetters of strife and warfare that have characterized the past. But armed conflicts today, as they have throughout history, continue to bring fear and horror to humanity, requiring our urgent involvement to try to prevent, contain and bring them to an end.

14. Since the creation of the United Nations in 1945, over 100 major conflicts around the world have left some 20 million dead. The United Nations was rendered powerless to deal with many of these crises because of the vetoes - 279 of them - cast in the Security Council, which were a vivid expression of the divisions of that period.

15. With the end of the cold war there have been no such vetoes since 31 May 1990, and demands on the United Nations have surged. Its security arm, once disabled by circumstances it was not created or equipped to control, has emerged as a central instrument for the prevention and resolution of conflicts and for the preservation of peace. Our aims must be:

To seek to identify at the earliest possible stage situations that

50 YEARS OF EFFORT FOR A BETTER WORLD

GEOTHERMIC WELL IN PRODUCTION

Electricity is an essential factor in the economic development of a country.

Empresa Nacional de Electricidad S.A. (ENDE), created over thirty three years ago, is responsible for the development of natural resources and the supply of electric power in the Republic of Bolivia.

Through the assistance of the United Nations and its agencies, ENDE has embarked upon a number of projects, including the pioneering geothermic project of Laguna Colorada which began in 1970 and involved exploratory missions and the drilling of 6 wells.

ENDE salutes the United Nations on its 50th Anniversary and is proud to commemorate the foundation of the organization and its efforts to promote development, health and education for all.

**EMPRESA NACIONAL
DE ELECTRICIDAD S.A.
ENDE**

Calle Colombia No. 0-0655
Tel. 59512 - Casilla No. 565
Fax. 42700
Cochabamba, Bolivia

could produce conflict, and to try through diplomacy to remove the sources of danger before violence results;

- Where conflict erupts, to engage in peacemaking aimed at resolving the issues that have led to conflict;
- Through peace-keeping, to work to preserve peace, however fragile, where fighting has been halted and to assist in implementing agreements achieved by the peace-makers;
- To stand ready to assist in peace-building in its differing contexts: rebuilding the institutions and infrastructures of nations torn by civil war and strife; and building bonds of peaceful mutual benefit among nations formerly at war;
- And in the largest sense, to address the deepest causes of conflict: economic despair, social injustice and political oppression. It is possible to discern an increasingly common moral perception that spans the world's nations and peoples, and which is finding expression in international laws, many owing their genesis to the work of this Organization.

16. This wider mission for the world Organization will demand the concerted attention and effort of individual States, of regional and non-governmental organizations and of all of the United Nations system, with each of the principal organs functioning in the balance and harmony that the Charter requires. The Security Council has been assigned by all Member States the primary responsibility for the maintenance of international peace and security under the Charter. In its broadest sense this responsibility must be shared by the General Assembly and by all the functional elements of the world Organization. Each has a special and indispensable role to play in an integrated approach to human security. The Secretary-General's contribution rests on the pattern of trust and cooperation established between him and the deliberative organs of the United Nations.

17. The foundation-stone of this work is and must remain the State. Respect for its fundamental sovereignty and integrity are crucial to any common international progress. The time of absolute and exclusive sovereignty, however, has passed; its theory was never matched by reality. It is the task of leaders of States today to understand this and to find a balance between the needs of good internal governance and the requirements of an ever more interdependent world. Commerce, communications and environmental matters transcend administrative borders; but inside those borders is where individuals carry out the first order of their economic, political and social lives. The United Nations has not closed its door. Yet if every ethnic, religious or linguistic group claimed statehood, there would be no limit to fragmentation and peace, security and economic well-being for all would become ever more difficult to achieve.

18. One requirement for solutions to these problems lies in commitment to human rights with a special sensitivity to those of minorities, whether ethnic, religious, social or linguistic. The League of Nations provided a machinery for the international protection of minorities. The General Assembly soon will have before it a declaration on the rights of minorities. That instrument, together with the increasingly effective machinery of the United Nations dealing with human rights, should enhance the situation of minorities as well as the stability of States.

19. Globalism and nationalism need not be viewed as opposing trends, doomed to spur each other on to extremes of reaction. The healthy globalization of contemporary life requires in the first instance solid identities and fundamental freedoms. The sovereignty, territorial integrity and independence of States within the established international system, and the principle of self-determination for peoples, both of great value and importance, must not be permitted to work against each other in the period ahead. Respect for democratic principles at all levels of social existence is crucial: in communities, within States and within the community of States. Our constant duty should be to maintain the integrity of each while finding a balanced design for all.

II. Definitions

20. THE TERMS preventive diplomacy, peacemaking and peace-keeping are integrally related and as used in this report are defined as follows:
- *Preventive diplomacy* is action to prevent disputes from arising between parties, to prevent existing disputes from escalating into conflicts and to limit the spread of the latter when they occur.
- *Peacemaking* is action to bring hostile parties to agreement, essentially through such peaceful means as those foreseen in Chapter VI of the Charter of the United Nations.
- *Peace-keeping* is the deployment of a United Nations presence in the field, hitherto with the consent of all the parties concerned, normally involving United Nations military and/or police personnel and frequently civilians as well. Peace-keeping is a technique that expands the possibilities for both the prevention of conflict and the making of peace.

21. The present report in addition will address the critically related concept of post-conflict *peace-building* - action to identify and support structures which will tend to strengthen and solidify peace in order to avoid a relapse into conflict. Preventive diplomacy seeks to resolve disputes before violence breaks out; peacemaking and peace-keeping are required to halt conflicts and preserve peace once it is attained. If successful, they strengthen the opportunity for post-conflict peace-building, which can prevent the recurrence of violence among nations and peoples.

22. These four areas for action, taken together, and carried out with the backing of all Members, offer a coherent contribution towards securing peace in the spirit of the Charter. The United Nations has extensive experience not only in these fields, but in the wider realm of work for peace in which these four fields are set. Initiatives on decolonization, on the environment and sustainable development, on population, on the eradication of disease, on disarmament and on the growth of international law - these and many others have contributed immeasurably to the foundations for a peaceful world. The world has often been rent by conflict and plagued by massive human suffering and deprivation. Yet it would have been far more so without the continuing efforts of the United Nations. This wide experience must be taken into account in assessing the potential of the United Nations in maintaining international security not only in its traditional sense, but in the new dimensions presented by the era ahead.

III. Preventive diplomacy

23. THE MOST desirable and efficient employment of diplomacy is to ease tensions before they result in conflict - or, if conflict breaks out, to act swiftly to contain it and resolve its underlying causes. Preventive diplomacy may be performed by the Secretary-General personally or through senior staff or specialized agencies and programmes, by the Security Council or the General Assembly, and by regional organizations in cooperation with the United Nations. Preventive diplomacy requires measures to create confidence; it needs early warning based on information gathering and informal or formal fact-finding; it may also involve preventive deployment and, in some situations, demilitarized zones.

MEASURES TO BUILD CONFIDENCE

24. Mutual confidence and good faith are essential to reducing the likelihood of conflict between States. Many such measures are available to Governments that have the will to employ them. Systematic exchange of military missions, formation of regional or subregional risk reduction centres, arrangements for the free flow of information, including the monitoring of regional arms agreements, are examples. I ask all regional organizations to consider what further confidence-building measures might be applied in their areas and to inform the United Nations of the results. I will undertake periodic consultations on confidence-building measures with parties to potential, current or past disputes and with regional organizations, offering such advisory assistance as the Secretariat can provide.

FACT FINDING

25. Preventive steps must be based upon timely and accurate knowledge of the facts. Beyond this, an understanding of developments and global trends, based on sound analysis, is required. And the willingness to take appropriate preventive action is essential. Given the economic and social roots of many potential conflicts, the information needed by the United Nations now must encompass economic and social trends as well as political developments that may lead to dangerous tensions.

a) An increased resort to fact finding is needed, in accordance with the Charter, initiated either by the Secretary-General, to enable him to meet his responsibilities under the Charter, including Article 99, or by the Security Council or the General Assembly. Various forms may be employed selectively as the situation requires. A request by a State for the sending of a United Nations fact-finding mission to its territory should be considered without undue delay.

b) Contacts with the Governments of Member States can provide the Secretary-General with detailed information on issues of concern. I ask that all Member States be ready to provide the information needed for effective preventive diplomacy. I will supplement my own contacts by regularly sending senior officials on missions for consultations in capitals or other locations. Such contacts are essential to gain insight into a situation and to assess its potential ramifications.

c) Formal fact-finding can be mandated by the Security Council or by the General Assembly, either of which may elect to send a mission under its immediate authority or may invite the Secretary-General to take the necessary steps, including the designation of a special envoy. In addition to collecting information on which a decision for further action can be taken, such a mission can in some instances help to defuse a dispute by its presence, indicating to the parties that the Organization, and in particular the Security Council, is actively seized of the matter as a present or potential threat to international security.

d) In exceptional circumstances the Council may meet away from Headquarters as the Charter provides, in order not only to inform itself directly, but also to bring the authority of the Organization to bear on a given situation.

EARLY WARNING

26. In recent years the United Nations system has been developing a valuable network of early warning systems concerning environmental threats, the risk of nuclear accident, natural disasters, mass movements of populations, the threat of famine and the spread of disease. There is a need, however, to strengthen arrangements in such a manner that information from these sources can be synthesized with political indicators to assess whether a threat to peace exists and to analyse what action might be taken by the United Nations to alleviate it. This is a process that will continue to require the close cooperation of the various specialized agencies and functional offices of the United Nations. The analyses and recommendations for preventive action that emerge will be made available by me, as appropriate, to the Security Council and other United Nations organs. I recommend in addition that the Security Council invite a reinvigorated and reconstructed Economic and Social Council to provide reports, in accordance with Article 65 of the Charter, on those economic and social developments that may, unless mitigated, threaten international peace and security.

27. Regional arrangements and organizations have an important role in early warning. I ask regional organizations that have not yet sought observer status at the United Nations to do so and to be linked, through appropriate arrangements, with the security mechanisms of this Organization.

PREVENTIVE DEPLOYMENT

28. United Nations operations in areas of crisis have generally been established after conflict has occurred. The time has come to plan for circumstances warranting preventive deployment, which could take place in a variety of instances and ways. For example, in conditions of national crisis there could be preventive deployment at the request of the Government or all parties concerned, or with their consent; in inter-State disputes such deployment could take place when two countries feel that a United Nations presence on both sides of their border can discourage hostilities; furthermore, preventive deployment could take place when a country feels threatened and requests the deployment of an appropriate United Nations presence along its side of the border alone. In each situation, the mandate and composition of the United Nations presence would need to be carefully devised and be clear to all.

29. In conditions of crisis within a country, when the Government requests or all parties consent, preventive deployment could help in a number of ways to alleviate suffering and to limit or control violence. Humanitarian assistance, impartially provided, could be of critical importance; assistance in maintaining security, whether through military, police or civilian personnel, could save lives and develop conditions of safety in which negotiations can be held; the United Nations could also help in conciliation efforts if this should be the wish of the parties. In certain circumstances, the United Nations may well need to draw upon the specialized skills and resources of various parts of the United Nations system; such operations may also on occasion require the participation of non-governmental organizations.

30. In these situations of internal crisis the United Nations will need to respect the sovereignty of the State; to do otherwise would not be in accordance with the understanding of Member States in accepting the principles of the Charter. The Organization must remain mindful of the carefully negotiated balance of the guiding principles annexed to General Assembly resolution 46/182 of 19 December 1991. Those guidelines stressed, *inter alia*, that humanitarian assistance must be provided in accordance with the principles of humanity, neutrality and impartiality; that the sovereignty, territorial integrity and national unity of States must be fully respected in accordance with the Charter of the United Nations; and that, in this context, humanitarian assistance should be provided with the consent of the affected country and, in principle, on the basis of an appeal by that country. The guidelines also stressed the responsibility of States to take care of the victims of emergencies occurring on their territory and the need for access to those requiring humanitarian assistance. In the light of these guidelines, a Government's request for United Nations involvement, or consent to it, would not be an infringement of that State's sovereignty or be contrary to Article 2, paragraph 7, of the Charter which refers to matters essentially within the domestic jurisdiction of any State.

31. In inter-State disputes, when both parties agree, I recommend that if the Security Council concludes that the likelihood of hostilities between neighbouring countries could be removed by the preventive deployment of a United Nations presence on the territory of each State, such action should be taken. The nature of the tasks to be performed would determine the composition of the United Nations presence.

32. In cases where one nation fears a cross-border attack, if the Security Council concludes that a United Nations presence on one side of the border, with the consent only of the requesting country, would serve to deter conflict, I recommend that preventive deployment take place. Here again, the specific nature of the situation would determine the mandate and the personnel required to fulfil it.

DEMILITARIZED ZONES

33. In the past, demilitarized zones have been established by agreement of the parties at the conclusion of a conflict. In addition to the deployment of United Nations personnel in such zones as part of peace-keeping operations, consideration should now be given to the usefulness of such zones as a form of preventive deployment, on both sides of a border, with the agreement of the two parties, as a means of separating potential belligerents, or on one side of the line, at the request of one party, for the purpose of removing any pretext for attack. Demilitarized zones would serve as symbols of the international community's concern that conflict be prevented.

IV. Peacemaking

34. BETWEEN the tasks of seeking to prevent conflict and keeping the peace lies the responsibility to try to bring hostile parties to agreement by peaceful means. Chapter VI of the Charter sets forth a comprehensive list of such means for the resolution of conflict. These have been amplified in various declarations adopted by the General Assembly, including the Manila Declaration of 1982 on the Peaceful Settlement of International Disputes and the 1988 Declaration on the Prevention and Removal of Disputes and Situations Which May Threaten International Peace and Security and on the Role of the United Nations in this Field. They have also been the subject of various resolutions of the General Assembly, including resolution 44/21 of 15 November 1989 on enhancing international peace, security and international cooperation in all its aspects in accordance with the Charter of the United Nations. The United Nations has had wide experience in the application of these peaceful means. If conflicts have gone unresolved, it is not because techniques for peaceful settlement were unknown or inadequate. The fault lies first in the lack of political will of parties to seek a solution to their differences through such means as are suggested in Chapter VI of the Charter, and second, in the lack of leverage at the disposal of a third party if this is the procedure chosen. The indifference of the international community to a problem, or the marginalization of it, can also thwart the possibilities of solution. We must look primarily to these areas if we hope to enhance the capacity of the Organization for achieving peaceful settlements.

35. The present determination in the Security Council to resolve international disputes in the manner foreseen in the Charter has opened the way for a more active Council role. With greater unity has come leverage and persuasive power to lead hostile parties towards negotiations. I urge the Council to take full advantage of the provisions of the Charter under which it may recommend appropriate procedures or methods for dispute settlement and, if all the parties to a dispute so request, make recommendations to the parties for a pacific settlement of the dispute.

36. The General Assembly, like the Security Council and the Secretary-General, also has an important role assigned to it under the Charter for the maintenance of international peace and security. As a universal forum, its capacity to consider and recommend appropriate action must be recognized. To that end it is essential to promote its utilization by all Member States so as to bring greater influence to bear in pre-empting or containing situations which are likely to threaten international peace and security.

37. Mediation and negotiation can be undertaken by an individual designated by the Security Council, by the General Assembly or by the Secretary-General. There is a long history of the utilization by the United Nations of distinguished statesmen to facilitate the processes of peace. They can bring a personal prestige that, in addition to their experience, can encourage the parties to enter serious negotiations. There is a wide willingness to serve in this capacity, from which I shall continue to benefit as the need arises. Frequently it is the Secretary-General himself who undertakes the task. While the mediator's effectiveness is enhanced by strong and evident support from the Council, the General Assembly and the relevant Member States acting in their national capacity, the good

offices of the Secretary-General may at times be employed most effectively when conducted independently of the deliberative bodies. Close and continuous consultation between the Secretary-General and the Security Council is, however, essential to ensure full awareness of how the Council's influence can best be applied and to develop a common strategy for the peaceful settlement of specific disputes.

THE WORLD COURT

38. The docket of the International Court of Justice has grown fuller but it remains an under-used resource for the peaceful adjudication of disputes. Greater reliance on the Court would be an important contribution to United Nations peacemaking. In this connection, I call attention to the power of the Security Council under Articles 36 and 37 of the Charter to recommend to Member States the submission of a dispute to the International Court of Justice, arbitration or other dispute settlement mechanisms. I recommend that the Secretary-General be authorized, pursuant to article 96, paragraph 2, of the Charter, to take advantage of the advisory competence of the Court and that other United Nations organs that already enjoy such authorization turn to the Court more frequently for advisory opinions.

39. I recommend the following steps to reinforce the role of the International Court of Justice:

(a) All Member States should accept the general jurisdiction of the International Court under Article 36 of its Statute, without any reservation, before the end of the United Nations Decade of International Law in the year 2000. In instances where domestic structures prevent this, States should agree bilaterally or multilaterally to a comprehensive list of matters they are willing to submit to the Court and should withdraw their reservations to its jurisdiction in the dispute settlement clauses of multilateral treaties;

(b) When submission of a dispute to the full Court is not practical, the Chambers jurisdiction should be used;

(c) States should support the Trust Fund established to assist countries unable to afford the cost involved in bringing a dispute to the Court, and such countries should take full advantage of the Fund in order to resolve their disputes.

AMELIORATION THROUGH ASSISTANCE

40. Peacemaking is at times facilitated by international action to ameliorate circumstances that have contributed to the dispute or conflict. If, for instance, assistance to displaced persons within a society is essential to a solution, then the United Nations should be able to draw upon the resources of all agencies and programmes concerned. At present, there is no adequate mechanism in the United Nations through which the Security Council, the General Assembly or the Secretary-General can mobilize the resources needed for such positive leverage and engage the collective efforts of the United Nations system for the peaceful resolution of a conflict. I have raised this concept in the Administrative Committee on Coordination, which brings together the executive heads of United Nations agencies and programmes; we are exploring methods by which the inter-agency system can improve its contribution to the peaceful resolution of disputes.

SANCTIONS AND SPECIAL ECONOMIC PROBLEMS

41. In circumstances when peacemaking requires the imposition of sanctions under Article 41 of the Charter, it is important that States confronted with special economic problems not only have the right to consult the Security Council regarding such problems, as Article 50 provides, but also have a realistic possibility of having their difficulties addressed. I recommend that the Security Council devise a set of measures involving the financial institutions and other components of the United Nations system that can be put in place to insulate States from such difficulties. Such measures would be a matter of equity and a means of encouraging States to cooperate with decisions of the Council.

USE OF MILITARY FORCE

42. It is the essence of the concept of collective security as contained in the Charter that if peaceful means fail, the measures provided in Chapter VII should be used, on the decision of the Security Council, to maintain or restore international peace and security in the face of a "threat to the peace, breach of the peace, or act of aggression". The Security Council has not so far made use of the most coercive of these measures - the action by military force foreseen in Article 42. In the situation between Iraq and Kuwait, the Council chose to authorize Member States to take measures on its behalf. The Charter, however, provides a detailed approach which now merits the attention of all Member States.

43. Under Article 42 of the Charter, the Security Council has the authority to take military action to maintain or restore international peace and security. While such action should only be taken when all peaceful means have failed, the option of taking it is essential to the credibility of the United Nations as a guarantor of international security. This will require bringing into being, through negotiations, the special agreements foreseen in Article 43 of the Charter, whereby Member States undertake to make armed forces, assistance and facilities available to the Security Council for the purposes stated in Article 42, not only on an ad hoc basis but on a permanent basis. Under the political circumstances that now exist for the first time since the Charter was adopted, the long-standing obstacles to the conclusion of such special agreements should no longer prevail. The ready availability of armed forces on call could serve, in itself, as a means of deterring breaches of the peace since a potential aggressor would know that the Council had at its disposal a means of response. Forces under Article 43 may perhaps never be sufficiently large or well enough equipped to deal with a threat from a major army equipped with sophisticated weapons. They would be useful, however, in meeting any threat posed by a military force of a lesser order. I recommend that the Security Council initiate negotiations in accordance with Article 43, supported by the Military Staff Committee, which may be augmented if necessary by others in accordance with Article 47, paragraph 2, of the Charter. It is my view that the role of the Military Staff Committee should be seen in the context of Chapter VII, and not that of the planning or conduct of peace-keeping operations.

PEACE-ENFORCEMENT UNITS

44. The mission of forces under Article 43 would be to respond to outright aggression, imminent or actual. Such forces are not likely to be available for some time to come. Cease-fires have often been agreed to but not complied with, and the United Nations has sometimes been called upon to send forces to restore and maintain the cease-fire. This task can on occasion exceed the mission of peace-keeping forces and the expectations of peace-keeping force contributors. I recommend that the Council consider the utilization of peace-enforcement units in clearly defined circumstances and with their terms of reference specified in advance. Such units from Member States would be available on call and would consist of troops that have volunteered for such service. They would have to be more heavily armed than peace-keeping forces and would need to undergo extensive preparatory training within their national forces. Deployment and operation of such forces would be under the authorization of the Security Council and would, as in the case of peace-keeping forces, be under the command of the Secretary-General. I consider such peace-enforcement units to be warranted as a provisional measure under Article 40 of the Charter. Such peace-enforcement units should not be confused with the forces that may eventually be constituted under Article 43 to deal with acts of aggression or with the military personnel which Governments may agree to keep on stand-by for possible contribution to peace-keeping operations.

45. Just as diplomacy will continue across the span of all the activities dealt with in the present report, so there may not be a dividing line between peacemaking and peace-keeping. Peacemaking is often a prelude to peace-keeping - just as the deployment of a United Nations presence in the field may expand possibilities for the prevention of conflict, facilitate the work of peacemaking and in many cases serve as a prerequisite for peace-building.

V. Peace-keeping

46. PEACE-KEEPING can rightly be called the invention of the United Nations. It has brought a degree of stability to numerous areas of tension around the world.

INCREASING DEMANDS

47. Thirteen peace-keeping operations were established between the years 1945 and 1987; 13 others since then. An estimated 528,000 military, police and civilian personnel had served under the flag of the United Nations until January 1992. Over 800 of them from 43 countries have died in the service of the Organization. The costs of these operations have aggregated some $8.3 billion till 1992. The unpaid arrears towards them stand at over $800 million, which represent a debt owed by the Organization to the troop-contributing countries. Peace-keeping operations approved at present are estimated to cost close to $3 billion in the current 12 month period, while patterns of payment are unacceptably slow. Against this, global defence expenditures at the end of the last decade had approached $1 trillion a year, or $2 million per minute.

48. The contrast between the costs of United Nations peace-keeping and the costs of the alternative, war - between the demands of the

SO THAT THEY MAY HAVE LIGHT, AND HAVE IT MORE ABUNDANTLY

The Electricity of Lebanon salutes the United Nations for 50 years of relentless efforts, so that the nations of the world remain united. One might wonder what is in common between the Electricity of Lebanon and the organization of the United Nations.  Aside from the fact that they both are noble institutions, keen on fulfilling their objectives while continuously pushing the limits, the similarity seems to stop here. Not quite. Because one fundamental task bonds the two institutions together. They both shed light, one on the present, the other on the future.

ELECTRICITE DU LIBAN

Organization and the means provided to meet them - would be farcical were the consequences not so damaging to global stability and to the credibility of the Organization. At a time when nations and peoples increasingly are looking to the United Nations for assistance in keeping the peace - and holding it responsible when this cannot be so - fundamental decisions must be taken to enhance the capacity of the Organization in this innovative and productive exercise of its function. I am conscious that the present volume and unpredictability of peace-keeping assessments poses real problems for some Member States. For this reason, I strongly support proposals in some Member States for their peace-keeping contributions to be financed from defence, rather than foreign affairs budgets and I recommend such action to others. I urge the General Assembly to encourage this approach.

49. The demands on the United Nations for peace-keeping, and peace-building, operations in the coming years continue to challenge the capacity, the political and financial will and the creativity of the Secretariat and Member States. Like the Security Council, I welcome the increase and broadening of the tasks of peace-keeping operations.

NEW DEPARTURES IN PEACE-KEEPING

50. The nature of peace-keeping operations has evolved rapidly in recent years. The established principles and practices of peace-keeping have responded flexibly to new demands of recent years, and the basic conditions for success remain unchanged: a clear and practicable mandate; the cooperation of the parties in implementing that mandate; the continuing support of the Security Council; the readiness of Member States to contribute the military, police and civilian personnel, including specialists, required; effective United Nations command at Headquarters and in the field; and adequate financial and logistic support. As the international climate has changed and peace-keeping operations are increasingly fielded to help implement settlements that have been negotiated by peacemakers, a new array of demands and problems has emerged regarding logistics, equipment, personnel and finance, all of which could be corrected if Member States so wished and were ready to make the necessary resources available.

PERSONNEL

51. Member States are keen to participate in peace-keeping operations. Military observers and infantry are invariably available in the required numbers, but logistic units present a greater problem, as few armies can afford to spare such units for an extended period. Member States were requested in 1990 to state what military personnel they were in principle prepared to make available; few replied. I reiterate the request to all Member States to reply frankly and promptly. Stand-by arrangements should be confirmed, as appropriate, through exchanges of letters between the Secretariat and Member States concerning the kind and number of skilled personnel they will be prepared to offer the United Nations as the needs of new operations arise.

52. Increasingly, peace-keeping requires that civilian political officers, human rights monitors, electoral officials, refugee and humanitarian aid specialists and police play as central a role as the military. Police personnel have proved increasingly difficult to obtain in the numbers required. I recommend that arrangements be reviewed and improved for training peace-keeping personnel - civilian, police, or military - using the varied capabilities of Member State Governments, of non-governmental organizations and the facilities of the Secretariat. As efforts go forward to include additional States as contributors, some States with considerable potential should focus on language training for police contingents which may serve with the Organization. As for the United Nations itself, special personnel procedures, including incentives, should be instituted to permit the rapid transfer of Secretariat staff members to service with peace-keeping operations. The strength and capability of military staff serving in the Secretariat should be augmented to meet new and heavier requirements.

LOGISTICS

53. Not all Governments can provide their battalions with the equipment they need for service abroad. While some equipment is provided by troop-contributing countries, a great deal has to come from the United Nations, including equipment to fill gaps in under-equipped national units. The United Nations has no standing stock of such equipment. Orders must be placed with manufacturers, which creates a number of difficulties. A pre-positioned stock of basic peace-keeping equipment should be established, so that at least some vehicles, communications equipment, generators, etc., would be immediately available at the start of an operation. Alternatively, Governments should commit themselves to keeping certain equipment, specified by the Secretary-General, on stand-by for immediate sale, loan or donation to the United Nations when required.

54. Member States in a position to do so should make air and sea-lift capacity available to the United Nations free of cost or at lower than commercial rates, as was the practice until recently.

VI. Post-conflict peace-building

55. PEACEMAKING and peace-keeping operations, to be truly successful, must come to include comprehensive efforts to identify and support structures which will tend to consolidate peace and advance a sense of confidence and well-being among people. Through agreements ending civil strife, these may include disarming the previously warring parties and the restoration of order, the custody and possible destruction of weapons, repatriating refugees, advisory and training support for security personnel, monitoring elections, advancing efforts to protect human rights, reforming or strengthening governmental institutions and promoting formal and informal processes of political participation.

56. In the aftermath of international war, post-conflict peace-building may take the form of concrete cooperative projects which link two or more countries in a mutually beneficial undertaking that can not only contribute to economic and social development but also enhance the confidence that is so fundamental to peace. I have in mind, for example, projects that bring States together to develop agriculture, improve transportation or utilize resources such as water or electricity that they need to share, or joint programmes through which barriers between nations are brought down by means of freer travel, cultural exchanges and mutually beneficial youth and educational projects. Reducing hostile perceptions through educational exchanges and curriculum reform may be essential to forestall a re-emergence of cultural and national tensions which could spark renewed hostilities.

57. In surveying the range of efforts for peace, the concept of peace-building as the construction of a new environment should be viewed as the counterpart of preventive diplomacy, which seeks to avoid the breakdown of peaceful conditions. When conflict breaks out, mutually reinforcing efforts at peacemaking and peace-keeping come into play. Once these have achieved their objectives, only sustained, cooperative work to deal with underlying economic, social, cultural and humanitarian problems can place an achieved peace on a durable foundation. Preventive diplomacy is to avoid a crisis; post-conflict peace-building is to prevent a recurrence.

58. Increasingly it is evident that peace-building after civil or international strife must address the serious problem of land mines, many tens of millions of which remain scattered in present or former combat zones. De-mining should be emphasized in the terms of reference of peace-keeping operations and is crucially important in the restoration of activity when peace-building is under way: agriculture cannot be revived without de-mining and the restoration of transport may require the laying of hard surface roads to prevent re-mining. In such instances, the link becomes evident between peace-keeping and peace-building. Just as demilitarized zones may serve the cause of preventive diplomacy and preventive deployment to avoid conflict, so may demilitarization assist in keeping the peace or in post-conflict peace-building, as a measure for heightening the sense of security and encouraging the parties to turn their energies to the work of peaceful restoration of their societies.

59. There is a new requirement for technical assistance which the United Nations has an obligation to develop and provide when requested: support for the transformation of deficient national structures and capabilities; and for the strengthening of new democratic institutions. The authority of the United Nations system to act in this field would rest on the consensus that social peace is as important as strategic or political peace. There is an obvious connection between democratic practices - such as the rule of law and transparency in decision-making - and the achievement of true peace and security in any new and stable political order. These elements of good governance need to be promoted at all levels of international and national political communities.

VII. Cooperation with regional arrangements and organizations

60. THE COVENANT of the League of Nations, in its Article 21, noted the validity of regional understandings for securing the maintenance of peace. The Charter devotes Chapter VIII to regional arrangements or agencies for dealing with such matters relating to the maintenance of international peace and security as are appropriate for regional action and consistent with the Purposes and Principles of the United Nations. The cold war impaired the proper use of Chapter VIII and indeed, in that era, regional arrangements worked on occasion against resolving disputes in the manner foreseen in the Charter.

61. The Charter deliberately provides no precise definition of regional arrangements and agencies, thus allowing useful flexibility for undertakings by a group of States to deal with a matter appropriate for regional action which also could contribute to the maintenance of international peace and security. Such associations or entities could include treaty-based organizations, whether created before or after the founding of the United Nations, regional organizations for mutual security and defence, organizations for general regional development or for cooperation on a particular economic topic or function, and groups created to deal with a specific political, economic or social issue of current concern.

62. In this regard, the United Nations has recently encouraged a rich variety of complementary efforts. Just as no two regions or situations are the same, so the design of cooperative work and its division of labour must adapt to the realities of each case with flexibility and creativity. In Africa, three different regional groups - the Organization of African Unity, the League of Arab States and the Organization of the Islamic Conference - joined efforts with the United Nations regarding Somalia. In the Asian context, the Association of South-East Asian Nations and individual States from several regions were brought together with the parties to the Cambodian conflict at an international conference in Paris, to work with the United Nations. For El Salvador, a unique arrangement - "The Friends of the Secretary-General" - contributed to agreements reached through the mediation of the Secretary-General. The end of the war in Nicaragua involved a highly complex effort which was initiated by leaders of the region and conducted by individual States, groups of States and the Organization of American States. Efforts undertaken by the European Community and its member States, with the support of States participating in the Conference on Security and Cooperation in Europe, have been of central importance in dealing with the crisis in the Balkans and neighbouring areas.

63. In the past, regional arrangements often were created because of the absence of a universal system for collective security; thus their activities could on occasion work at cross-purposes with the sense of solidarity required for the effectiveness of the world Organization. But in this new era of opportunity, regional arrangements or agencies can render great service if their activities are undertaken in a manner consistent with the Purposes and Principles of the Charter, and if their relationship with the United Nations, and particularly the Security Council, is governed by Chapter VIII.

64. It is not the purpose of the present report to set forth any formal pattern of relationship between regional organizations and the United Nations, or to call for any specific division of labour. What is clear, however, is that regional arrangements or agencies in many cases possess a potential that should be utilized in serving the functions covered in this report: preventive diplomacy, peace-keeping, peacemaking and post-conflict peace-building. Under the Charter, the Security Council has and will continue to have primary responsibility for maintaining international peace and security, but regional action as a matter of decentralization, delegation and cooperation with United Nations efforts could not only lighten the burden of the Council but also contribute to a deeper sense of participation, consensus and democratization in international affairs.

65. Regional arrangements and agencies have not in recent decades been considered in this light, even when originally designed in part for a role in maintaining or restoring peace within their regions of the world. Today a new sense exists that they have contributions to make. Consultations between the United Nations and regional arrangements or agencies could do much to build international consensus on the nature of a problem and the measures required to address it. Regional organizations participating in complementary efforts with the United Nations in joint undertakings would encourage States outside the region to act supportively. And should the Security Council choose specifically to authorize a regional arrangement or organization to take the lead in addressing a crisis within its region, it could serve to lend the weight of the United Nations to the validity of the regional effort. Carried forward in the spirit of the Charter, and as envisioned in Chapter VIII, the approach outlined here could strengthen a general sense that democratization is being encouraged at all levels in the task of maintaining international peace and security, it being essential to continue to recognize that the primary responsibility will continue to reside in the Security Council.

VIII. Safety of personnel

66. WHEN United Nations personnel are deployed in conditions of strife, whether for preventive diplomacy, peacemaking, peace-keeping, peace-building or humanitarian purposes, the need arises to ensure their safety. There has been an unconscionable increase in the number of fatalities. Following the conclusion of a cease-fire and in order to prevent further outbreaks of violence, United Nations guards were called upon to assist in volatile conditions in Iraq. Their presence afforded a measure of security to United Nations personnel and supplies and, in addition, introduced an element of reassurance and stability that helped to prevent renewed conflict. Depending upon the nature of the situation, different configurations and compositions of security deployments will need to be considered. As the variety and scale of threat widens, innovative measures will be required to deal with the dangers facing United Nations personnel.

67. Experience has demonstrated that the presence of a United Nations operation has not always been sufficient to deter hostile action. Duty in areas of danger can never be risk-free; United Nations personnel must expect to go in harm's way at times. The courage, commitment and idealism shown by United Nations personnel should be respected by the entire international community. These men and women deserve to be properly recognized and rewarded for the perilous tasks they undertake. Their interests and those of their families must be given due regard and protected.

68. Given the pressing need to afford adequate protection to United Nations personnel engaged in life-endangering circumstances, I recommend that the Security Council, unless it elects immediately to withdraw the United Nations presence in order to preserve the credibility of the Organization, gravely consider what action should be taken towards those who put United Nations personnel in danger. Before deployment takes place, the Council should keep open the option of considering in advance collective measures, possibly including those under Chapter VII when a threat to international peace and security is also involved, to come into effect should the purpose of the United Nations operation systematically be frustrated and hostilities occur.

IX. Financing

69. A CHASM has developed between the tasks entrusted to this Organization and the financial means provided to it. The truth of the matter is that our vision cannot really extend to the prospect opening before us as long as our financing remains myopic. There are two main areas of concern: the ability of the Organization to function over the longer term; and immediate requirements to respond to a crisis.

70. To remedy the financial situation of the United Nations in all its aspects, my distinguished predecessor repeatedly drew the attention of Member States to the increasingly impossible situation that has arisen and, during the forty-sixth session of the General Assembly, made a number of proposals. Those proposals which remain before the Assembly, and with which I am in broad agreement, are the following:

- *Proposal one.* This suggested the adoption of a set of measures to deal with the cash flow problems caused by the exceptionally high level of unpaid contributions as well as with the problem of inadequate working capital reserves:

(a) Charging interest on the amounts of assessed contributions that are not paid on time;

(b) Suspending certain financial regulations of the United Nations to permit the retention of budgetary surpluses;

(c) Increasing the Working Capital Fund to a level of $250 million and endorsing the principle that the level of the Fund should be approximately 25 per cent of the annual assessment under the regular budget;

(d) Establishment of a temporary Peace-keeping Reserve Fund, at a level of $50 million, to meet initial expenses of peace-keeping operations pending receipt of assessed contributions;

(e) Authorization to the Secretary-General to borrow commercially, should other sources of cash be inadequate.

- *Proposal two.* This suggested the creation of a Humanitarian Revolving Fund in the order of $50 million, to be used in emergency humanitarian situations. The proposal has since been implemented.

- *Proposal three.* This suggested the establishment of a United Nations Peace Endowment Fund, with an initial target of $1 billion. The Fund would be created by a combination of assessed and voluntary contributions, with the latter being sought from Governments, the private sector as well as individuals. Once the Fund reached its target level, the proceeds from the investment of its principal would be used to finance the initial costs of authorized peace-keeping operations, other conflict resolution measures and related activities.

71. In addition to these proposals, others have been added in recent months in the course of public discussion. These ideas include: a levy on arms sales that could be related to maintaining an Arms Register by the United Nations; a levy on international air travel, which is dependent on the maintenance of peace; authorization for the United Nations to borrow from the World Bank and the International Monetary Fund - for peace and development are

interdependent; general tax exemption for contributions made to the United Nations by foundations, businesses and individuals; and changes in the formula for calculating the scale of assessments for peace-keeping operations.

72. As such ideas are debated, a stark fact remains: the financial foundations of the Organization daily grow weaker, debilitating its political will and practical capacity to undertake new and essential activities. This state of affairs must not continue. Whatever decisions are taken on financing the Organization, there is one inescapable necessity: Member States must pay their assessed contributions in full and on time. Failure to do so puts them in breach of their obligations under the Charter.

73. In these circumstances and on the assumption that Member States will be ready to finance operations for peace in a manner commensurate with their present, and welcome, readiness to establish them, I recommend the following:

(a) Immediate establishment of a revolving peace-keeping reserve fund of $50 million;

(b) Agreement that one third of the estimated cost of each new peace-keeping operation be appropriated by the General Assembly as soon as the Security Council decides to establish the operation; this would give the Secretary-General the necessary commitment authority and assure an adequate cash flow; the balance of the costs would be appropriated after the General Assembly approved the operation's budget;

(c) Acknowledgement by Member States that, under exceptional circumstances, political and operational considerations may make it necessary for the Secretary-General to employ his authority to place contracts without competitive bidding.

74. Member States wish the Organization to be managed with the utmost efficiency and care. I am in full accord. I have taken important steps to streamline the Secretariat in order to avoid duplication and overlap while increasing its productivity. Additional changes and improvements will take place. As regards the United Nations system more widely, I continue to review the situation in consultation with my colleagues in the Administrative Committee on Coordination. The question of assuring financial security to the Organization over the long term is of such importance and complexity that public awareness and support must be heightened. I have therefore asked a select group of qualified persons of high international repute to examine this entire subject and to report to me. I intend to present their advice, together with my comments, for the consideration of the General Assembly, in full recognition of the special responsibility that the Assembly has, under the Charter, for financial and budgetary matters.

X. An agenda for peace

75. THE NATIONS and peoples of the United Nations are fortunate in a way that those of the League of Nations were not. We have been given a second chance to create the world of our Charter that they were denied. With the cold war ended we have drawn back from the brink of a confrontation that threatened the world and, too often, paralysed our Organization.

76. Even as we celebrate our restored possibilities, there is a need to ensure that the lessons of the past four decades are learned and that the errors, or variations of them, are not repeated. For there may not be a third opportunity for our planet which, now for different reasons, remains endangered.

77. The tasks ahead must engage the energy and attention of all components of the United Nations system - the General Assembly and other principal organs, the agencies and programmes. Each has, in a balanced scheme of things, a role and a responsibility.

78. Never again must the Security Council lose the collegiality that is essential to its proper functioning, an attribute it has gained after such trial. A genuine sense of consensus deriving from shared interests must govern its work, not the threat of the veto or the power of any group of nations. And it follows that agreement among the permanent members must have the deeper support of the other members of the Council, and the membership more widely, if the Council's decisions are to be effective and endure.

79. The Summit Meeting of the Security Council of 31 January 1992 provided a unique forum for exchanging views and strengthening cooperation. I recommend that the Heads of State and Government of the members of the Council meet in alternate years, just before the general debate commences in the General Assembly. Such sessions would permit exchanges on the challenges and dangers of the moment and stimulate ideas on how the United Nations may best serve to steer change into peaceful courses. I propose in addition that the Security Council continue to meet at the Foreign Minister level, as it has effectively done in recent years, whenever the situation warrants such meetings.

80. Power brings special responsibilities, and temptations. The powerful must resist the dual but opposite calls of unilateralism and isolationism if the United Nations is to succeed. For just as unilateralism at the global or regional level can shake the confidence of others, so can isolationism, whether it results from political choice or constitutional circumstance, enfeeble the global undertaking. Peace at home and the urgency of rebuilding and strengthening our individual societies necessitates peace abroad and cooperation among nations. The endeavours of the United Nations will require the fullest engagement of all its Members, large and small, if the present renewed opportunity is to be seized.

81. Democracy within nations requires respect for human rights and fundamental freedoms, as set forth in the Charter. It requires as well a deeper understanding and respect for the rights of minorities and respect for the needs of the more vulnerable groups of society, especially women and children. This is not only a political matter. The social stability needed for productive growth is nurtured by conditions in which people can readily express their will. For this, strong domestic institutions of participation are essential. Promoting such institutions means promoting the empowerment of the unorganized, the poor, the marginalized. To this end, the focus of the United Nations should be on the "field", the locations where economic, social and political decisions take effect. In furtherance of this I am taking steps to rationalize and in certain cases integrate the various programmes and agencies of the United Nations within specific countries. The senior United Nations official in each country should be prepared to serve, when needed, and with the consent of the host authorities, as my Representative on matters of particular concern.

82. Democracy within the family of nations means the application of its principles within the world Organization itself. This requires the fullest consultation, participation and engagement of all States, large and small, in the work of the Organization. All organs of the United Nations must be accorded, and play, their full and proper role so that the trust of all nations and peoples will be retained and deserved. The principles of the Charter must be applied consistently, not selectively, for if the perception should be of the latter, trust will wane and with it the moral authority which is the greatest and most unique quality of that instrument. Democracy at all levels is essential to attain peace for a new era of prosperity and justice.

83. Trust also requires a sense of confidence that the world Organization will react swiftly, surely and impartially and that it will not be debilitated by political opportunism or by administrative or financial inadequacy. This presupposes a strong, efficient and independent international civil service whose integrity is beyond question and an assured financial basis that lifts the Organization, once and for all, out of its present mendicancy.

84. Just as it is vital that each of the organs of the United Nations employ its capabilities in the balanced and harmonious fashion envisioned in the Charter, peace in the largest sense cannot be accomplished by the United Nations system or by Governments alone. Non-governmental organizations, academic institutions, parliamentarians, business and professional communities, the media and the public at large must all be involved. This will strengthen the world Organization's ability to reflect the concerns and interests of its widest constituency, and those who become more involved can carry the word of United Nations initiatives and build a deeper understanding of its work.

85. Reform is a continuing process, and improvement can have no limit. Yet there is an expectation, which I wish to see fulfilled, that the present phase in the renewal of this Organization should be complete by 1995, its fiftieth anniversary. The pace set must therefore be increased if the United Nations is to keep ahead of the acceleration of history that characterizes this age. We must be guided not by precedents alone, however wise these may be, but by the needs of the future and by the shape and content that we wish to give it.

86. I am committed to broad dialogue between the Member States and the Secretary-General. And I am committed to fostering a full and open interplay between all institutions and elements of the Organization so that the Charter's objectives may not only be better served, but that this Organization may emerge as greater than the sum of its parts. The United Nations was created with a great and courageous vision. Now is the time, for its nations and peoples, and the men and women who serve it, to seize the moment for the sake of the future.

Fully aware of the link between efficient transportation and economic growth, the highest priority has been given to road rehabilitation and road maintenance.

Whilst resources are being increased to upgrade the ageing transportation infrastructure, the sheer scale of investment required has meant that the government is committed to achieving a high level of private sector participation.

With the institutional capacity at Ghana Highway Authority being strengthened, activity will be concentrated on the building and re-building of long-neglected roads with new projects programmed to come on stream.

A more unified and long-term approach to the management and financing of the road sector, particularly with regard to expenditure control, cost recovery and the financing of road maintenance, will ensure that the objective of an efficient and effective road transport system can now be realized.

Head Office - P.O. Box 1641, Accra, Ghana

Tel: 233 (21) 66591-4/64627-9/64620

Telegrams/Cablegrams: HIGHWAYS

The UN community ~ *the associations and committees*

WORLD FEDERATION OF UNITED NATIONS ASSOCIATIONS (WFUNA)

FEDERATION MONDIALE DES ASSOCIATIONS POUR LES NATIONS UNIES (FMANU)

PALAIS DES NATIONS, 1211 GENEVE 10, SUISSE

TEL: (+4122) 733 07 30 FAX: (+4122) 733 48 38

cables: WORFEDUNA GENEVA, telex: 41 29 62 UNO CH (WFUNA)

OFFICERS OF THE FEDERATION

PRESIDENT

Ms. Androula Vassiliou (Cyprus)
P.O. Box 2098, Nicosia, Cyprus

VICE PRESIDENTS

Dr. Ervin Gombos (Hungary)
c/o UNA-Hungary (see further for UNA address)

Ms. June Lambert (Ireland)
c/o UNA-Ireland (see further for UNA address)

Dr. Yadav Prasad Pant (Nepal)
c/o UNA-Nepal (see further for UNA address)

Dame Laurie Salas, DBE,QSO (New Zealand)
c/o UNA New-Zealand (see further for UNA address)

Ms. Rena Shashua-Hasson (Israel)
4 Hapalmach Street,
Ramat-Hasharon 47 203, Israel

CHAIRMAN OF THE EXECUTIVE COMMITTEE

Mr. Geoffrey Grenville-Wood (Canada)
43, Florence Street, Ottawa,
Ontario K2P OW6, Canada

VICE-CHAIRMEN OF THE EXECUTIVE COMMITTEE

Amb. Omran El-Shafei (Egypt)
27 Yathreb Street, Dokki
Cairo, Egypt

Mr. Xie Qimei (China)
c/o UNA-China
(see further for UNA address)

TREASURER

Mr. L.H. Horace Perera (Sri Lanka)
c/o WFUNA

SECRETARY-GENERAL

Dr. Marek Hagmajer (Poland)
c/o WFUNA

MEMBERS OF THE EXECUTIVE COMMITTEE

Mr. Glenn Bowen (Jamaica)
c/o Alpart, Spur Tree, Jamaica, W.I.

Prof. Dr Erica-Irene A. Daes (Greece)
20ch. François-Lehmann
1218 Grand-Saconnex, Switzerland

Dr. Haluk Gerger (Turkey)
Atac Sokak, 71/22
06420 Ankara, Turkey

Dr. (Mme) Cécile Goldet (France)
8 Avenue Simon Bolivar
75019 Paris, France

Mr. Malcolm C. Harper (United Kingdom)
c/o UNA-United Kingdom (see further for UNA address)

M. Malamine Kourouma (Sénégal)
c/o Faculté des Sciences Juridiques et Economiques, Université Cheikh Anta Diop
B.P. 5005, Dakar, Senegal

Mr. Gregory M. Kovrizhenko (Russian Federation)
c/o UNA-Russian Federation (see further for UNA address)

Mr. Joachim Krause (Germany)
c/o UNA-Germany (see further for UNA address)

Ms. Usha Krishna Kumar (India)
19, Teen Murti Marg
New Delhi 110 011, India

Prof. Ved P. Nanda (USA)
College of Law, University of Denver
1900 Olive Street, Denver CO 80220, USA

Mr. Francesc Noguero i Vallverdú (Spain)
c/o UNA-Spain (see further for UNA address)

Dr. Luis Alberto Padilla Menendez (Guatemala)
c/o UNA-Guatemala (see further for UNA address)

Mr. Roger Shipton, O.A.M. (Australia)
P.O.B. 374, North Melbourne 3051
Victoria, Australia

Ms. Tina Uwechue (Nigeria)
P.O. Box 662, Lagos, Nigeria

ISMUN President : Mr. Bright O. Akwetey,
Attorney-General Department,
P.O. Box M 221, Accra, Ghana

SECRETARIAT

Mr. Mike Awua-Asamoa,
Deputy Secretary-General
Director, WFUNA Regional Office for Africa
P.O. Box 2329, Accra, Ghana

Mr. Sitaram Sharma,
Deputy Secretary-General
Director, WFUNA Regional Office for Asia and the Pacific, Tower House, 2A,
Chowringhee Square (2nd fl.)
Calcutta 700 069, India

Ms. Annabelle Wiener,
Deputy Secretary-General
Director, WFUNA Office at UN Headquarters,
Room DC 1-1177, United Nations, New York,
N.Y. 10017, U.S.A.

Ms. Andree Y. Piaget,
Assistant Secretary-General
c/o WFUNA

Mr. Ricardo Dominicé,
Co-ordinator for Latin America
c/o WFUNA

HONORARY PRESIDENTS

Mr. Hilary G. Barratt-Brown
Pedruxella Gran, Pollensa, Mallorca, Balearic Islands, Spain

Ms. Angie Brooks Randolph
c/o Ministry for Foreign Affairs, Monrovia, Liberia

Ms. P.H. Graamans
102 Kringloop, Amstelveen, Netherlands

Mr. Mogens Hasdorf
Platanvej 28, 1, 1810 Frederiksberg C, Denmark

Prof. Dr. Klaus Hufner
c/o Frei Universität Berlin, Boltzmann-Strasse 20, Berlin, Germany

Amb. Aly Khalil
78 Nile Street, Orman, 12311 Guiza, Egypt

Mr. Zentaro Kosaka
c/o UNA-Japan (see further for UNA address)

Mr. Bennard Kwami Kuma
c/o Tesano Textiles Ltd, P.O. Box 5696, Accra, Ghana

S.E. M.Kéba Mbaye
Rue "G", angle rue Léon Gontran Damas,
B.P. 5865, Dakar-Fann, Sénégal

H.E. Mr. Nelson Mandela
Office of the President
Tuynhuys Private Bag X1000
Cape Town 8000 South Africa

Ms. Winnie Mandela
Private Bag X889
Pretoria 0001, South Africa

Mr. Ram Niwas Mirdha, M.P.
7, Lodhi Estate
New Delhi 110 003, India

Professor Dr. Grigory I. Morozov
c/o UNA-Russian Federation (see further for UNA address)

Mr. L.H. Horace Perera
22, Avenue Luserna
1203 Geneva, Switzerland

Ms. Hilkka Pietila
Jussarenkuja 5N 134, 00840 Helsinki, Finland

Mr. Douglas G. Roche
8923 Strathearn Drive, N.W.
Edmonton, Alberta T6C 4C8, Canada

S.E. M. Leopold Sedar Senghor
1, Square de Tocqueville
75017 Paris, France

Academician Professor Dr. Mihály Simai
World Institute for Development Economics Research
Katajanokanlaituri 6 B,
00160 Helsinki, Finland

Mr. Francis H. H. Strasser-King
c/o UNA-Sierra Leone (see further for UNA address)

Mr. Maurice F. Strong
Chairman, C.E.O., Ontario Hydro
700 University Ave.
Toronto, Ontario M5G 1X6, Canada

Mr. Michael A. Tryantafyllides
Former Attorney-General of the Republic of
Cyprus, P.O. Box 652, Nicosia, Cyprus

Mr. Sidney H. Willner
One Sutton Place South
New York, N.Y. 10022-2471, U.S.A.

MEMBER UNITED NATIONS ASSOCIATIONS

ARGENTINA
Asociación pro Naciones Unidas de
Argentina c/o Centro de Informaciones de
Naciones Unidas para Argentina y Uruguay
Junin 1940, 1° piso, (1113) Buenos Aires
Argentina (Republic of)
FAX:(+541) 804 75 45

AUSTRALIA
United Nations Association of Australia
15 Moorhouse Street
Armadale, Vic 3143
Australia (Commonwealth of)
TEL:(+613) 822 71 48 FAX:(+613) 329 86 29

AUSTRIA
Oesterreichische Liga für die Vereinten
Nationen, Annagasse 5, 1010 Vienna, Austria
(Republic of)
TEL:(+431) 513 08 37

BANGLADESH
United Nations Association of Bangladesh
55 Dilkusha Commercial Area (1st floor)
Dhaka 2, Bangladesh (People's Republic of)
TEL:(+8802) 256 850

BARBADOS
United Nations Association of Barbados
9 Bamboo Ridge, Holders
St. James, Barbados
FAX:(+1809) 432 1947

BELARUS
United Nations Association of Belarus
24-A, Internatsionalnaya Street, 1st Fl.
220050 Minsk, Belarus (Republic of Belarus)
TEL:(+70172) 27 54 44 FAX:(+70172) 27 57 69

BELGIUM
Vereniging voor de Verenigde Naties
VUB Centrum voor UNO-Recht
Pleinlaan 2, 1050 Bruxelles
Belgique (Royaume de)
TEL:(+322) 512 17 07

BHUTAN
United Nations Association of Bhutan
Ministry of Foreign Affairs, Thimphu
Bhutan (Kingdom of)
FAX:(+975) 22 459

BULGARIA
United Nations Association of Bulgaria
12 Vassil Aprilov Street, Sofia 1504
Bulgaria (Republic of)
TEL:(+3592) 465 495

CANADA
United Nations Association in Canada
900-130 Slater, Ottawa, Ontario K1P 6E2
Canada
TEL:(+1613) 232 57 51 FAX:(+1613) 563 24 55

CHILE
Asociación Chilena para Naciones Unidas Lda.
Brown Norte 379, Nuñoa, Santiago
Chile (Republic of)
TEL:(+562) 223 48 68 FAX:(+562) 274 31 50

CHINA
United Nations Association of China
71 Nanchizi, Beijing 100 006
China (People's Republic of)
TEL:(+861) 512 0585 FAX:(+861) 513 1831

CONGO
Association Congolaise pour les Nations Unies
c/o Centre d'Information des Nations Unies
B.P. 13 210, Brazzaville, Congo
(République du)
TEL/FAX:(+242) 83 1000

CROATIA
Udruzenje za Ujedinjene Narode Republike
Hrvatske, Gornje Prekrizje 51
41000 Zagreb, Croatia (Republic of)
FAX:(+385) 41 273 933

CUBA
Asociación Cubana de las Naciones Unidas
J No. 514, Esq. 25, Vedado, Havana,
Cuba (Republic of)
TEL:(+537) 32 47 23
FAX:(+537) 33 31 39/30 08

CYPRUS
United Nations Association of Cyprus
(Mitsis Building No. 3, Corner Makarios
and Evagoras Ave, 2nd fl., office 202)
P.O. Box 1508, Nicosia, Cyprus (Republic of)
TEL:(+3572) 443 598 FAX:(+3572) 44 15 60

DENMARK
FN-forbundet Skindergade 26, 1.
1159 Copenhagen K, Denmark (Kingdom of)
TEL:(+45) 33 12 39 39 FAX:(+45) 33 12 10 58

EGYPT
Egyptian United Nations Association
28 Talaat Harb Street, flat 710
Cairo, Egypt (Arab Republic of)
TEL:(+202) 746 217 FAX:(+202) 346 9025

FINLAND
Suomen YK-Liitto, Unioninkatu 45 B
00170 Helsinki 17, Finland (Republic of)
TEL:(+3580) 135 1402/1521
FAX:(+3580) 135 2173

FRANCE
Association Française pour les Nations Unies
1, Avenue de Tourville, 75007 Paris
France (République Française)
TEL:(+331) 45 55 71 73
FAX:(+331) 45 56 19 88

GERMANY
Deutsche Gesellschaft für die Vereinten
Nationen, Dag-Hammarskjold-Haus
Poppelsdorfer Allee 55, D-53115 Bonn,
Germany (Federal Republic of)
TEL:(+49228) 213 646 FAX:(+49228) 217 492

GHANA
United Nations Association of Ghana
P.O. Box 2329, Accra, Ghana (Republic of)
TEL:(+23321) 664 531 FAX:(+23321) 772 642

GREECE
Greek Association for the United Nations
Megaron "Parnassos"
Plateia Karytsi 8, 105 61 Athens
Greece (Hellenic Republic)
TEL:(+301) 721 6284

GUATEMALA
Asociación Guatemalteca pro-Naciones
Unidas
la. Calle 9-52, Zona 1, 01001 Guatemala City
Guatemala (Republic of)
TEL:(+5022) 28 260 FAX:(+5022) 531 532

GUINEA
Association Guinéenne pour les Nations Unies
Ministère de la Communication
B.P. 2675, Conakry, Guinée (République de)
TEL:(+224) 44 42 88 FAX:(+224) 44 46 46

HONG KONG
United Nations Association of Hong Kong
343-349 Nathan Road, G.P.O. Box 2135
Kowloon, Hong Kong
TEL:(+852) 3-771 8367/328 615
FAX:(+852) 782 1334

HUNGARY
Magyar ENSZ Tarsasag
Andrassy ut. 124, 1062 Budapest VI
Hungary (Republic of)
TEL/FAX:(+361) 131 21 24

ICELAND
United Nations Association of Iceland
P.O. Box 679, 121 Reykjavik
Iceland (Republic of)
TEL:(+3541) 625 322 FAX:(+3541) 625 313

INDIA
Indian Federation of UN Associations (IFUNA)
12 Janpath Lane "Hutments"(Behind Central
Cottage Industries Emporium)
New Delhi 110 001
India (Republic of)
TEL:(+9111) 3322944/3327791

INDONESIA
Himpunan Perserikatan Bangsa-Bangsa
82 Jalan Raya Cikini, Jakarta Pusat 10330
Indonesia (Republic of)
TEL:(+62 21) 314 2605 FAX:(+62 21) 310 7734

IRELAND
Irish United Nations Association
3/4 South Leinster Street
Dublin 2, Ireland
TEL:(+3531) 702 21 85

ISLE OF MAN
United Nations Association of the Isle of Man
Wellington House, Market Street, Douglas
Isle of Man (British Isles)
TEL:(+44624) 624 364 FAX:(+44624) 626 186

ISRAEL
United Nations Association of Israel
P.O. Box 331, Jerusalem 91002
Israel (State of)
FAX:(+9722) 66 03 70

ITALY
Società Italiana per l'Organizzazione
Internazionale
Palazzetto di Venezia, Via San Marco 3
00186 Roma, Italy (Italian Republic)
TEL:(+396) 679 3566/679 3949
FAX:(+396) 678 9102

JAMAICA
United Nations Association of Jamaica
33 Anthurium Drive, MONA, Kingston 6
Jamaica
TEL:(+1809) 927 65 94 FAX:(+1809) 962 93 33

JAPAN
United Nations Association of Japan, Inc.
5th fl., Nippon Bldg., Room 521
6-2 Ohtemachi, 2-chome
Chiyoda-ku, Tokyo 100, Japan
TEL:(+813) 3270 4731/5
FAX:(+813) 3270 4735

KENYA
United Nations Association of Kenya
P.O. Box 73710, Nairobi, Kenya (Republic of)
TEL:(+2542) 337 582/339 000
FAX:(+2542) 333 448

LATVIA
United Nations Association of Latvia
Skunu Iela 12/14, Riga, 1050
Latvia (Republic of)
TEL:(+371) 2 - 224 188 FAX:(+371) 2 - 284 510

LESOTHO
United Nations Association of Lesotho
c/o UN Information Centre, P.O. Box 301
Maseru 100, Lesotho (Kingdom of)

LITHUANIA
United Nations Association of Lithuania
Kalvariju 172-81, Vilnius 2042
Lithuania (Republic of)
FAX:(+3702) 77 66 91

LUXEMBOURG
Association Luxembourgeoise pour les Nations
Unies
99 Route d'Arlon, 1140 Luxembourg
Grand-Duché de Luxembourg
TEL:(+352) 454 606 FAX:(+352) 455 314

MALAYSIA
United Nations Association of Malaysia
P.O. Box 12424, 50778 Kuala Lumpur
Malaysia
TEL:(+603) 282 9291/293 9366
FAX:(+603) 282 9319/293 9430

MALI
Association Malienne pour les Nations Unies
Boîte Postale 78, Bamako, Mali (Republic of)
TEL:(+223) 227 860

MAURITIUS
United Nations Association of Mauritius
P.O. Box 401, Port Louis, Mauritius
TEL:(+2308) 0145

MEXICO
Asociación Mexicana para las Naciones
Unidas, A.C.
Apdo Postal 19-666, 03910 Mexico, D.F.
Mexico (United Mexican States)
TEL:(+525) 664 2728 FAX:(+525) 664 3039

MONGOLIA
Association Mongole pour les Nations Unies
Boîte Postale 363, Ulaanbaatar 44, Mongolie
TEL:(+976) 26 981 FAX:(+976) 1 -32 00 45

NEPAL
United Nations Association of Nepal
Post Box No. 3257, Baluwater-4, Kathmandu
Nepal (Kingdom of)
TEL:(+9771) 41 49 14/22 64 22

NETHERLANDS
Nederlandse Vereniging voor de Verenigde
Naties
Alexanderstraat 20-22, 2514JM The Hague
Netherlands (Kingdom of the)
TEL:(+3170) 342 0351 FAX:(+3170) 342 0359

NEW ZEALAND
United Nations Association of New Zealand
P.O. Box 11 750, Wellington, New Zealand
TEL:(+644) 382 8783 FAX:(+644) 479 3415

NIGERIA
United Nations Association of Nigeria
P.O. Box 54423, Falomo, Ikoyi, Lagos
Nigeria (Federal Republic of)
FAX:(+2341) 66 36 21

NORWAY
FN-Sambandet i Norge
Storgt. 33 A, 0184 Oslo, Norway (Kingdom of)
TEL:(+472) 22 09 170 FAX:(+472) 22 08 142

PAKISTAN
Pakistan United Nations Association
D-19, Block 4, Gulshan-i-Iqbal, Karachi
75300 Pakistan (Islamic Republic of)
TEL:(+9221) 520 080

PANAMA
Asociación Panameña por los Principios
Universales de las Naciones Unidas
(A.P.P.U.N.U.)
Apdo. Postal 10885, Estafeta Universitaria
Panama (Republic of)
TEL:(+507) 64 17 47 FAX:(+507) 64 17 31

PERU
Asociación pro Naciones Unidas del Perú
Castilla 1313, Arequipa, Peru (Republic of)
TEL:(+51-54) 212 031

PHILIPPINES
United Nations Association of the Philippines
Eulogio "Amang" Rodriguez, Institute of
Science and Technology
Nagtahan, Sampaloc, Manila
Philippines (Republic of the)

POLAND
Polskie Towarzystwo Przyjaciół ONZ
Al Niepodległości 10
60-967 Poznań, Poland (Republic of)
TEL:(4861) 699 261-ext. 1509
FAX:(4861) 668 924

REPUBLIC OF KOREA
United Nations Association of the Republic of
Korea
115-3 Kwonnong-Dong, Chongro-ku
Seoul 110-380, Korea (Republic of)
TEL:(822) 764 8998 FAX:(822) 763 8463

ROMANIA
Asociatia Pentru Natiunile Unite Din
Romania
Bd. Magheru 22 - 1st fl., Sector 1, Bucharest
Romania
TEL:(+400) 596 820

RUSSIAN FEDERATION
Association for the United Nations in the
Russian Federation
36 Prospect Mira, 129010 Moscow
Russian Federation
TEL:(+7095) 280 3358 FAX:(+7095) 200 4250

SENEGAL
Association Sénégalaise pour les Nations
Unies
Palais de Justice, Boîte Postale 9003, Dakar
Sénégal (République du)

SIERRA LEONE
Sierra Leone United Nations Association
P.O. Box 632, Freetown
Sierra Leone (Republic of)
TEL:(+23222) 25 832

SINGAPORE
Pertubohan Bangsa-Bangsa Bersatu Singapura
P.O. Box 351, Tanglin Post Office
Singapore 9124, Singapore (Republic of)
TEL:(+65) 772 37 07 FAX:(+65) 773 29 80

SLOVENIA
United Nations Association of Slovenia
Box 210, Ljubljana, Slovenia (Republic of)
TEL:(+3861) 210 708 FAX:(+3861) 210 708

SPAIN
Asociación para la Naciones Unidas en España
Calle Fontanella 14, 1°, la, 08010 Barcelona
Spain (Kingdom of)
TEL:(+343) 301 3990/301 3198
FAX:(+343) 317 5768

SRI LANKA
UN Association in the Democratic
Socialist Republic of Sri Lanka
Thirty Nine Upon One
Cyril Jansz Mawatha
UNASL Panadura Sri Lanka (Democratic
Socialist Republic of)
TEL:(+9434) 65 41 23
FAX:(+9434) 33 16 17 & 65 20 45

SWEDEN
Svenska FN-Forbundet
(Skolgränd 2), Box 15115, 104 65 Stockholm
Sweden (Kingdom of)
TEL:(+468) 6449 835 FAX:(+468) 6418 876

SWITZERLAND
Liaison FMANU
Société Suisse - Nations Unies 7, Chemin
Grosse Pierre, 1110 Morges, Suisse
(Confédération Suisse)
TEL:(+4121) 801 8838

THAILAND
United Nations Association of Thailand
c/o Ministry of Foreign Affairs
Sri-ayadhya Road, Bangkok 10400
Thailand (Kingdom of)
TEL:(+662) 246 42 82

TUNISIA
Association Tunisienne pour les Nations
Unies
c/o Ministere des Affaires Etrangères
Place de la Kasbah, Tunis
Tunisie (République Tunisienne)

TURKEY
Birlesmis Milletler Turk Dernegi
Arjantin Caddesi, Halici Sokak 8/1
Gaziosmanpasa, 06700 Ankara
Turkey (Republic of)
TEL:(+90312) 272 216

UGANDA
United Nations Association of Uganda
P.O. Box 14058 Kampala,
Uganda (Republic of)
TEL:(+25641) 234 177/235 543

UNITED KINGDOM
UN Association of the United Kingdom of
Great Britain and Northern Ireland
3 Whitehall Court, London SW1A 2EL
United Kingdom
TEL:(+44171) 930 2931/2
FAX:(+44171) 930 5893

UNITED REPUBLIC OF TANZANIA
United Nations Association of Tanzania
P.O. Box 9224, United Republic of Tanzania
TEL:(+25551) 23 655/31 683

UNITED STATES OF AMERICA
United Nations Association of the U.S.A.
485 Fifth Avenue, New York,
N.Y. 10017-6104, U.S.A
TEL:(+1212) 697 3232 FAX:(+1212) 682 9185

YUGOSLAVIA
Yugoslav UN Association
Makedonska Street 22/III, 11000 Belgrade
Yugoslavia (Federal Republic of)
TEL:(+38111) 326 073 FAX:(+38111) 138 331

ZAIRE
Association Zairoise pour les Nations Unies
Boîte Postale 9628, Kinshasa 1
Zaire (République du)

ZAMBIA
United Nations Association of Zambia
c/o Geography Department
University of Zambia, P.O. Box 32379
Lusaka, Zambia (Republic of)
TEL:(+2601) 254 406 FAX:(+2601) 253 952

ZIMBABWE
Zimbabwe United Nations Association
P.O. Box 14, Gweru, Zimbabwe (Republic of)
TEL:(+263) 41 54 2531/2 FAX:(+263) 54 51638

**INTERNATIONAL YOUTH AND
STUDENT MOVEMENT FOR THE UNITED
NATIONS (ISMUN)**
c/o Palais des Nations, 1211 Geneva 10
Switzerland
TEL:(+4122) 798 5850/798 8400
FAX:(+4122) 733 48 38

ZAMBIA TELECOMMUNICATIONS COMPANY LIMITED

As the reshaping of the country's infrastructure continues apace, the private sector is being further encouraged to play a key role in stimulating efficiency and higher productivity.

With a commitment to a programme of reform together with the current monetary and fiscal policies, Zambia's main objectives are to maintain stability and create the platform for sustained economic growth and social development.

The expansion and modernization of the country's telecommunications infrastructure is a cornerstone of this development strategy.

Greater liberalization and the policy of privatization will accelerate the introduction of new technologies, providing better and more flexible telephone services.

Not only will there be greater access to a basic level of communications capability, opportunities also exist to improve quality and performance.

The development of the telecommunications sector is critical to the competitiveness and productivity of the nation, providing, as it will, a vital service linking Zambia to the emerging global economy.

The rapidly changing world of telecommunications is full of hope and promise. Zambia Telecommunications share in that vision for the future.

Provident House, P.O. Box 71630, Ndola, Zambia
Tel. 260 (2) 611333 : Telex ZA 30360 : Fax. 260 (2) 615855

INTERNATIONAL ASSOCIATE
Fédération Internationale des Corps et
Associations Consulaires (F.I.C.A.C.)
Aurehojvej 11, 2900 Hellerup
Denmark (Kingdom of)
TEL:(+45) 316 26 358 FAX:(+45) 316 27 476

COLLECTIVE ASSOCIATE
Organization for Defending Victims of
Violence
P.O. Box 16765-911, Tehran
Iran (Islamic Republic of)

**NATIONAL COMMITTEES ESTABLISHED
FOR UN50**

Algeria
NATIONAL COMMITTEE OF ALGERIA
FOR UN50
6, rue Ibn El-Batran, El Mouradia, Alger
TEL: (213) 2 60 25 25/692744
FAX: (213) 2 69 21 61

Argentina
NATIONAL COMMITTEE OF ARGENTINA
FOR UN50
c/o The CARI, Uruguay Street 1037, 1 piso,
Buenos Aires 1616
TEL:(54) 1 811-0071 FAX: (54) 1 111-835

Australia
AUSTRALIAN NATIONAL COMMITTEE
FOR UN50
c/o UNA - Australia, P.O. Box 374, North
Melbourne, VIC 3051
TEL: (61) 3 329-611 FAX: (61) 3 329-8629

Austria
NATIONAL COMMITTEE OF AUSTRIA
FOR UN50
c/o Federal Chancellery, Ballhausplatz 2,
A-1014 Vienna
TEL: (43) 1 53115-0 FAX: (43) 1535453-0

Bahamas
NATIONAL COMMITTEE OF THE
BAHAMAS FOR UN50
P.O. Box 3746, Nassau
TEL: (809) 322 7624/5 FAX: (809) 328 8212

Bangladesh
NATIONAL COMMITTEE OF
BANGLADESH FOR UN50
Ministry of Foreign Affairs, Segun Segun
Bagicha, Dhaka 1000

Belarus
NATIONAL COMMITTEE OF BELARUS
FOR UN50
Minsk

Belgium
BELGIAN NATIONAL COMMITTE FOR
UN50
Rue des Quatre Bras 2, 1000 Bruxelles
TEL: (32) 2 516 8111 FAX: (32) 2 511 6385

Benin
COMITE NATIONAL PREPARATOIRE DU
CINQUANTIEME ANNIVERSAIRE DE
L'ONU
PO Box 318, Cotonou
TEL: (229) 300 245 FAX: (229) 300 400

Bhutan
NATIONAL COMMITTEE OF BHUTAN
FOR UN50
Thimphu
TEL: (975) 2 22359 FAX: (975) 2 22458

Bulgaria
NATIONAL COMMITTEE OF BULGARIA
FOR UN50
Ministry of Foreign Affairs, Alexander Jendov
Street, No. 2, Sofia 113
TEL: (359) 2 71431
FAX: (359) 2 700536/803761

Cambodia
COMITE PERMANENT D'ORGANISATION
DES FETES NATIONALES ET
INTERNATIONALES
Cabinet of the King, Royal Palace,
Phnom Penh
TEL: (855) 23 26802 FAX: (855) 23 26801

Canada
CANADIAN COMMITTEE FOR THE 50TH
OF THE UN
130 rue Slater Street, Suite 900, Ottawa,
Ontario K1P 6E2
TEL: (613) 232-5751 FAX: (613) 594-2948

Chile
NATIONAL COMMITTEE OF CHILE FOR
UN50
c/o Ministry of Foreign Affairs, Santiago
TEL: (56) 2 6982501/2
FAX: (56) 2 6994202/681272

Costa Rica
NATIONAL COMMITTEE OF COSTA RICA
FOR UN50
c/o Universidad Para La Paz, Apartado 138,
Ciudad Colon
TEL: (506) 49 1072 FAX: (506) 49 1929

Croatia
NATIONAL COMMITTEE OF CROATIA
FOR UN50
c/o Ministry of Culture and Education, Trg
Bruze, 6, 41000 Zagreb
TEL: (385) 41-410-449 FAX: (385) 41-410-421

Cuba
NATIONAL COMMITTEE OF CUBA FOR
UN50
Ministry of Foreign Affairs, Calzada y G,
La Habana
TEL: (53) 7 329264 FAX: (53) 7 327942

Cyprus
NATIONAL COMMITTEE OF CYPRUS
FOR UN50
Nicosia

Egypt
NATIONAL COMMITTEE OF EGYPT FOR
UN50
Ministry of Foreign Affairs, Maspiro, Cairo
TEL: (20) 2 574-9848 FAX: (20) 2 574-9808

Finland
NATIONAL COMMITTEE OF FINLAND
FOR UN50
c/o Ministry of Foreign Affairs, Meriaasarmi
Merikasaeminkatu, 5F, PL-176, 00161 Helsinki
TEL: (35) 80 134151 FAX: (35) 80 629840

France
COMITE NATIONAL PREPARATOIRE
EN VUE DE LA CELEBRATION DU
CINQUANTIENE ANNIVERSAIRE DE L'ONU
Ministère des Affaires Etrangères, Quai
de Orsay, Paris
TEL: (47) 66 77 88 FAX: (47) 53 57 58

Germany
DEUTSCHE GESELLSCHAFT FÜR DIE
VEREINTEN NATIONEN
Dag-Hammarskjold-Haus, Poppelsdorfer Allee
55, D-53115 Bonn
TEL: (49) 228 21 38 48 FAX: (49) 228 21 74 92

Ghana
NATIONAL COMMITTEE OF GHANA FOR
UN50
Ministry of Foreign Affairs, Box M 53, Accra
TEL: (233) 21 665-491 FAX: (233) 21 665-363

Greece
NATIONAL COMMITTEE OF GREECE FOR
UN50
c/o Ministry of Foreign Affairs, Akmidias 1,
Athens

Guyana
NATIONAL COMMITTEE OF GUYANA
FOR UN50
c/o Ministry of Foreign Affairs,
254 New Garden Street, Georgetown
TEL: (59) 22 57404 FAX: (59) 22 59192

Honduras
NATIONAL COMMITTEE OF HONDURAS
FOR UN50
Avenida Juan Pablo 11, Tegucigalpa
TEL: (504) 314200 FAX: (504) 310097

India
NATIONAL COMMITTEE OF INDIA FOR
UN50
Ministry of External Affairs, New Delhi, 110011
TEL: (91) 11 301-2292 FAX: (91) 11 301-0680

Indonesia
NATIONAL COMMITTEE OF INDONESIA
FOR UN50
Ministry of Foreign Affairs, Int'l Org.,
Jalan Taman, Pejambon 6, Jakarta, Pusat
TEL: (62) 21 384-9350 Ext. 4026

Iran
NATIONAL COMMITTEE OF IRAN FOR
UN50
c/o Ministry of Foreign Affairs, Tehran

Italy
COMITATO NAZIONALE PER IL
CINQUANTENARIO ONU
c/o Ministero degli Affari Esteri-DGAP,
Piazzale della Farnesina, Roma
TEL: (39) 6 36 91 22 63 FAX: (39) 6 36 91 42 58

Jamaica
NATIONAL COMMITTEE OF JAMAICA
FOR UN50
Ministry of Foreign Affairs, 21 Dominica
Drive, Kingston 5
TEL: (809) 926-4220 FAX: (809) 929 6733

Jordan
NATIONAL COMMITTEE OF JORDAN
FOR UN50
Ministry of Foreign Affairs, Amman
TEL: (962) 6 644-361 FAX: (962) 6 648-825

Kazakhstan
NATIONAL COMMITTEE OF
KAZAKHSTAN FOR UN50
House of Parliament, Jeltoksan Street 167,
Almacy
TEL: (7) 3272-623103

Kuwait
NATIONAL COMMITTEE OF KUWAIT
FOR UN50
c/o Permanent Mission of Kuwait to UN
321 East 44th Street, New York, NY 10017,
USA
TEL: (212) 973-4300
FAX: (212) 661-7263 - 370-1733

Kyrgyzstan
NATIONAL COMMITTEE OF
KYRGYZSTAN FOR UN50

Lao
NATIONAL COMMITTEE OF LAO FOR
UN50
c/o Permanent Mission of Lao to the UN
317 East 51st Street, New York, NY 10022,
USA

Libya
NATIONAL COMMITTEE OF LIBYA FOR
UN50
The General People's Committee for Foreign
Liaison and Int'l Cooperation, Tripoli
TEL: 218 2 32458

Liechtenstein
NATIONAL COMMITTEE OF
LIECHTENSTEIN FOR UN50
c/o Permanent Mission of Liechtenstein
405 Lexington Avenue, 43rd floor, New York,
NY 10174-4301, USA
TEL: (212) 599-0220 FAX: (212) 599-0064

Luxembourg
NATIONAL COMMITTEE OF
LUXEMBOURG FOR UN50
c/o Minstère des Affaires Etrangères,
Luxembourg

Malaysia
NATIONAL COMMITTEE OF MALAYSIA
FOR UN50
Ministry of Foreign Affairs, Wisma Putra,
50602 Kuala Lumpur
TEL: (603) 248-8088 FAX: (603) 242-4551

Malta
NATIONAL COMMITTEE OF MALTA FOR
UN50
Ministry of Foreign Affairs, Merchants Street,
Valletta
TEL: (356) 235635 FAX: (356) 237822

Mexico
NATIONAL COMMITTEE OF MEXICO
FOR UN 50TH
Ministry of Foreign Relations, Rirdo Flores
Magon 1, Tlatelco, Mexico D.F.CD06995

Mongolia
NATIONAL COMMITTEE OF MONGOLIA
FOR UN50
Ministry of External Affairs, Ulaanbaatar

Namibia
NATIONAL COMMITTEE OF NAMIBIA
FOR UN50
Ministry of Foreign Affairs, Government Bldg.,
PB 13347, Windhoek
TEL: (264) 61 282 9111
FAX: (264) 61 282 2239-37

Nigeria
NATIONAL COMMITTEE OF NIGERIA
FOR UN50
c/o Ministry of Foreign Affairs, Wuse Zone 3,
PO Box 130, Garki, Abuja

Norway
NATIONAL COMMITTEE OF NORWAY
FOR UN50
Ministry of Foreign Affairs, PO Box 8114,
DEP 0032 Oslo
TEL: (47) 22 349580 FAX: (47) 22 343 600

Pakistan
NATIONAL COMMITTEE OF PAKISTAN
FOR UN50
Ministry of Foreign Affairs, Islamabad
TEL: (925) 1 211-942 FAX: (925) 1 820-420

People's Republic of China
NATIONAL COMMITTEE OF CHINA FOR
UN 50TH
Ministry of Foreign Affairs, 225 Chao Nei
Street, Beijing 100701
TEL: (861) 5134521 FAX: (861) 5130368

Peru
NATIONAL COMMITTEE OF PERU FOR
UN50
Ministry of Foreign Affairs, Jiron Ucayali 363,
Lima 1
TEL: (511) 4 27 38 60 FAX: (511) 4 32 32 66

Philippines
NATIONAL COMMITTEE OF THE
PHILIPPINES FOR UN50
Department of Foreign Affairs,
2330 Roxas Road, Manila

Poland
THE POLISH NATIONAL COMMITTEE
FOR UN50
Ministry of Foreign Affairs, UN Sys., Dep,
Al. Szucha 23, Warsaw
TEL: (48) 2 623-9400 FAX: (48) 2 628-5578

Portugal
NAT'L COMMITTEE OF REPUBLIC OF
PORTUGAL FOR UN50
c/o Ministry of Foreign Affairs, Largo do
Rilvas, 1300 Lisboa, Portugal
TEL: (351) 1 604930 FAX: (351) 1 397-2812

Republic of Korea
NAT'L COMMITTEE OF REPUBLIC OF
KOREA FOR UN50
16th fl., Daewoo Foundation Bldg., 526,
Namdaemun-Ro 5 Ka, Chung-Ku, Seoul
TEL: (82) 2 774-9891 FAX: (82) 2 774-9894

Republic of Moldova
NAT'L COMMITTEE OF REPUBLIC OF
MOLDOVA FOR UN50
Piata Marii Adunarai Nitionali 1, Chisinau,
Republic of Moldova
TEL: (373) 2 233728/233940
FAX: (373) 2 232-302

Romania
NATIONAL COMMITTEE OF ROMANIA
FOR UN50
c/o Chamber of Deputies, Bucharest
TEL: (40) 1 613-1450 FAX: (40) 1 312-2436

Russian Federation
RUSSIAN FEDERATION NAT'L
COMMITTEE FOR UN50
Ministry of Foreign Affairs, Smolenskaya
Senneya Square 32/34, Moscow
TEL: (7) 95 2444737 FAX: (7) 95 2442203

Senegal
NATIONAL COMMITTEE OF SENEGAL
FOR UN50
Ministère des Affaires Etrangères et des
Sénégalais de l'Extérieur
BP 4044, Place de l'Indépendance, Dakar
TEL: (221) 238488

Singapore
NATIONAL COMMITTEE OF SINGAPORE
FOR UN50
Ministry of Foreign Affairs, 250 North Bridge
Road, 39 Raffles City Tower, Singapore 0617
TEL: (65) 3305600 FAX: (65) 3381908

Slovenia
NATIONAL COMMITTEE OF SLOVENIA
FOR UN50
Ministry of Foreign Affairs, Gregorciceva 25,
61000 Ljubljana
TEL: (386) 61 1250 300 FAX: (386) 61 213 357

Spain
NATIONAL COMMITTEE OF SPAIN FOR
UN50
c/o Ministry of Foreign Affairs, Plaza de Santa
Cruz, Madrid 28012
TEL: (34) 1 266-3925 FAX: (34) 1 266-5461

Sri Lanka
NATIONAL COMMITTEE OF SRI LANKA
FOR UN50
c/o Ministry of Foreign Affairs, 1 Republic
Square, Colombo

Sudan
NATIONAL COMMITTEE OF SUDAN FOR
UN50
c/o Ministry of Foreign Affairs, Khartoum

Sweden
NATIONAL COMMITTEE OF SWEDEN
FOR UN50
Box 16 121, Stockholm
TEL: (46) 8 7866000 FAX: (46) 8 7231176

Syrian Arab Republic
NATIONAL COMMITTEE OF SYRIA FOR
UN50
c/o Ministry of Information, Damascus
TEL: (963) 11 662 0052

Tajikistan
NATIONAL COMMITTEE OF TAJIKISTAN
FOR UN50
42 Rudaki, Dushanbe
TEL: (7) 3772 23-2804 FAX: (7) 3772 23-2964

Thailand
NATIONAL COMMITTEE OF THAILAND
FOR UN50
Government House, Thanon Nakhon
Pathom, Bangkok 10300
TEL: (66) 2 282-8134 FAX: (66) 2 282-9543

The Netherlands
NATIONAL COMMITTEE OF THE
NETHERLANDS FOR UN50
P.O. Box 80125, 3508 TC Utrecht
TEL: (30) 53 92 97 FAX: (30) 53 92 93

Trinidad & Tobago
NATIONAL COMMITTEE OF TRINIDAD
& TOBAGO FOR UN50
c/o Ministry of Foreign Affairs, Queens Park
West, Port-of-Spain

Tunisia
NATIONAL COMMITTEE OF TUNISIA
FOR UN50
Ministère des Affaires Etrangères, Place du
Gouvernment, La Kasbah, Tunis
TEL: (216) 1 567-388 FAX: (216) 1 260-531

Turkey
NATIONAL COMMITTEE OF TURKEY
FOR UN50
Ministry of Foreign Affairs, Balgat, Ankara
TEL: (90) 312 287-1665 FAX: (90) 312 287-3869

Ukraine
NATIONAL COMMITTEE OF THE
UKRAINE FOR UN50
Ministry of Foreign Affairs, Mikhailivska
Square 1, Kiev 252001

United Kingdom
UK COMMITTEE FOR THE UN 50TH
ANNIVERSARY
c/o UNA-UK, 3 Whitehall Court, London,
SW1A 2EL

USA
NATIONAL COMMITTEE OF THE USA
FOR UN50
Permanent Mission of the US to the UN
799 United Nations Plaza, New York, NY
10017-7671

Yemen
NATIONAL COMMITTEE OF YEMEN
FOR UN50
Ministry of Foreign Affairs, Sana
TEL: (967) 20 25 45/47
FAX: (967) 276-556 or 289-540